IMAGES of America

NUTLEY

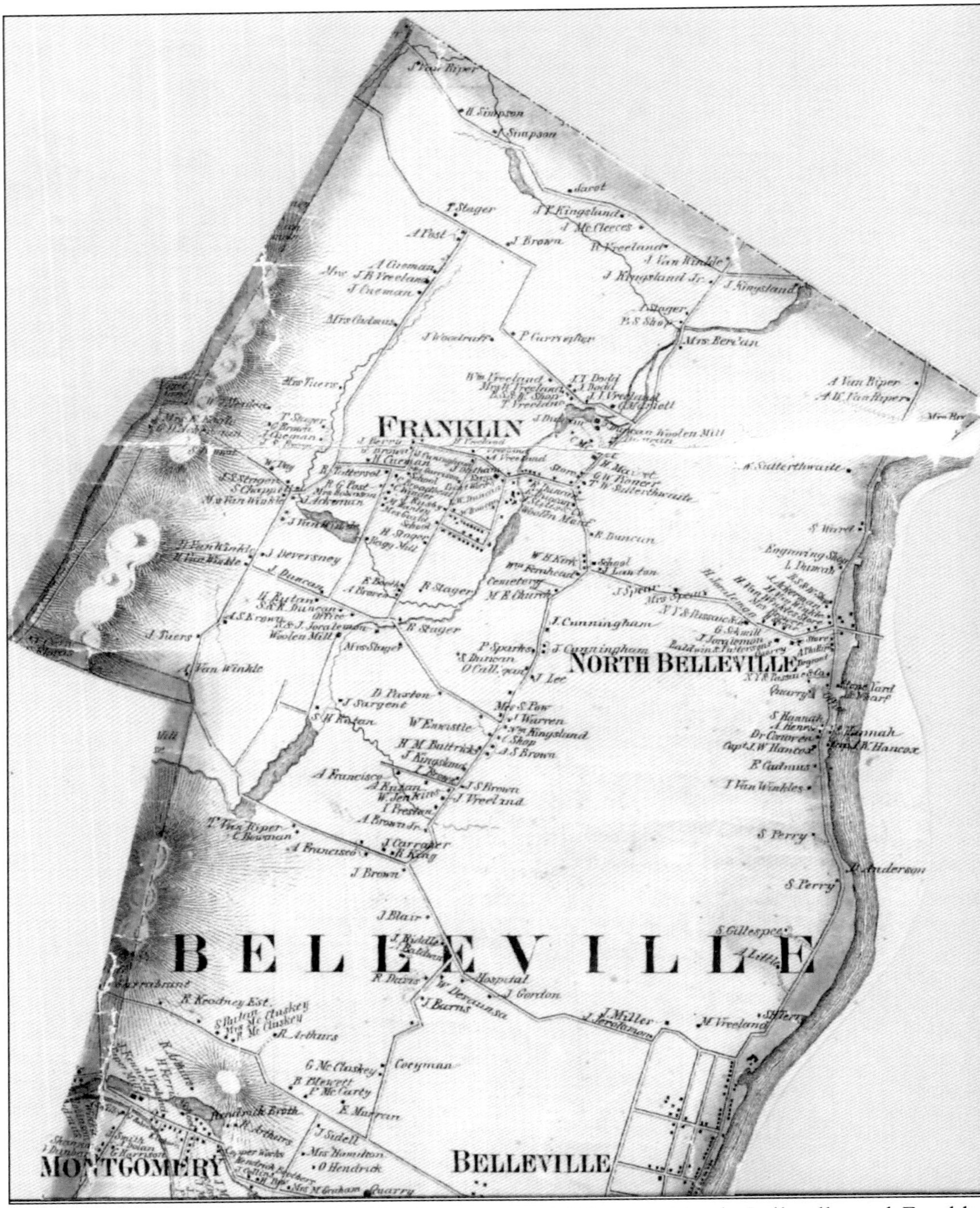

This image shows a section of Belleville from an 1859 map. North Belleville and Franklin were two districts of the town at that time. Within fifteen years, Franklin would break away to become its own township and the area that we call Nutley today.

IMAGES
of America

NUTLEY

John Demmer

ARCADIA
PUBLISHING

ISBN 978-0-7385-6253-7

Published by Arcadia Publishing
Charleston, South Carolina

Printed in the United States of America

Library of Congress Catalog Card Number: 2008932277

For all general information contact Arcadia Publishing at:
Telephone 843-853-2070
Fax 843-853-0044
E-mail sales@arcadiapublishing.com
For customer service and orders:
Toll-Free 1-888-313-2665

Visit us on the Internet at www.arcadiapublishing.com

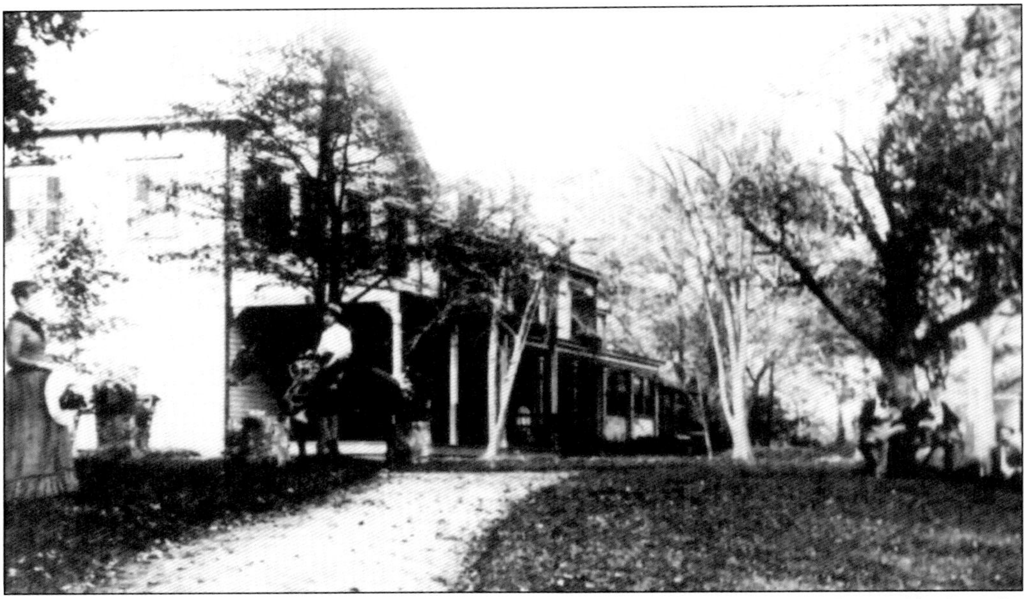

The Van Zandt house, also known as Bend View and the Wheeler Hotel, is traditionally thought to have been built by Jacob Vreeland in 1702. It began as a small brownstone house that was later entirely encased in future wooden additions. The house stood near the banks of the Passaic River near the Clifton town line and was once a rest stop for travelers.

Contents

Acknowledgments

The author would like to thank all those who contributed their time and effort in the making of this book. Community pride and spirit was evident with the scores of phone calls and letters received from people willing to share their own little bit of Nutley history. It was only with their assistance that such a project could be undertaken successfully. Many thanks to Anthony Andriola; Jim and Sue Armstrong; the Backstreet Gourmet; Judge and Mrs. Stanley Bedford; Edith and Elsie Bragger; James William Brenner; John Brinckmann; Larry Calabro (in Memory of James Hamlisch); Daniel Caplan; William Christian; Frank Cocchiola; Mark Conca; Giovanni Conturso; Michele Derosa; Sal Dimichino; Express Press; Lynn Falduto; Tony Forte; Gary Furnari; Michael C. Gabriele; Joe and Barbara Gallagher; John and Wilma Gantner; Dan and Maria Geltrude; Edward Hamm Jr.; Phil Harms; Maxine Hoffer; Hoffmann-la Roche; Holy Family Roman Catholic Church; Anthony Iannarone; William J. Jernick; Rev. William A. Krepps; Cynthia Land; Helen Maguire; Maps of Antiquity; Gary Mayer; Mrs. Julia Nakamura; Newark Public Library, New Jersey Room; Annmarie Nicolette; North Jersey Chapter of the National Railway Historical Society; Nutley Camera; Nutley Fire Department; Nutley Historical Society; Nutley Police Department; Nutley Free Public Library; the *Nutley Sun*; Nutley Town Hall; Carmen Orechio; Frank Orechio; Charlie Piro; Lois Plinio; Mr. And Mrs. Plishka; Mrs. Ann Rabinowitz; Vincent Ritacco; Saint Paul's Congregational Church; Fred Scalera; Ira Siegel; Beverly Simko; Gary and Janet Sprong; Jackie Shaughnessy/Stoppy; Mr. and Mrs. William J. Smith; Mr. and Mrs. Clem Tennis; Lynn Vigeant; Mr. and Mrs. Frank Viola; Michele Viscel; David Wilson; Fred Windheim; and James Zoccoli.

Special thanks to James Challes for his tireless research of the *Nutley Sun* microfilms; first citizen, former Mayor Harry Chenoweth, whose extensive collection of artifacts and stories were made available to me; and Fred and Jeanne Van Steen for reviewing this work in manuscript.

Introduction

Nutley is a community of about 30,000 people located in Essex County, New Jersey, at the foot of the Orange Mountains. Situated on the west bank of the Passaic River, it was part of the original land grant that Robert Treat secured from a group of Native Americans in 1666. Known then as Newark, this large land area would go through a series of boundary transformations, establishing the town limits that we are familiar with today. The first of these boundary changes happened when Bloomfield, which included the lands of Belleville and Nutley, broke away from the Newark tract in 1812. By 1839, the area of Belleville and its northern section, known as North Belleville or Franklinville, separated itself from Bloomfield. In the 1870s, there was a feeling that the residents of the northern end of Belleville were not receiving fair representation in town government. There was also a similar view that this section was not equally treated in regard to fund appropriations for its development. These factors led to the separation of Franklin (Nutley) from Belleville, officially recorded in 1874 and approved with supplements on February 25, 1875.

Within Franklin's boundaries were three distinct sections of town: Avondale on the east side; Nutley, roughly the north-central part; and Franklin on the west side of town. Avondale was best known for its quarries, which were along River Road near Park Avenue. The quarries brought Italian immigrants to the area, many of whom lived in the vicinity of Roma and Humbert Streets. When the railroad was brought through town in the late 1860s, many of the Irish railroad workers settled in the Avondale section of town as well. The Nutley portion of town was the first business district. The mills run by the Duncan and Stitts families brought in many English textile workers. The area around Passaic Avenue and Chestnut Street was heavily concentrated with a variety of retail stores. The lands of Franklin on the west side of town were, for the most part, still farmlands and great wooded fields. This side of town, especially near Franklin Avenue, would eventually win in the bid to become the town center. In 1887, the U.S. Post Master General approved the change of the postmark from Franklin to Nutley; however, the township would not make Nutley the official name until 1902.

One of Nutley's key features is the Third River, which flows throughout the town and was responsible for powering Nutley's various mill operations. As a result of the mills and quarries, the town grew rapidly. Nutley's true residential growth was due to early real estate developers. Names like Barney, Hay, and Lambert dominate most maps of the Nutley area from around the turn of the century. These men realized the importance of Nutley as a community, which could offer a country-like environment with links to large cities such as Paterson, Newark, and New York. It was during these years that many of the large elaborate homes in town were built on large lots. From then on, Nutley has continued to grow and prosper, offering pleasant residential areas and space for industry and local businesses to thrive.

This book was printed to preserve some of the local history through vintage images, for those not familiar with Nutley's story. It relies on the written and recollected stories of some of Nutley's residents, and while it is believed to be as accurate as possible, it should be remembered that the same story can be told in many ways. Nutley has far too much history to be contained in any one book, but I have tried to represent a little bit of everything in this work. It should also be noted that there will be some spelling variations of certain local names. The most notable of these variations is found in the spelling of the word "yantacaw."

Before European settlers came to this area, Native American tribes were very prominent. Tribes like the Delawares, Iroquois, and Hackensacks ruled over most of New Jersey. A branch of the Delawares, called the Lenni Lenape, populated the lands of Essex and Passaic Counties. It was probably the Lenni Lenape term "kante kaey" that became corrupted into the word yantacaw and all of its variations (yountakah, yantico, etc.). Kante kaey was the name for the ceremonial dance that the tribe held in the area of the former ITT properties in Nutley and Clifton, where the Yantacaw (Third River) empties into the Passaic River. The ceremony was a celebration of the harvest and its bounty.

Along with the photographic views of Nutley that will be presented in this book are the names of early residents that today are commonly known as street names. Families like the Vreelands, Van Ripers, Stagers, Speers, Kingslands, Blums, Booths, Chappells, Duncans, and several others were very important because they were the original roots of this community. It was their decision to go beyond simply finding a place to live, and to develop the area into a town that they could call home, one that would appeal to future generations. It is important to realize that the town you live in, wherever it may be, is the product of people who worked together to provide a place their families could be proud of. I invite all who read this book to take some time out and drive around town to see what things have changed and admire those that have not.

John F. Demmer II

One

Quarries, Mills, and Factories

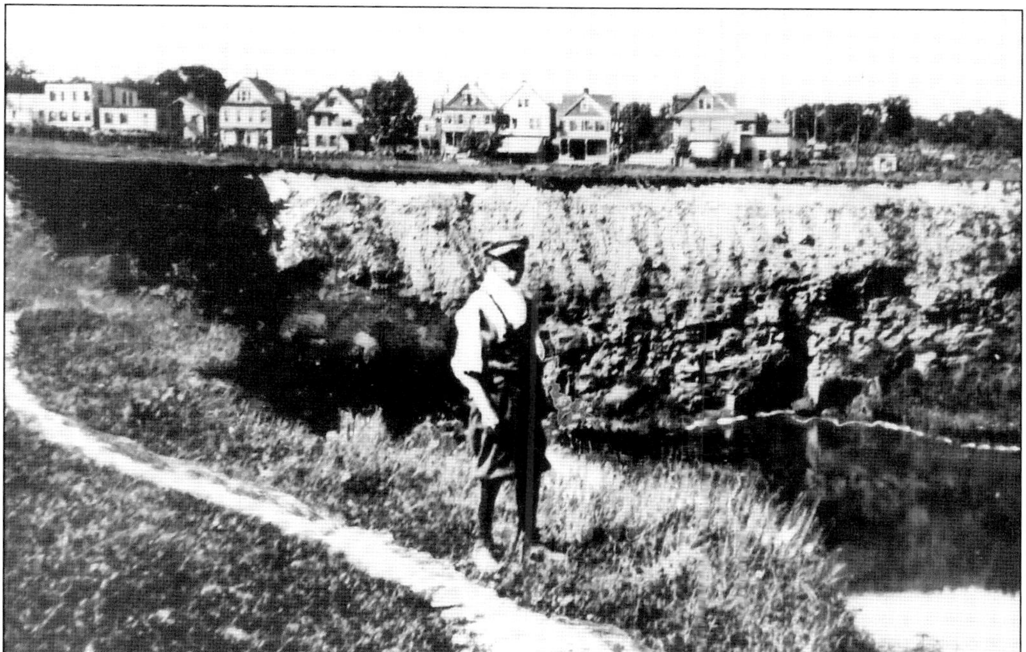

This gentleman is standing roughly where the Rets building is today on Park Avenue near Washington Avenue, *c.* 1915. The view is looking northward across the street. The beginnings of Humbert and Roma Streets are visible between the houses. The quarry was filled with water by this time.

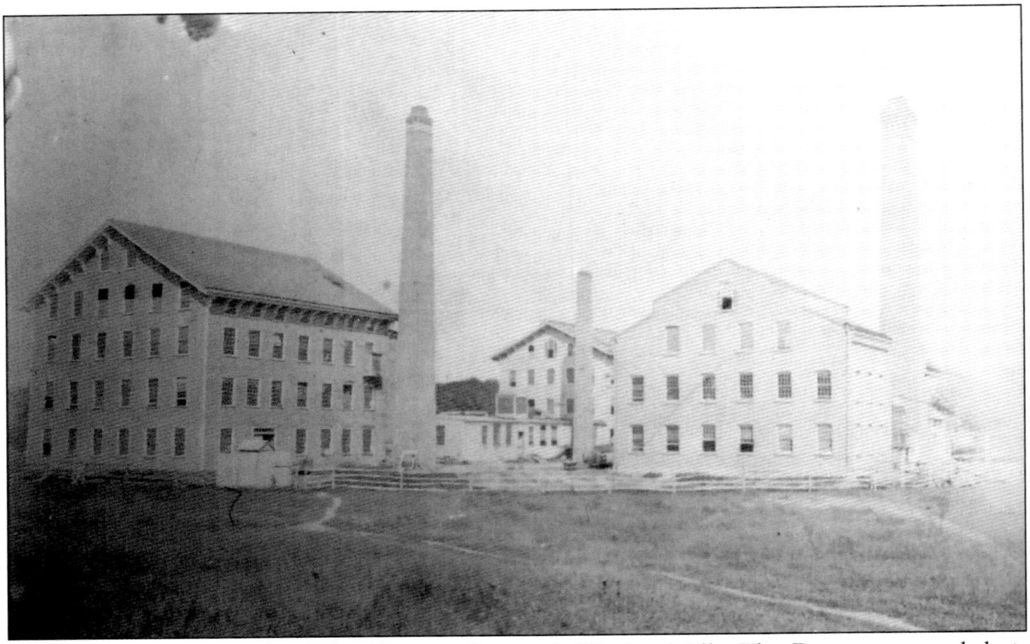

This is a view of several mill buildings at Duncan's Woolen Mills. The Duncans started their manufacturing dynasty at the foot of Grant Avenue near the Passaic River and made block-printed handkerchiefs and scarves. Another mill producing cotton goods was built near the area known as the Mudhole (Cotton Mill Pond).

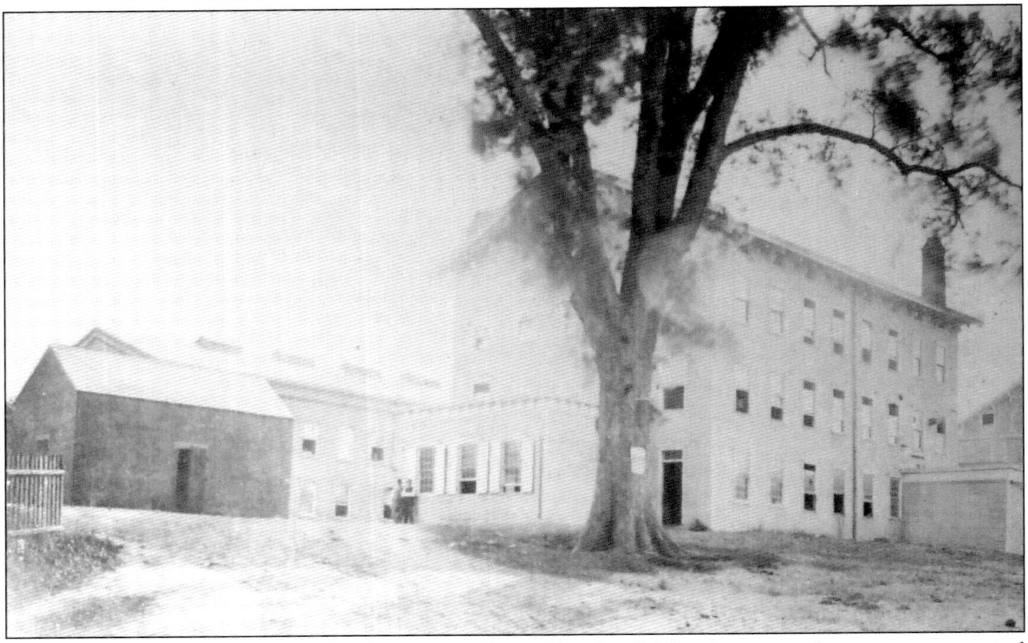

Pictured here is a view of the the long-gone Essex Woolen Mills; the grounds are now occupied by the library, town hall, high school, and oval. There was also another mill north of Chestnut Street at Third River and one at Harrison Street by the A&P store. These mills were all run by various members of the Duncan family.

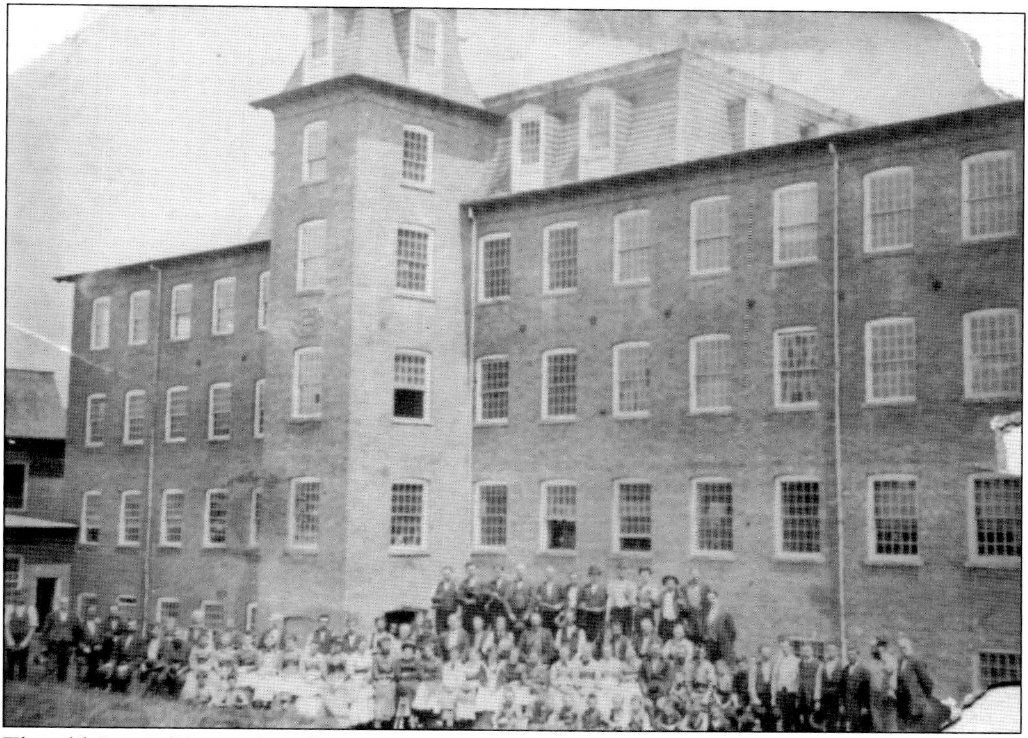

The old Stitt's (Yantico) Mill once stood where Vincent Church is presently located. The mill was right across the street from the Duncan Mill complex, of which the town hall building was a part. Stitt's Mill was so well known and traveled to that the Nutley Train Station was referred to as Stitt's Station for a time.

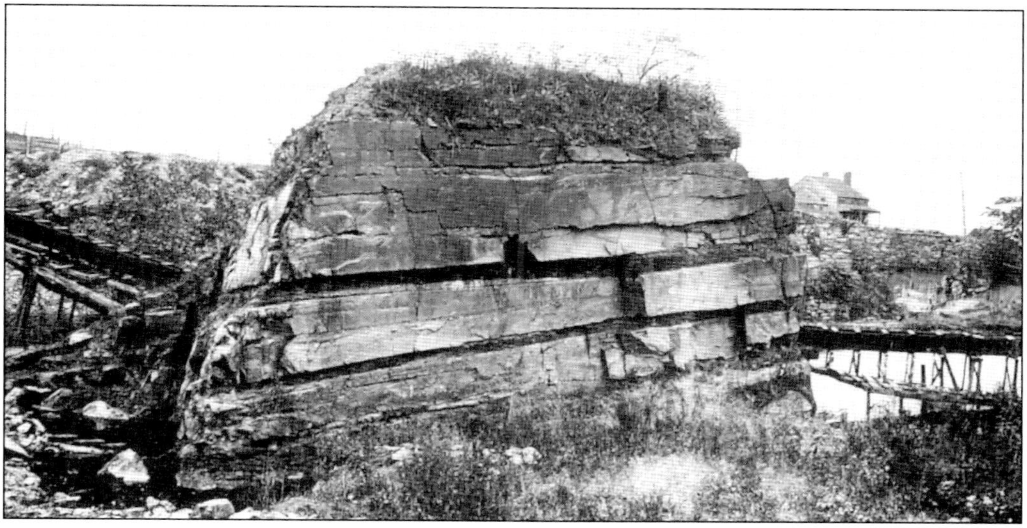

Lone Rock was a part of the quarry in Avondale (East Nutley). The quarry was excavated, leaving this 45-foot-high monolith standing. You can see the softer bands of material in between various layers of the fine brownstone that was used in many homes and buildings both here and in New York.

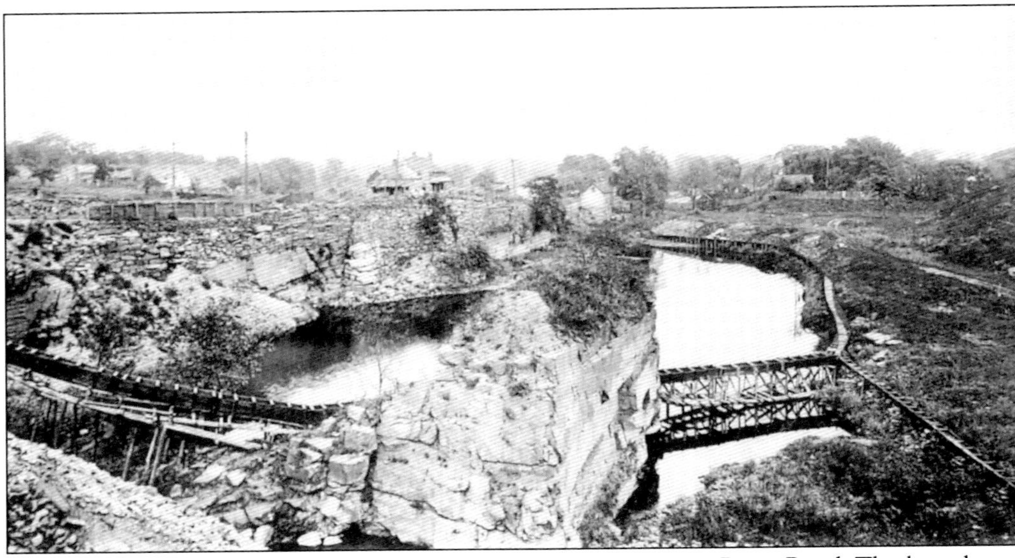

This abandoned quarry was on the south side of Park Avenue near River Road. The large house sits on the other side of the street. The wood structure built around the quarry is a water sluiceway coming from Darby Brook, which originated from the ground spring at Park Avenue near Whitford Avenue.

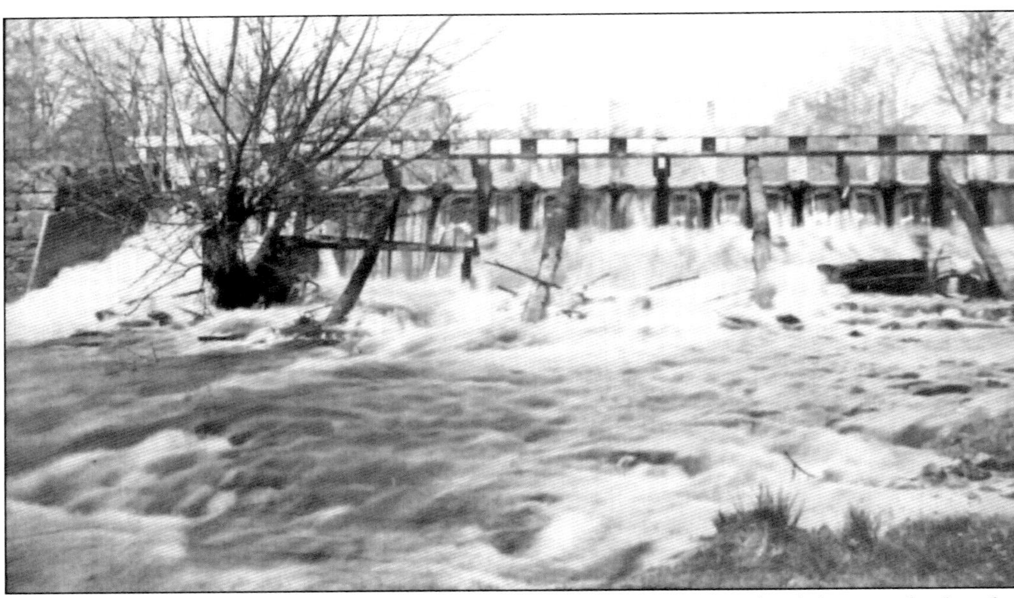

On July 1, 1897, the Yantacaw Dam, located at Third River near Vreeland Avenue, broke after heavy flood waters weakened the structure. The 1898 annual township committee report stated that $124.48 was spent to repair the failing dam. In the 1899 report, Mr. E.E. Faith, the health inspector, reported that the dam was removed completely.

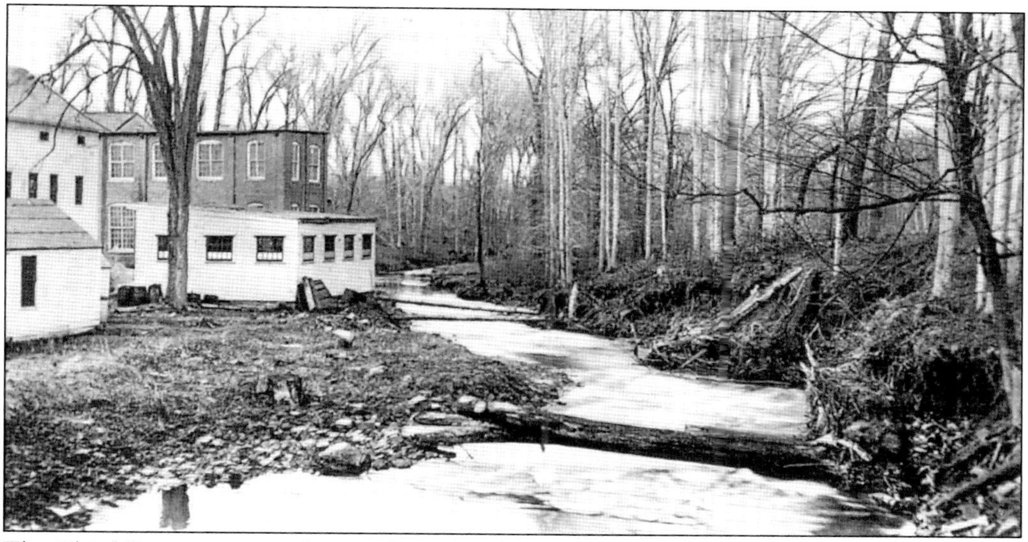

The Third River was a vital part of many mills and factories in town. This 1907 view shows the river heading north after passing under the Kingsland Avenue Bridge. This site was the location of the Kingsland Paper Mills. In 1909, the White Spring Paper Mills operated on the same site.

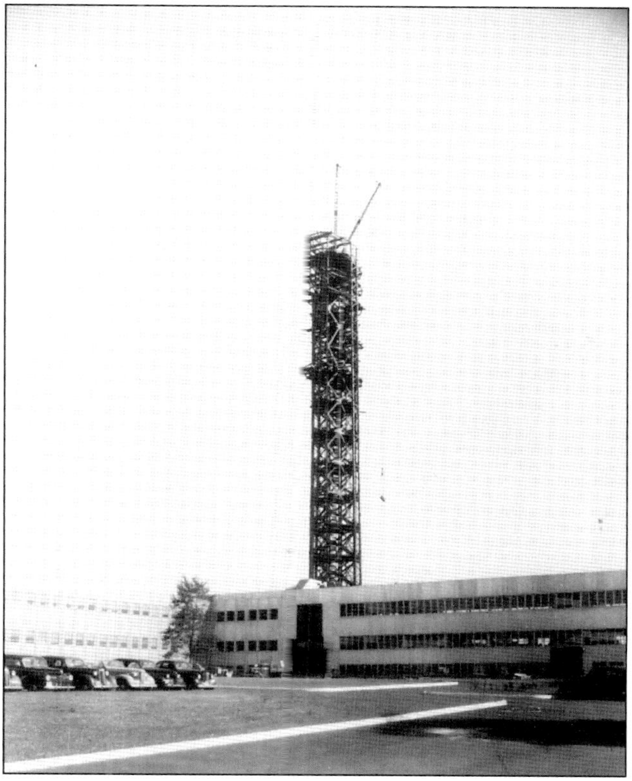

The former site of the Yountakah Country Club was purchased and developed by ITT Corporation in 1945. Its famous 300-foot tall microwave research tower, which has recently been demolished, is shown here during its construction.

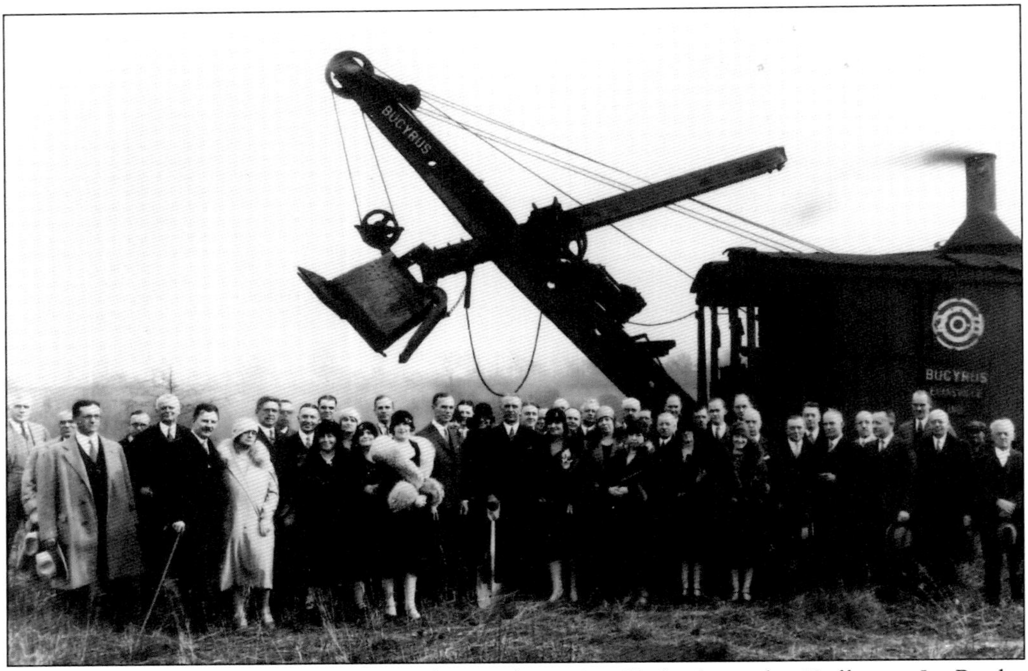

After searching for a suitable site to relocate their New York plant, the Hoffmann-La Roche Company decided on a piece of property at the northwest side of Nutley. This photograph shows the ground-breaking ceremony, which took place on November 17, 1928. The plant was in full operation by June of 1929.

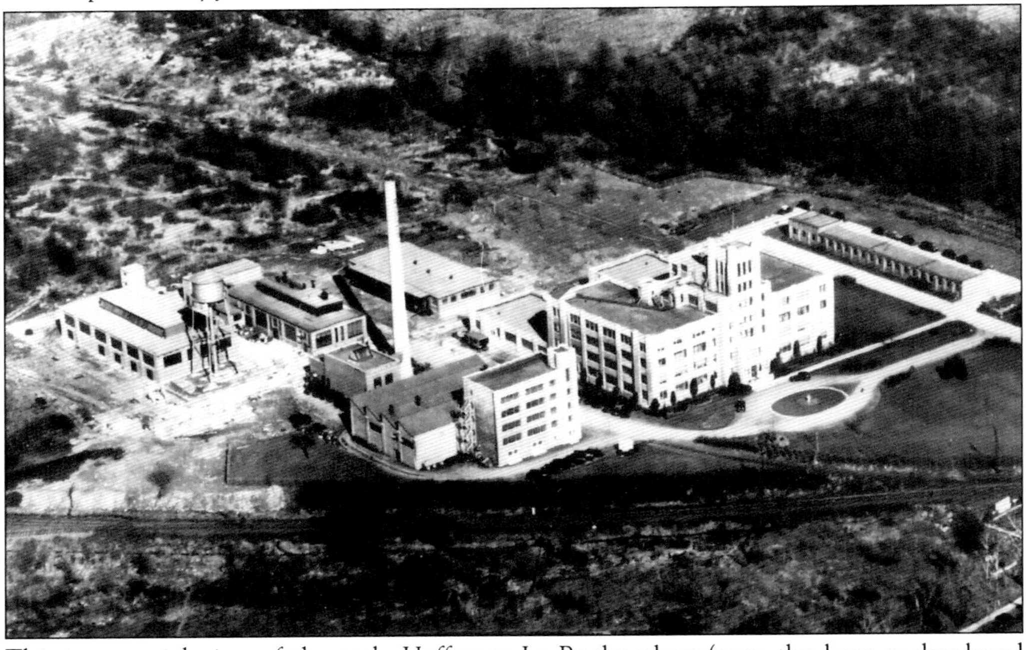

This is an aerial view of the early Hoffmann-La Roche plant (note the large undeveloped section behind old Building One). The plant was built near the former site of the Eaton Stone Quarry, where Mr. Stone also had the winter headquarters for his circus.

You could once see the large brick chimney of a factory if you stood above the falls and looked north across Kingsland Avenue. On that site, J. and R. Kingsland ran their paper manufacturing company. They later merged with George La Monte and Son in 1905; eventually all paper manufacturing was done at La Monte's plant further up the road.

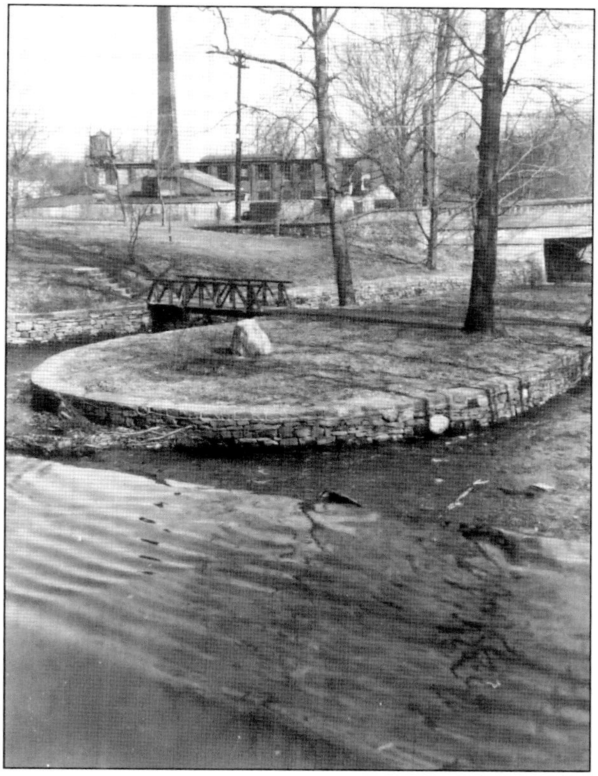

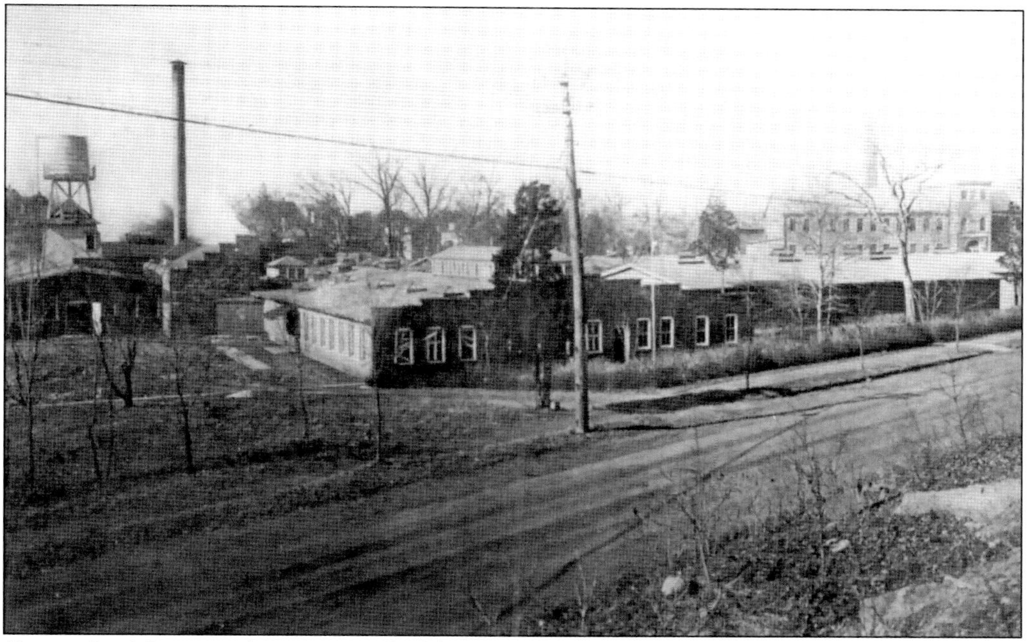

George La Monte and Son was a highly successful safety paper business with an enormous manufacturing plant at 299 Kingsland Avenue. Safety paper was invented due to a need for safeguarding bank notes, documents, and checks from being forged.

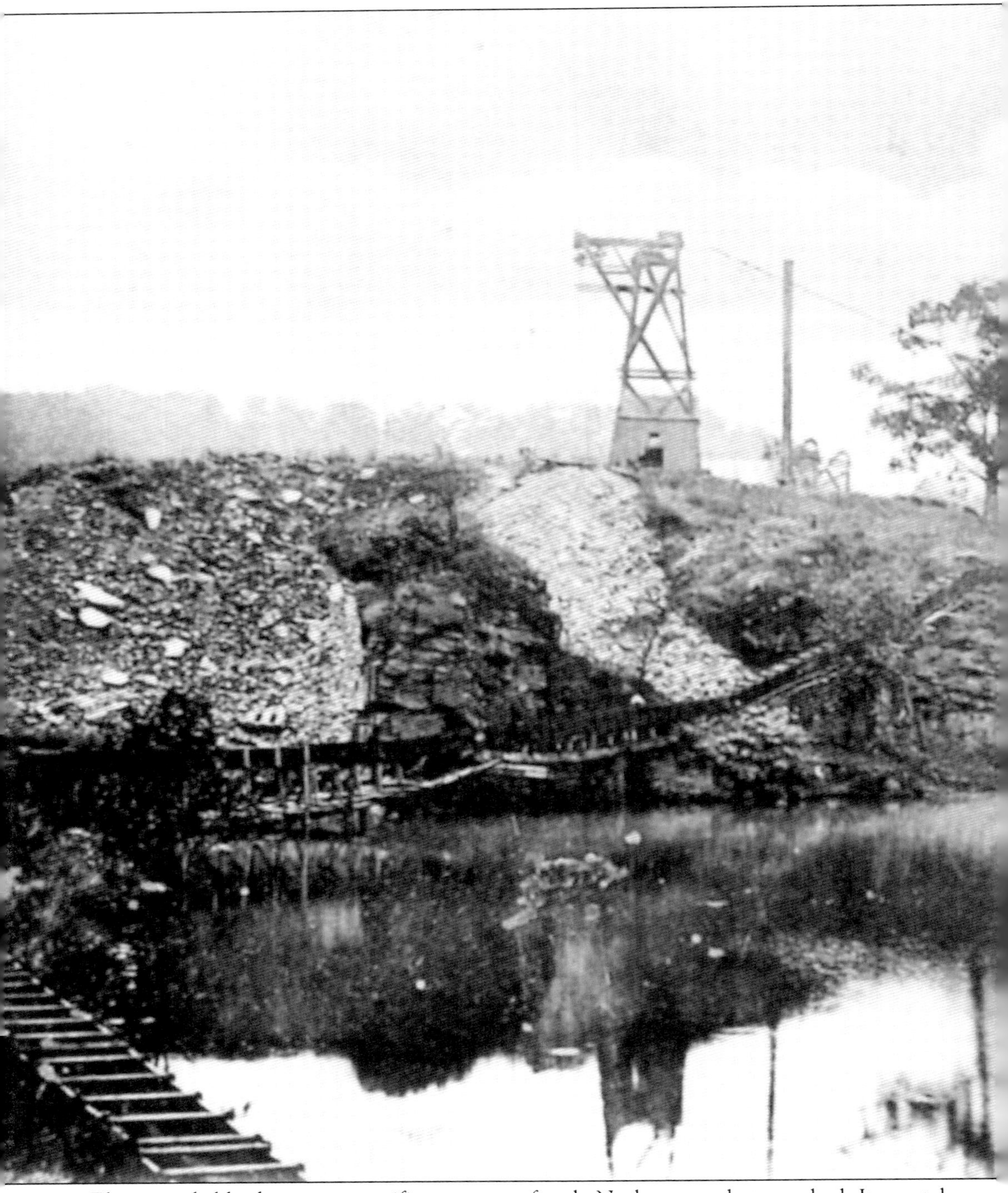

This is probably the most magnificent scene of early Nutley ever photographed. It was taken from River Road, looking west. The house shown on the right was on the north side of Park Avenue (Avondale Road). The wooden wall in front of the house was built to prevent people from falling into the hole. Early newspaper reports showed this to be an ongoing problem, with drowning victims occasionally having to be brought to the water's surface by using dynamite.

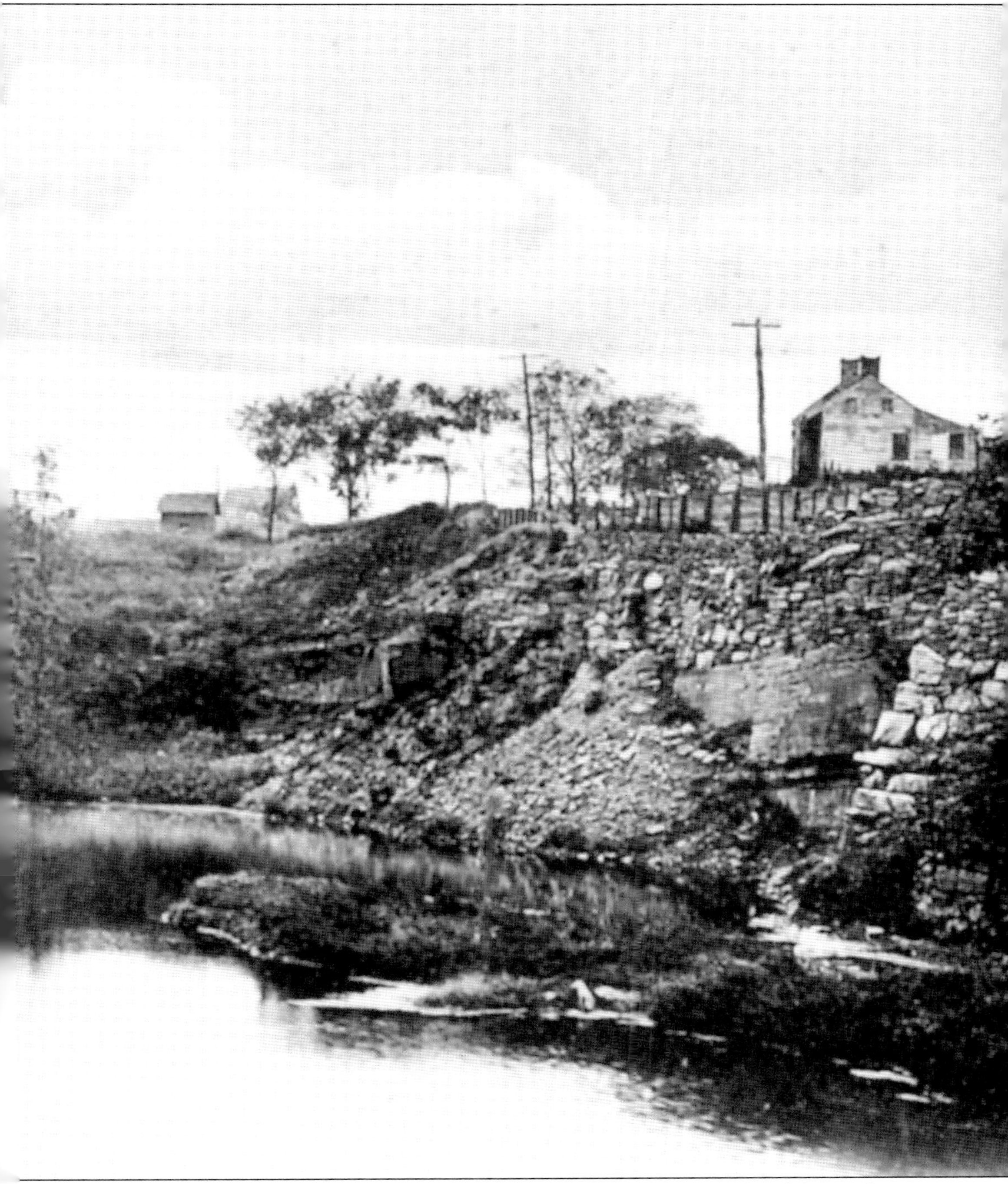

The odd-looking structure to the left of center is a cable hoist tower used to lift out the cut stone. During the quarry's use, some of the men were crushed by falling rock; a cemetery was laid out specifically for these men, located on the south side of Park Avenue near the present tennis courts. It is not known if there are any bodies still buried there.

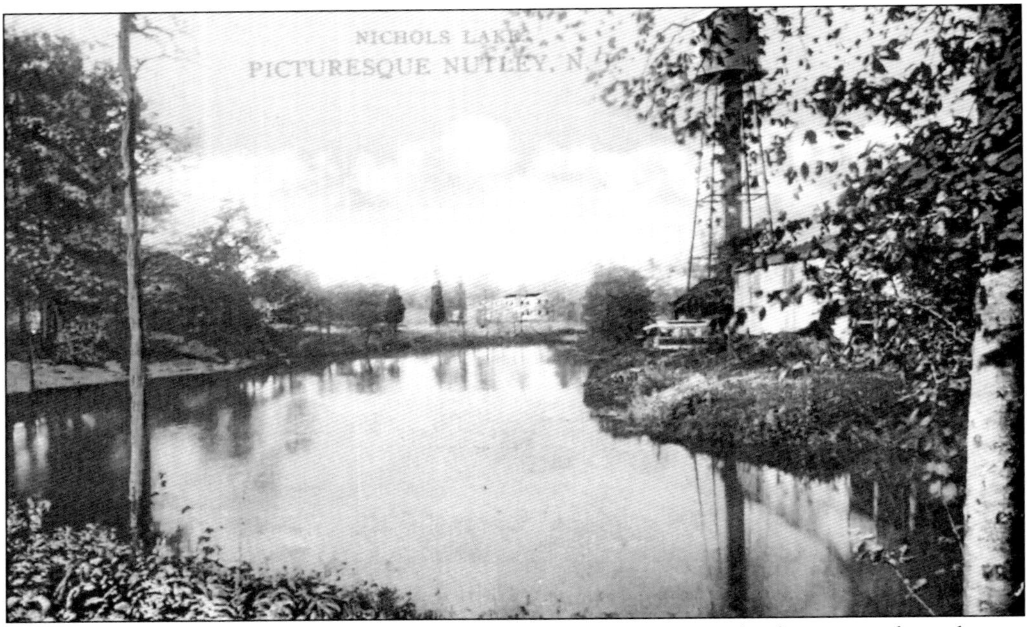

This photograph shows Nichol's Lake just before the falls, *c.* 1910. The factory on the right was located in the area where the *Nutley Sun* offices are today. Nichols Hat Factory was here and provided Nutley with its first electric service as of October 11, 1893. A contract with the town allowed the Nichols plant to power a hundred electric street lights for one year, starting on May 1, 1894, for $2,000.

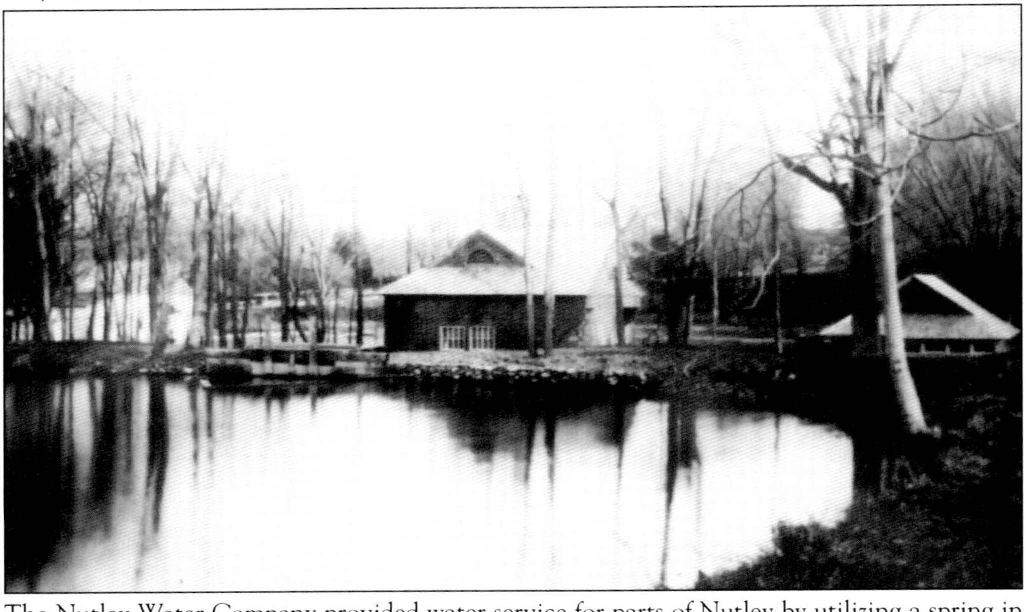
The Nutley Water Company provided water service for parts of Nutley by utilizing a spring in the Mudhole area near Passaic and Vreeland Avenues. The town bought the rights to the spring but soon decided to contract with the East Jersey Water Co. for municipal water service. The pumphouse building shown here was brought up the hill and is now the second floor of 407 Passaic Avenue.

Two

Town and Country (Clubs)

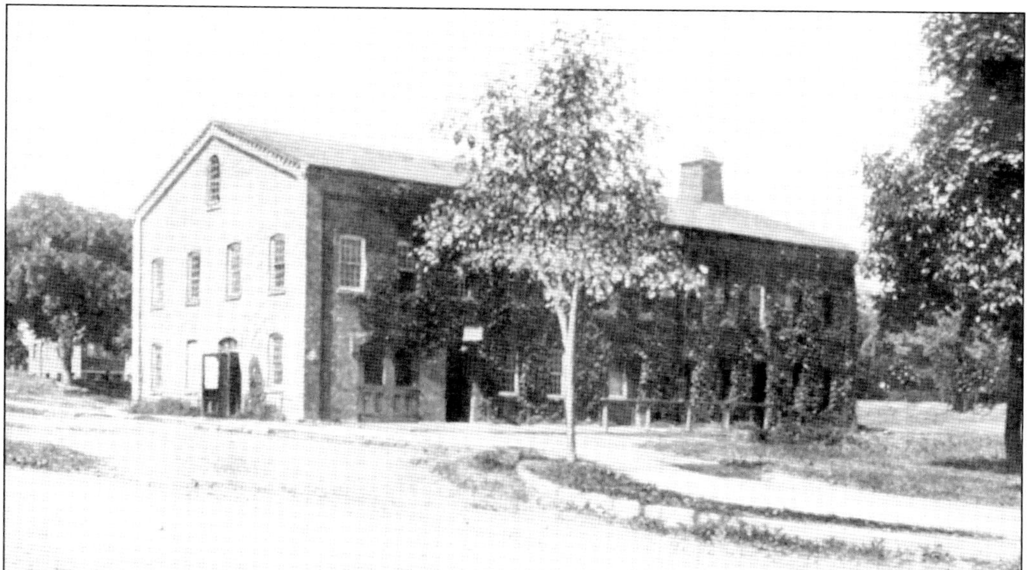

This building, now known as Nutley Town Hall, has had a long, illustrious career. Originally built as one of the mill buildings for the Essex Woolen Mills, it has housed school classes, a post office, a jail, a bank, and a fire department. A fire on February 8, 1904, destroyed the roof of the old two-story building, which led to its next transformation.

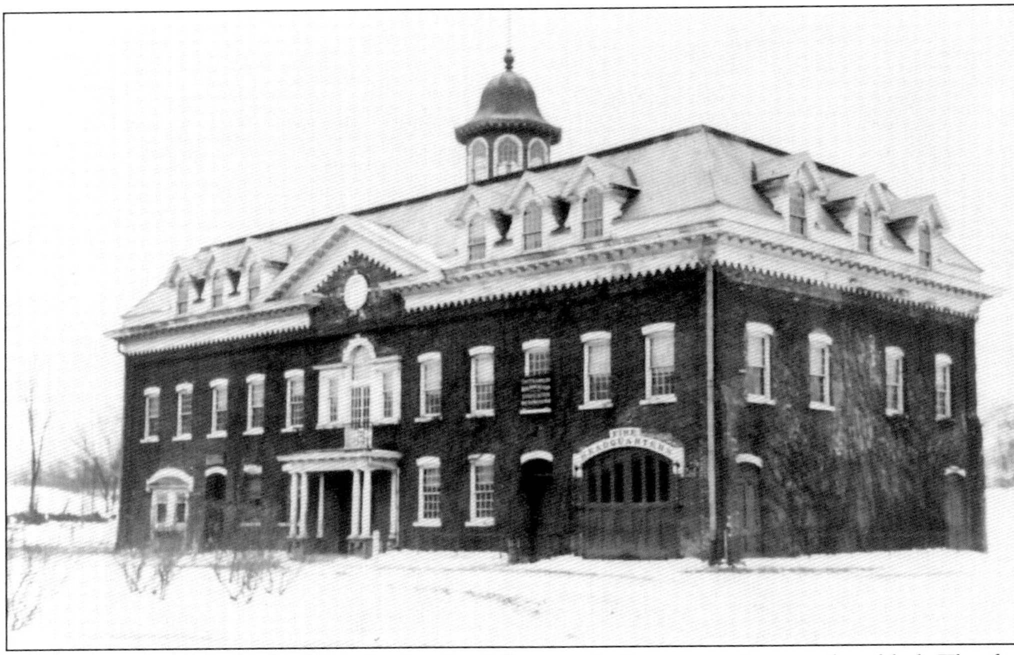

After the 1904 fire, the building had a third floor with dormers and a cupola added. The fire headquarters of Yantacaw Hose were on the right, and a jail facility was provided; they remained there until a new public safety building was built across the street in 1929.

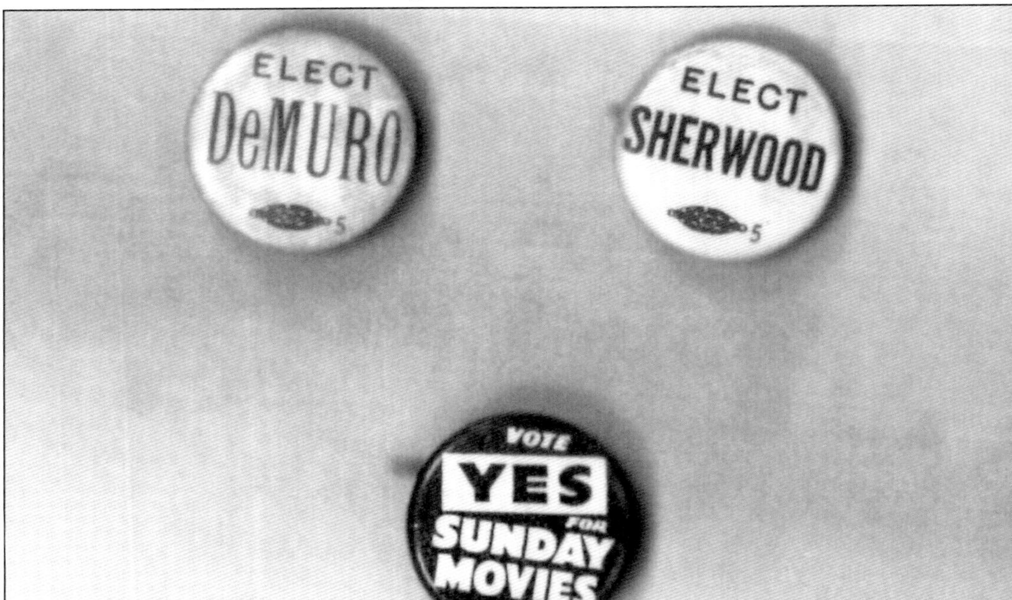

Some early propaganda items are shown here urging people to get out to vote. The year that these buttons were made voters could chose De Muro or Sherwood for commissioner and also decide the Sunday movie issue. Blue laws prevented the showing of movies on Sunday, but this unpopular ruling was eventually repealed.

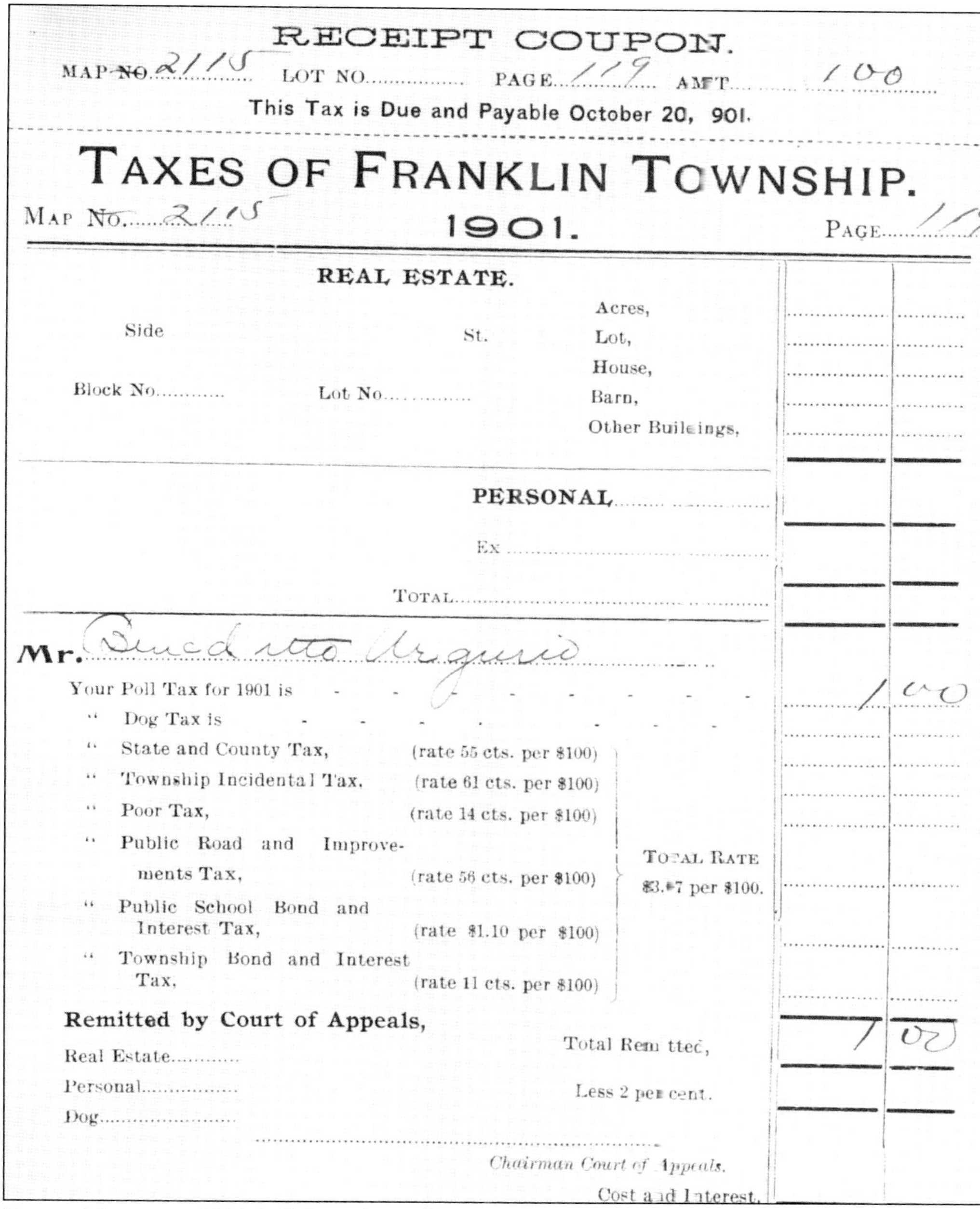

RECEIPT COUPON.

MAP NO. 2115 LOT NO.............. PAGE 119 AMT. 1 00

This Tax is Due and Payable October 20, 1901.

TAXES OF FRANKLIN TOWNSHIP.

MAP NO. 2115 **1901.** PAGE 119

REAL ESTATE.

Side St. Acres,
Lot,
House,
Block No........... Lot No........... Barn,
Other Buildings,

PERSONAL.........

Ex ....

TOTAL..........

Mr. Benedetto Urguria

Your Poll Tax for 1901 is		1	00
" Dog Tax is			
" State and County Tax,	(rate 55 cts. per $100)		
" Township Incidental Tax,	(rate 61 cts. per $100)		
" Poor Tax,	(rate 14 cts. per $100)		
" Public Road and Improvements Tax,	(rate 56 cts. per $100)		
" Public School Bond and Interest Tax,	(rate $1.10 per $100)		
" Township Bond and Interest Tax,	(rate 11 cts. per $100)		

TOTAL RATE $3.07 per $100.

Remitted by Court of Appeals,

Real Estate..........
Personal..........
Dog..........

Total Remitted, 1 00

Less 2 per cent.

....
Chairman Court of Appeals.

Cost and Interest.

Pictured here is a 1901 bill for a $1 poll tax. Poll tax was required to be paid in order for a resident to be able to vote on local issues. The bill head states, "Township of Franklin" because Nutley was not the town's name until 1902. The envelope for this piece is interesting because it is from Dr. Van Riper of Nutley, New Jersey, and there are two postmarks: one postmark from Nutley and the other from Avondale. Consequently, in this one piece, all three sections of town are represented. The stationery used is also interesting; the watermark on the bill shows that it was made by the Kingsland Paper Company, and the envelope has light printing on it reading, "safety paper." Both of these marks are tied into the La Monte Company of Nutley, which merged with the Kingsland Paper Company and invented banker's safety paper.

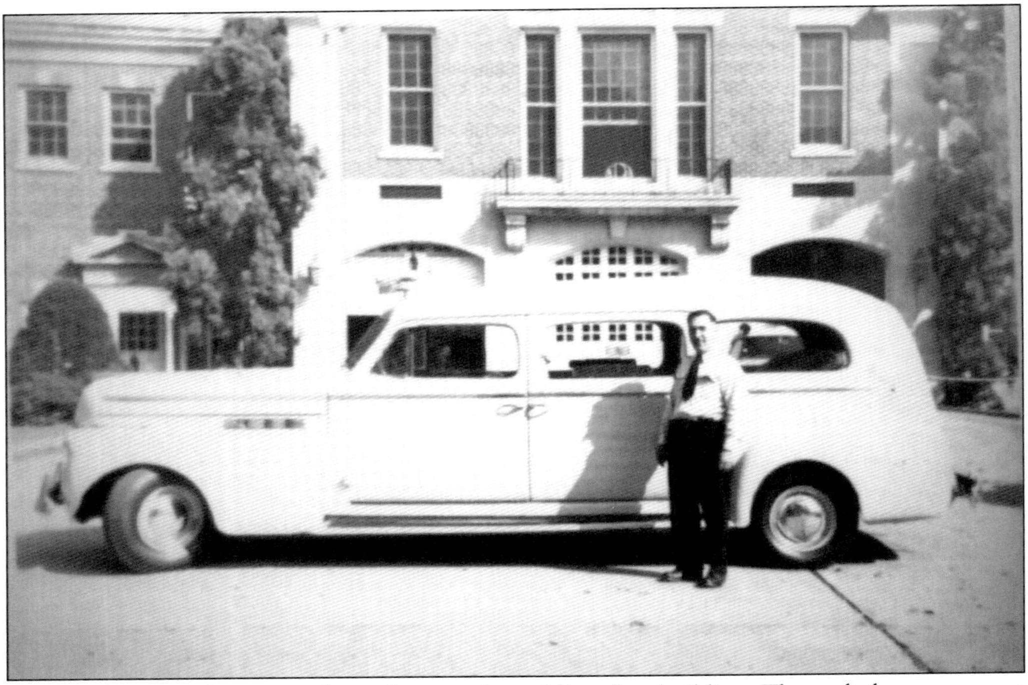

"Jimmy the Cop" Ritacco is shown here at the public safety building. The ambulance was part of the public safety unit until 1953, when the volunteer emergency squad was established. In June 1952, this ambulance caught fire on its way to Clara Maass Hospital in Belleville.

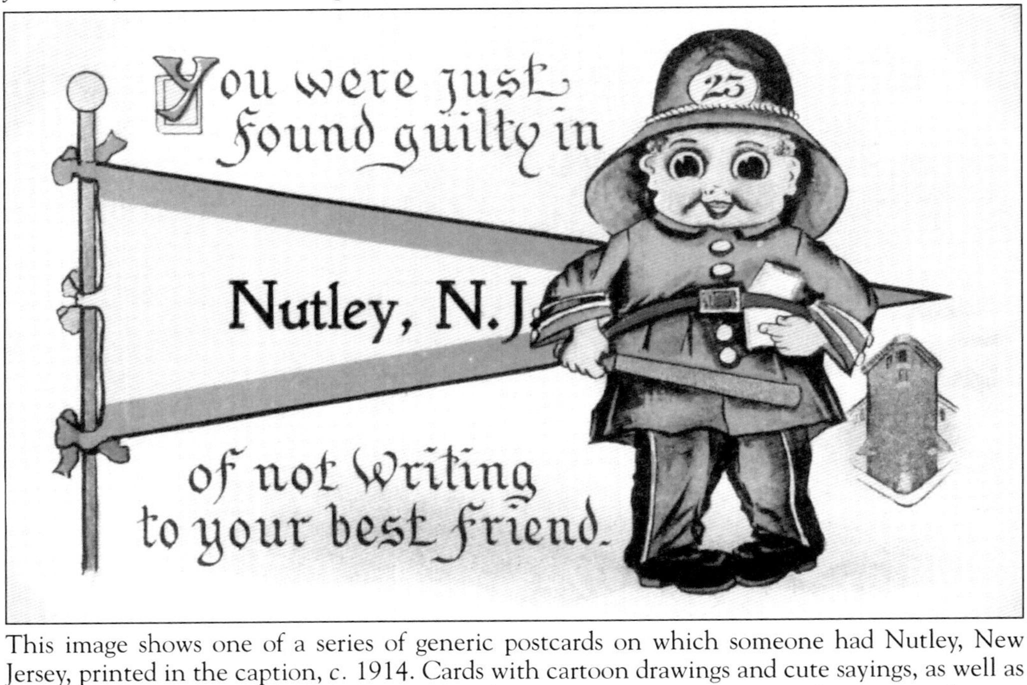

This image shows one of a series of generic postcards on which someone had Nutley, New Jersey, printed in the caption, *c.* 1914. Cards with cartoon drawings and cute sayings, as well as postcards with very nondescript country road views, were quite common; for an extra fee you could have your town name inserted on them.

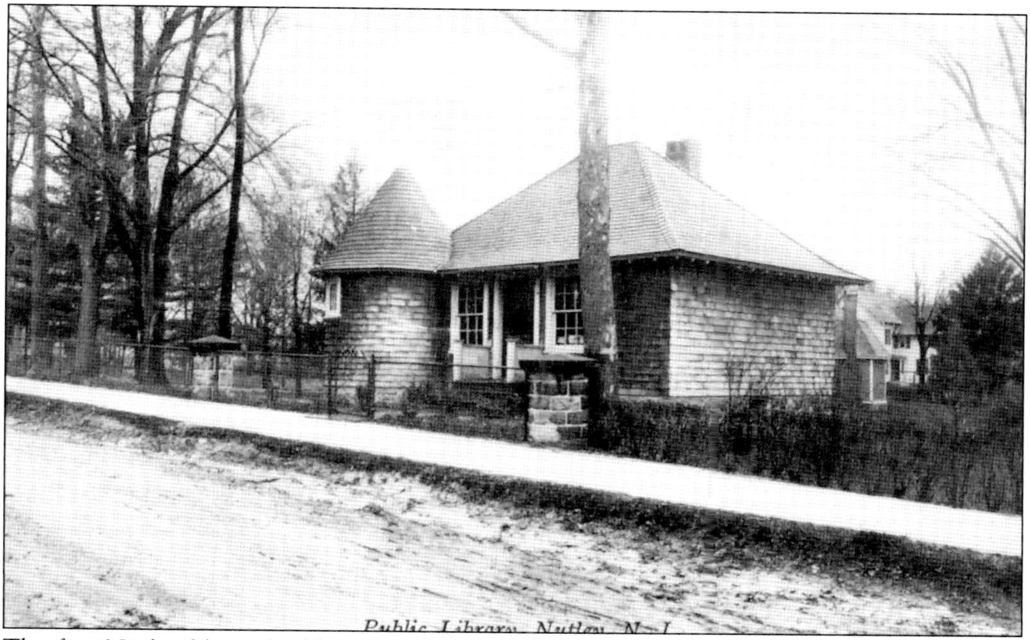

The first Nutley library building was constructed at 381 Passaic Avenue in 1904 as a private library. In 1913, plans were made to build a new public library at a different location.

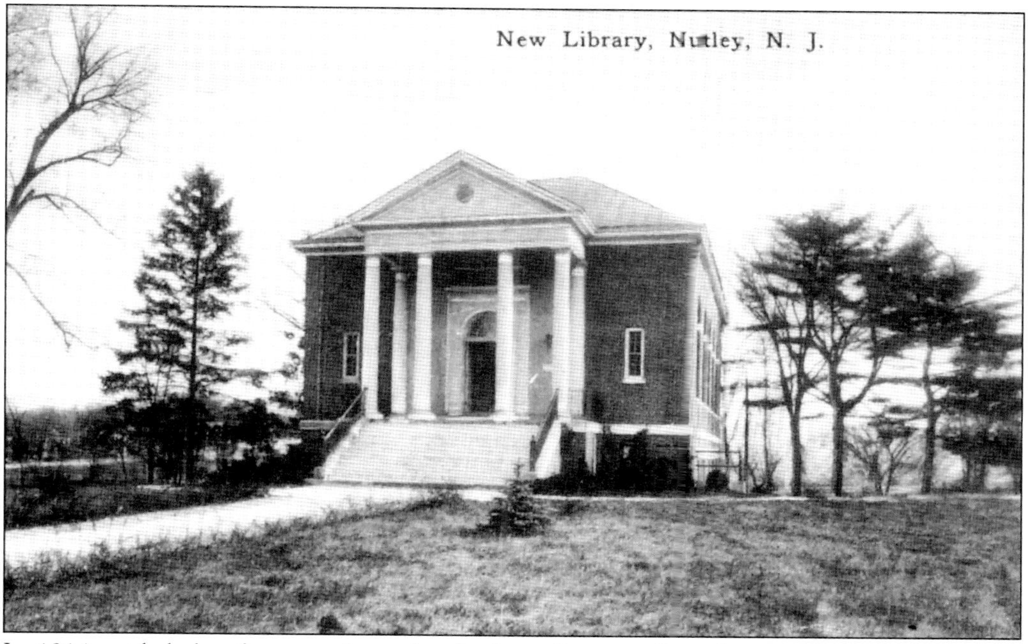

In 1914, with help of a grant from the Andrew Carnegie Foundation, the new Free Public Library of Nutley was built. It occupied the knoll where Mr. Henry Duncan built his house, from which he could look over his mill yards. This library also outgrew its space, and in 1939 an addition was approved and started.

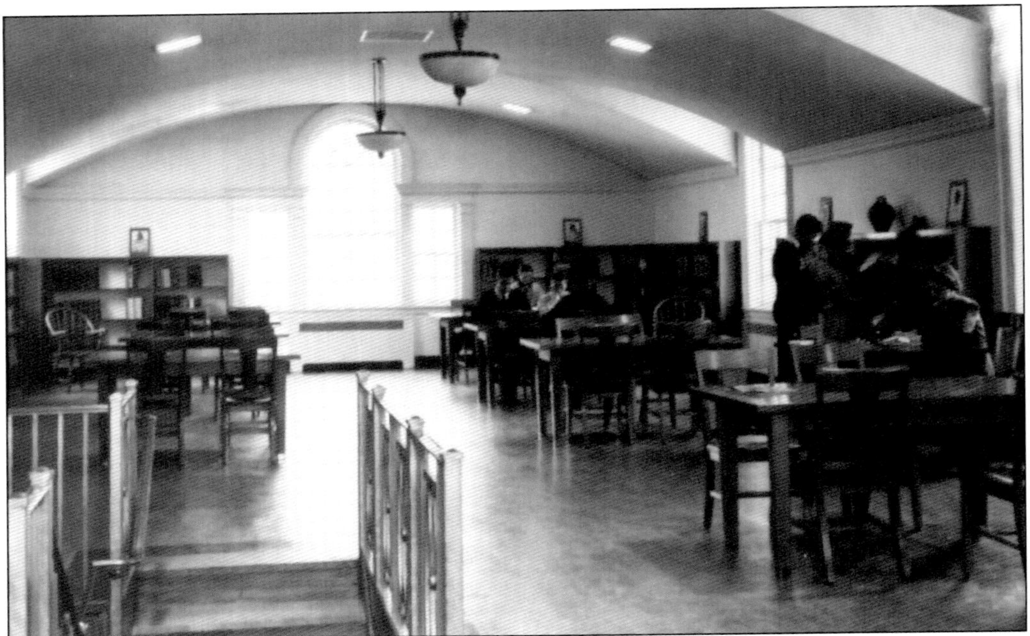

This is an early photograph of the second-floor interior of the Nutley Public Library. The original arched ceiling collapsed in 1980 during the night, without causing injury to anyone. It is hard to believe that this small area with its few bookshelves is part of the present library, which currently has over 90,214 books available for public use.

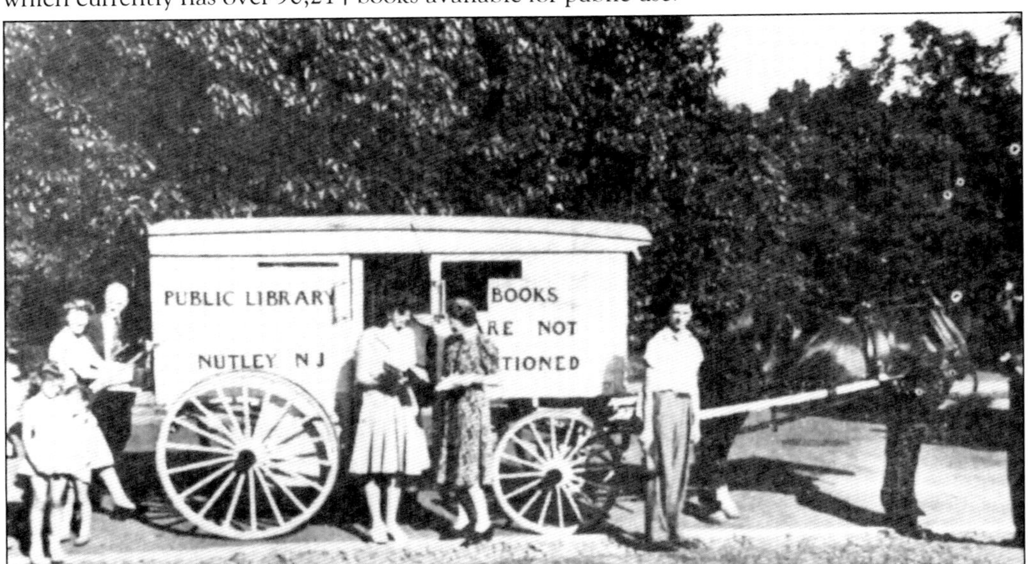

The Nutley Library developed a book wagon service for the town during the ban on pleasure driving, which occurred during World War II. The converted milk wagon would make a trip every Friday night from 5:30 to 8:30 pm to different areas of town. The cart was the delight of many children and was pulled by "Teddy the library horse."

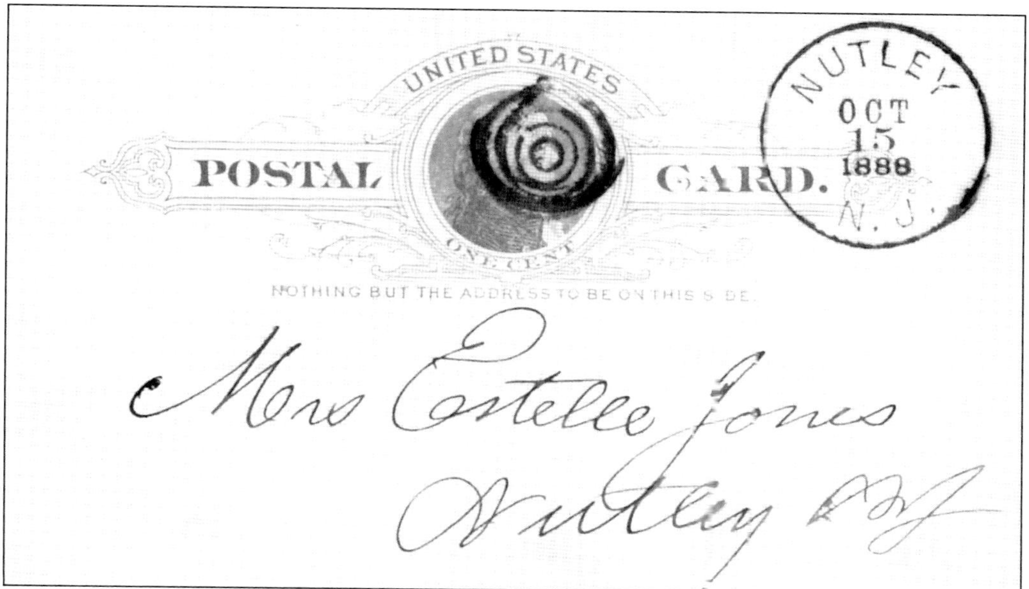

Mail service has been available in Nutley (Franklin) since 1849. A Congressional act on February 11, 1887, changed the cancellation stamp from Franklin to Nutley. It was fifteen years before the town would officially change its name to the same. This postcard is one of the oldest known examples of the new "Nutley" stamp cancellation. It is dated October 15, 1888.

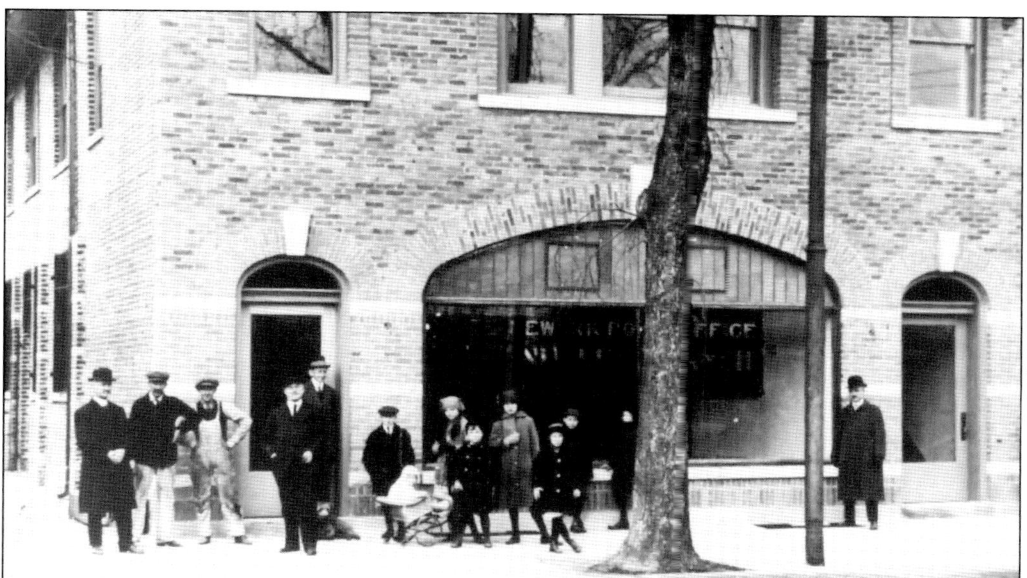

Pictured here is the Nutley Post Office, which was designed by William Lambert and built by his Nutley Realty Company in 1915. This branch was used until 1927, when Nutley's next post office was built at 383 Franklin Avenue. This building is now the Plaza Bootery at 483 Franklin Avenue.

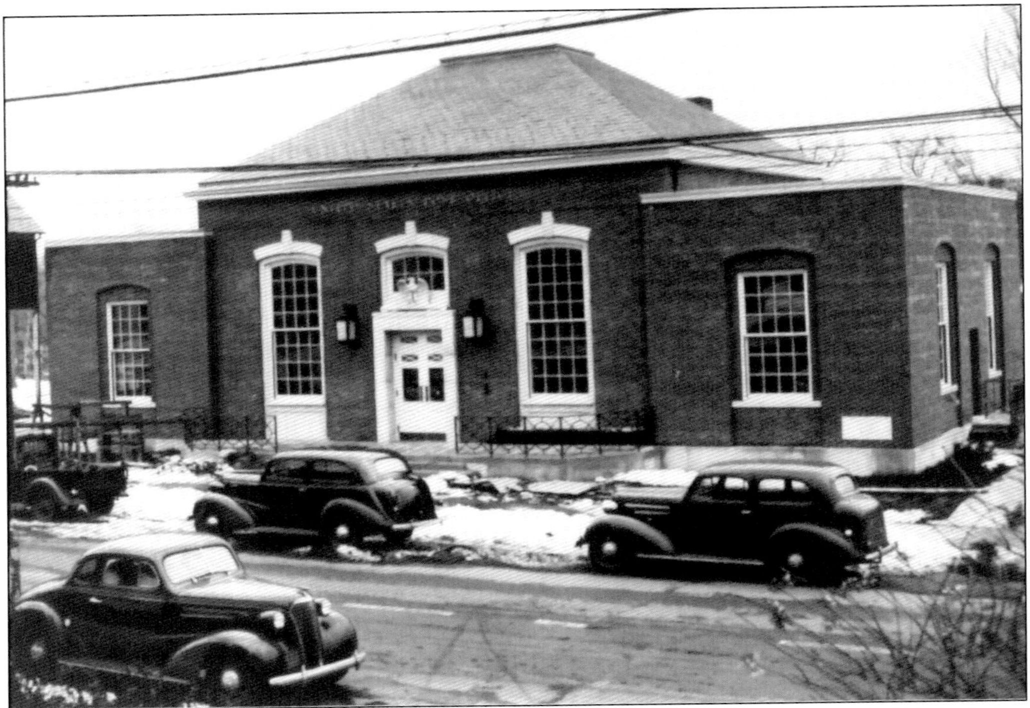

This street scene from the 1940s occurred outside the new post office building (constructed in 1940) on Franklin Avenue. The trolley tracks that once ran down the center of the street were gone by this time, as Nutley residents were increasingly using their own vehicles to get around town.

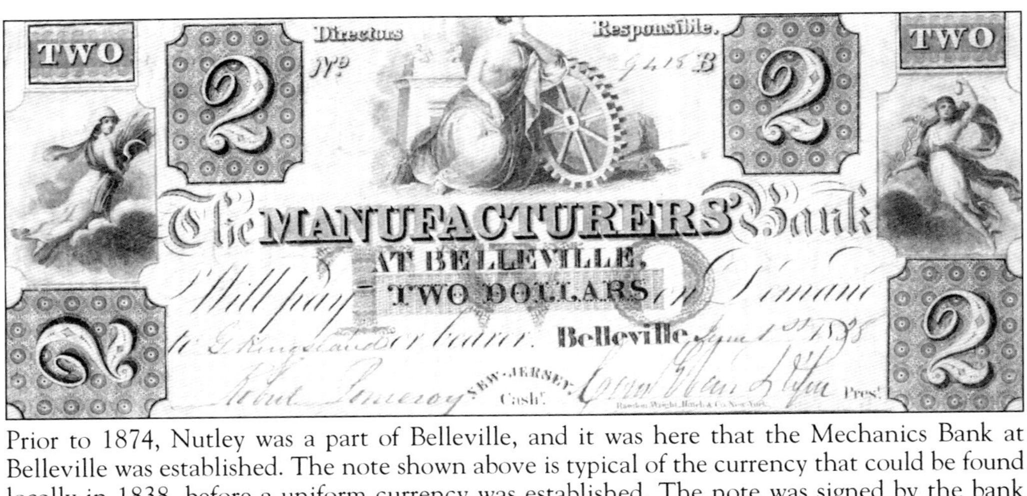

Prior to 1874, Nutley was a part of Belleville, and it was here that the Mechanics Bank at Belleville was established. The note shown above is typical of the currency that could be found locally in 1838, before a uniform currency was established. The note was signed by the bank representatives, as well as the receiver of the note, Mr. G. Kingsland.

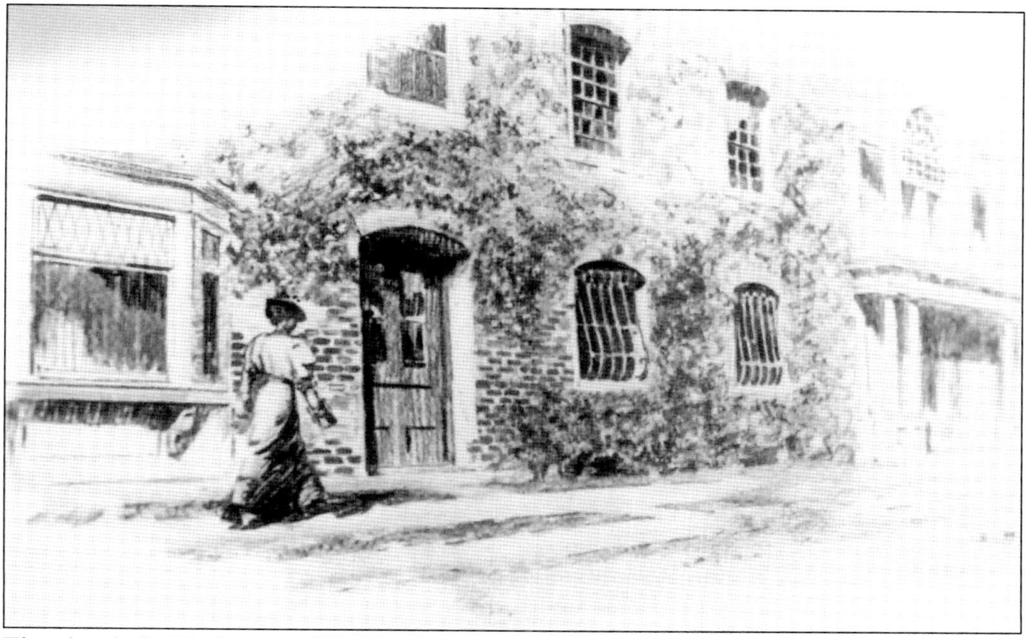

This sketch, by Nutley artist I.B. Hazelton, is of the Bank of Nutley when it was located at the town hall. Formed in 1906, the bank's first president was Bird W. Spencer. As revenues grew, a proposal was made to find a more suitable structure for banking purposes.

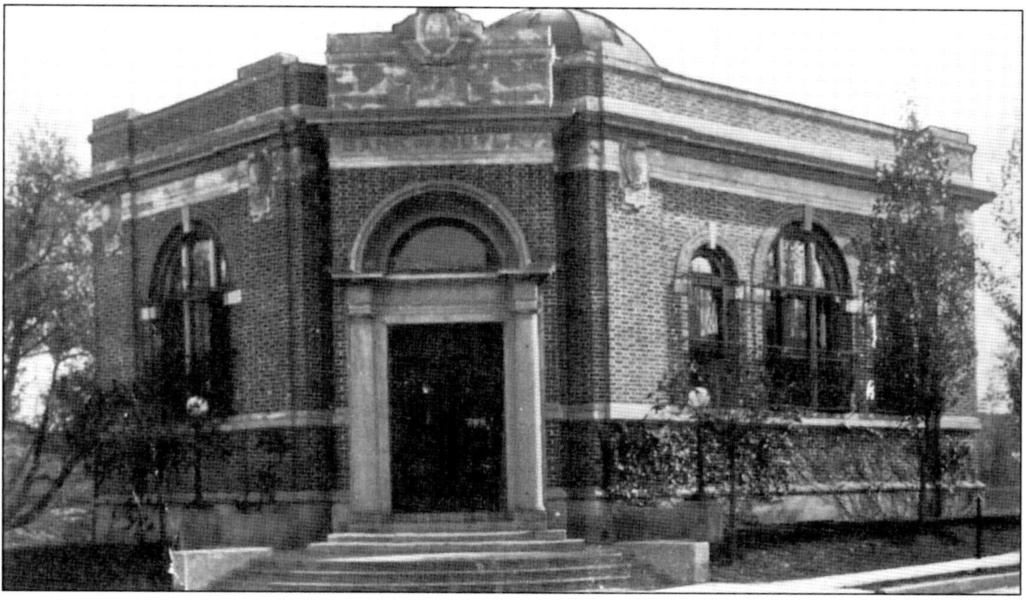

In 1910, the Bank of Nutley moved into its newly constructed building on the corner of Chestnut Street and Vincent Place. It conducted business here for sixteen years before moving again. This building also housed the offices of the *Nutley Sun* for a time and is today an ophthalmologist's office.

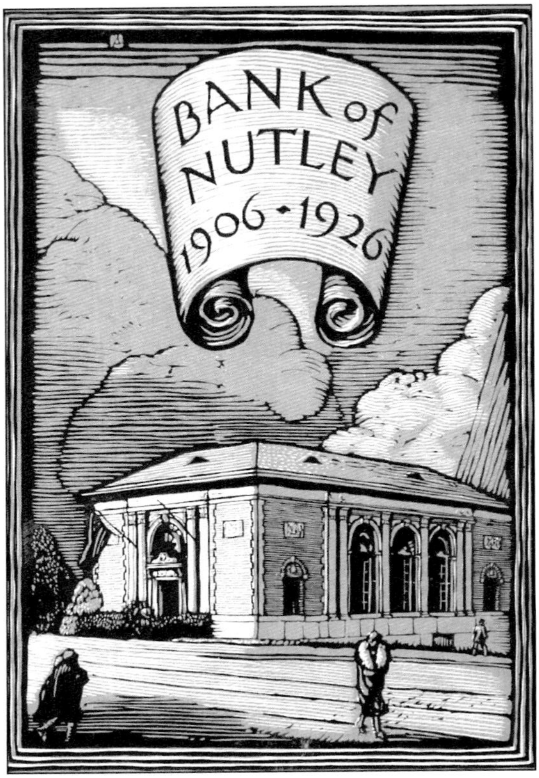

After the house on the corner of Franklin Avenue and Chestnut Street was moved, the Bank of Nutley built a new facility in 1926. The new building cost $149,000, and the bank had resources of over $3,334,500. This book was a promotional item issued by the bank in 1926.

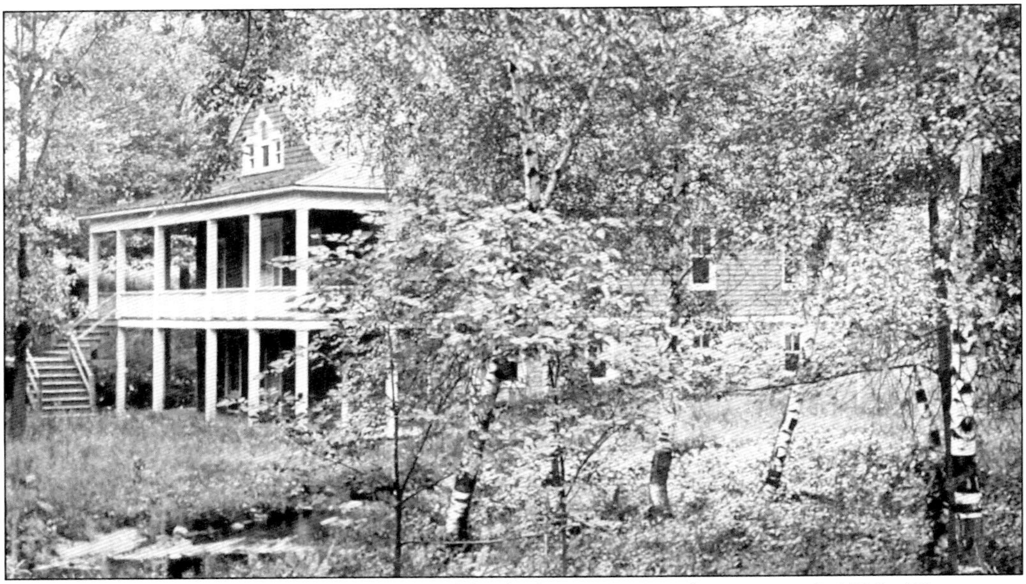

The Fortnightly Club was designed and built by W.A. Lambert around 1900. The group was organized in 1898 and held bi-monthly dances and bowling games. As the interest in dancing faded, the club was used for social events, billiards, and card games. The building also served as Saint Paul's parish house and most recently as the Italian American Club at 640 Franklin Avenue.

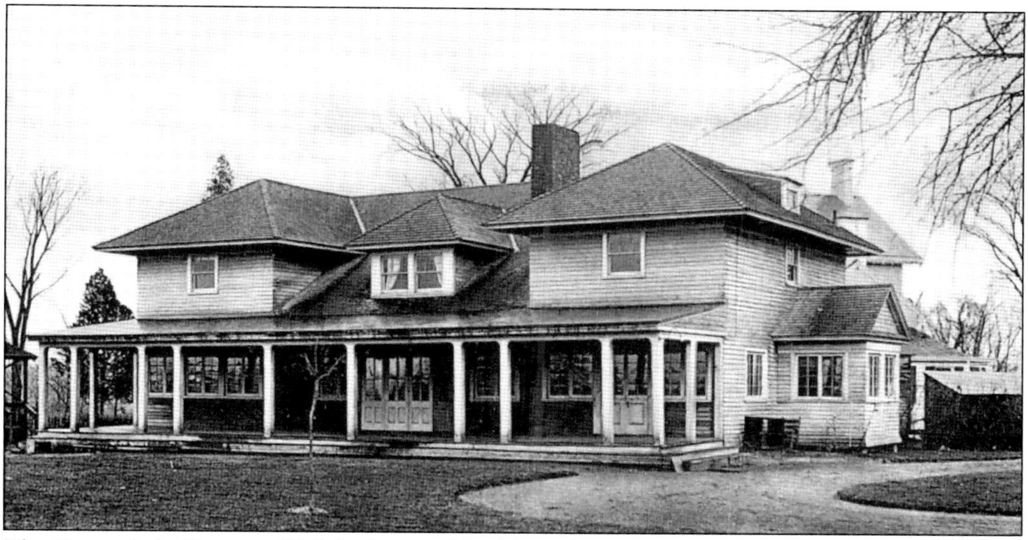

The Yountakah Country Club had several buildings located on the grounds during its hey-day. This is one of the club buildings located on the former ITT property on River Road. Many club and town events were held at the clubhouse.

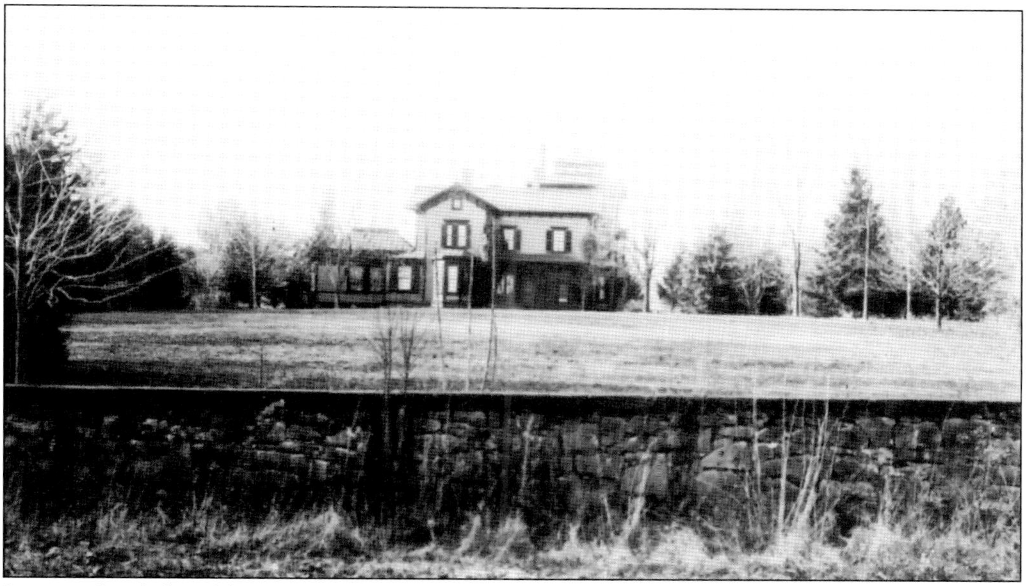

Just north of the old Nutley manor house was this large home known as the Larkin house. An 1890 map shows that the land around this mansion was known as "Meadowside." Both the Nutley manor and the Larkin house were part of the Satterthwaite estate (on the former ITT property) in 1890. The Larkin house was later used as a clubhouse for the Yountakah Country Club.

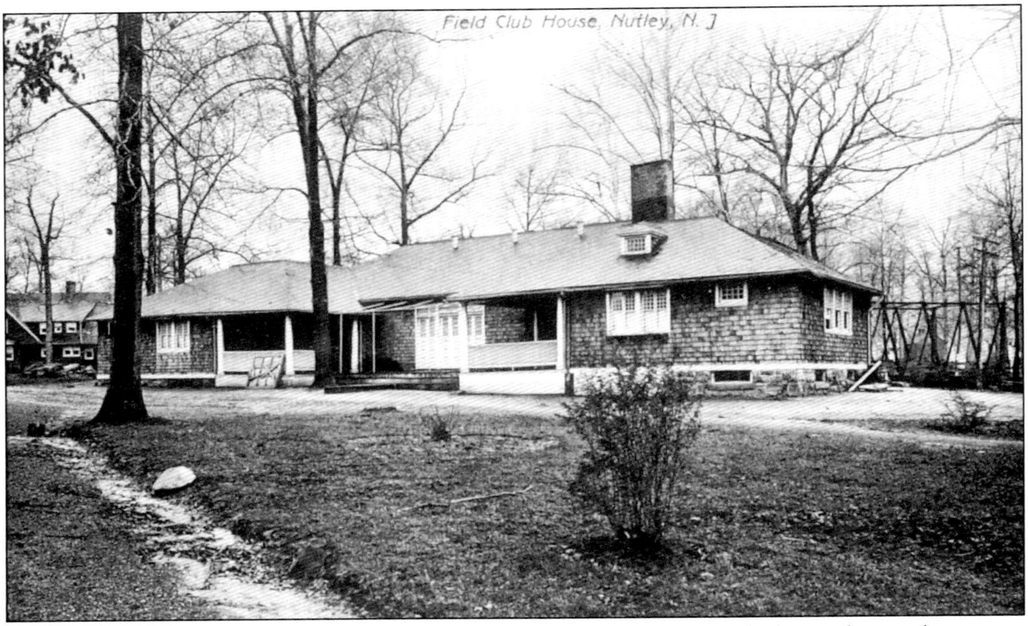

Another popular organization around town was the Nutley Field Club, located near the corner of Nutley Avenue and Tennis Place. John Vernou Bouvier Jr., the grandfather of Jacqueline Bouvier Kennedy Onassis, was a past president of this club.

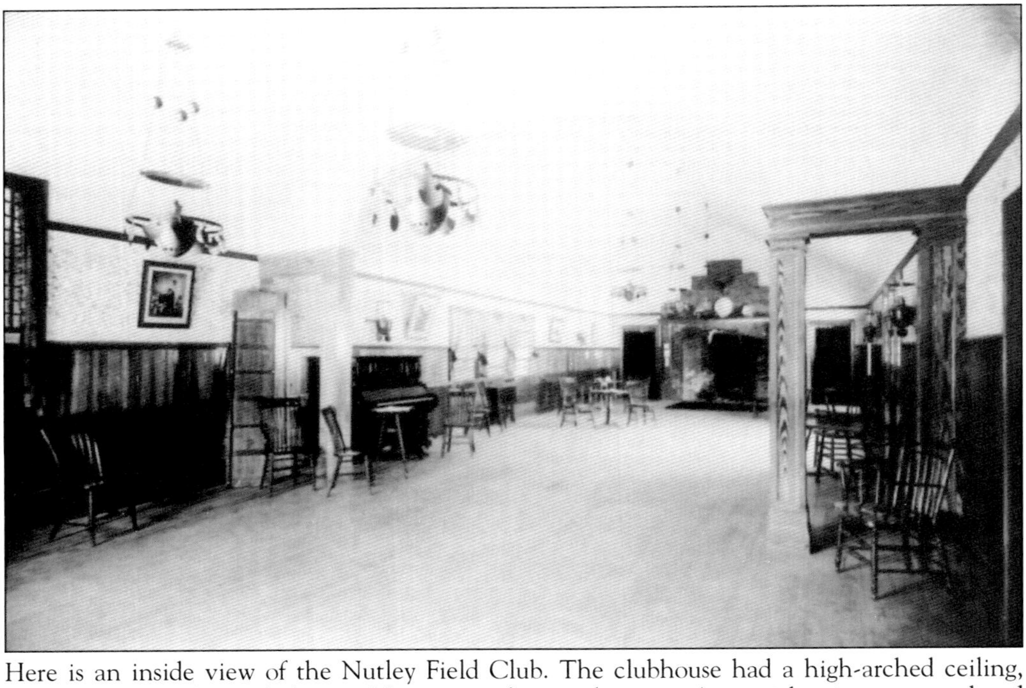

Here is an inside view of the Nutley Field Club. The clubhouse had a high-arched ceiling, wood-paneled walls, and plenty of floor space for social events. An upright piano was on hand for musical entertainment, and a grand fireplace provided heat and atmosphere.

Three

Fire and Brimstone

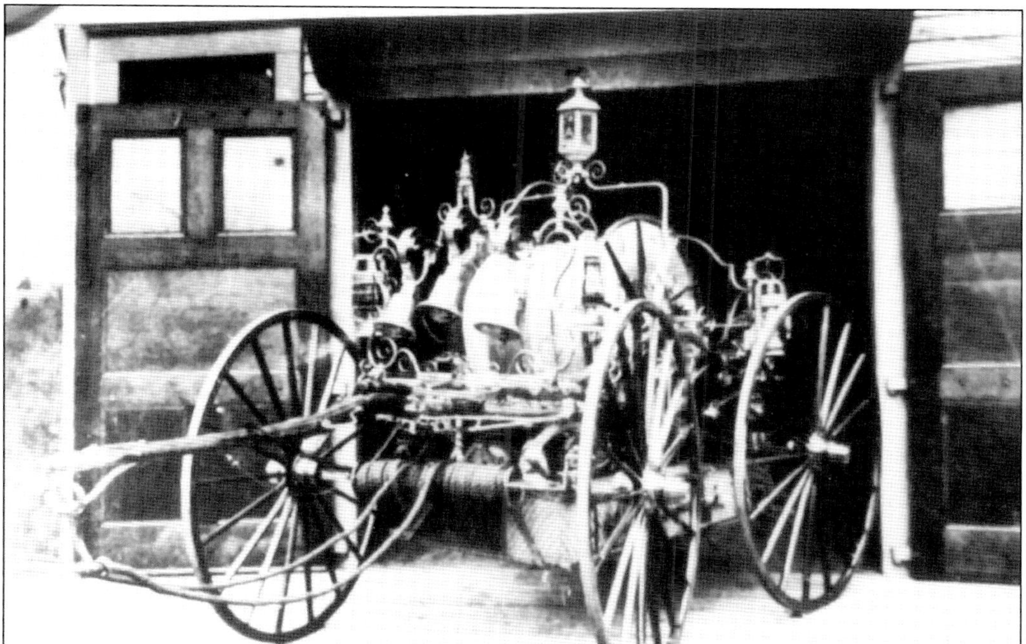

This hose cart was obtained by Yantacaw Hose and Truck Company in 1894. It was built in 1865 and was used by several other towns before being purchased by Nutley. It took six men to pull the cart, with another riding the step brake at the rear. The company also had a horse-drawn chemical wagon.

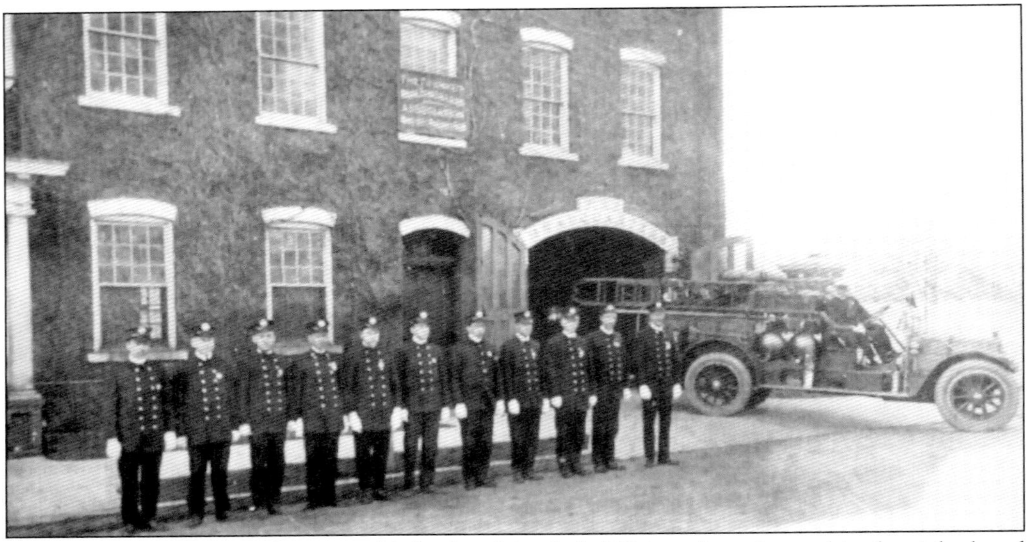

Yantacaw Hose and Truck was established on March 5, 1894, and was housed in the right-hand side of the town hall. It received the first motorized fire vehicle in Nutley on February 8, 1911. The truck was built by the Pope Hartford Company, and was considered top of the line for the day. It even had specific design changes made by Nutley fireman Harry Stager.

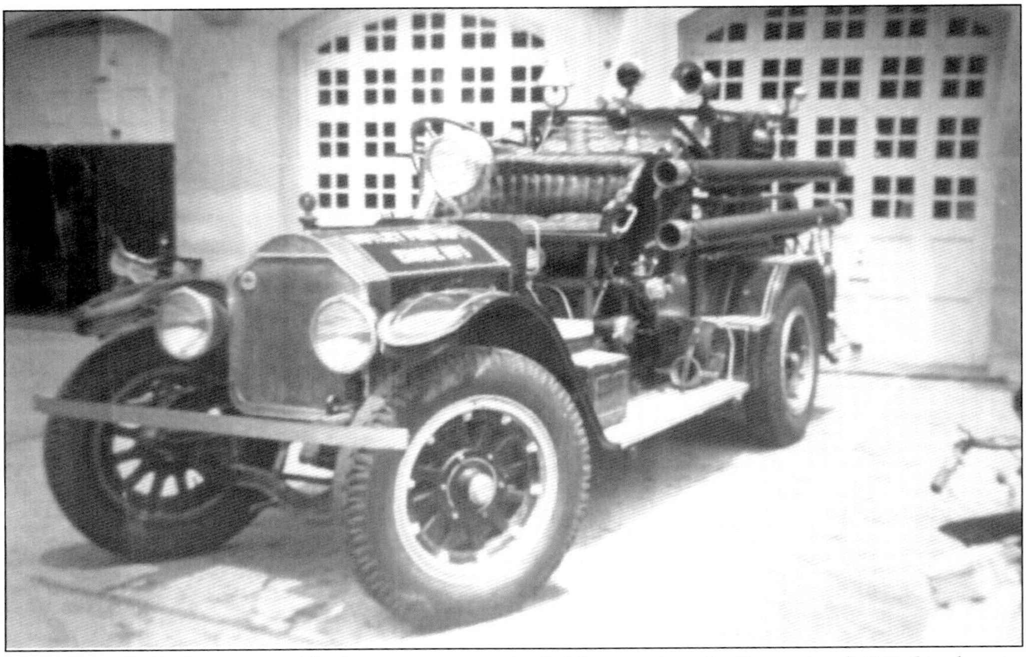

By 1925, all firehouses in Nutley were motorized. Hoses #1 and #2 received R.E.O. chassis, to which their old horse-drawn trucks were adapted. Yantacaw took possession of the 1924 American La France pumper truck shown here. Nutley now had a fully modernized fire department.

This little booklet was printed by the W.C. Ryan Press of Nutley. It contained the bylaws for the hose company. In 1896, the equipment of that company included one hose cart with cover, three wrenches, one play pipe, 75 feet of rope, two lanterns, and two cranks for the reel. The company consisted of two officers and twenty-four men.

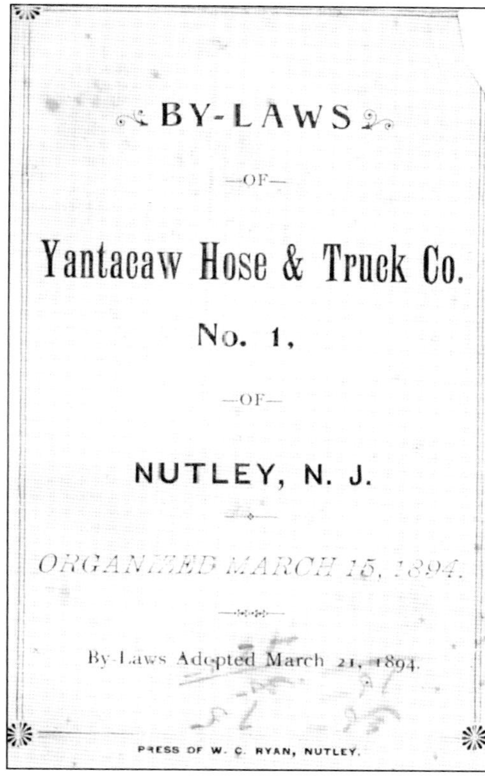

BY-LAWS

—OF—

Yantacaw Hose & Truck Co.

No. 1,

—OF—

NUTLEY, N. J.

ORGANIZED MARCH 15, 1894.

By-Laws Adopted March 21, 1894.

PRESS OF W. C. RYAN, NUTLEY.

Avondale Hook and Ladder Company was formed in 1895 to better serve the east side of town. They were first located out of a barn on Weston Street and had no meeting place of their own until their present firehouse on Park Avenue was built in 1898. This 1911 photograph shows the men of the company with their two-horsepower hose-and-ladder cart.

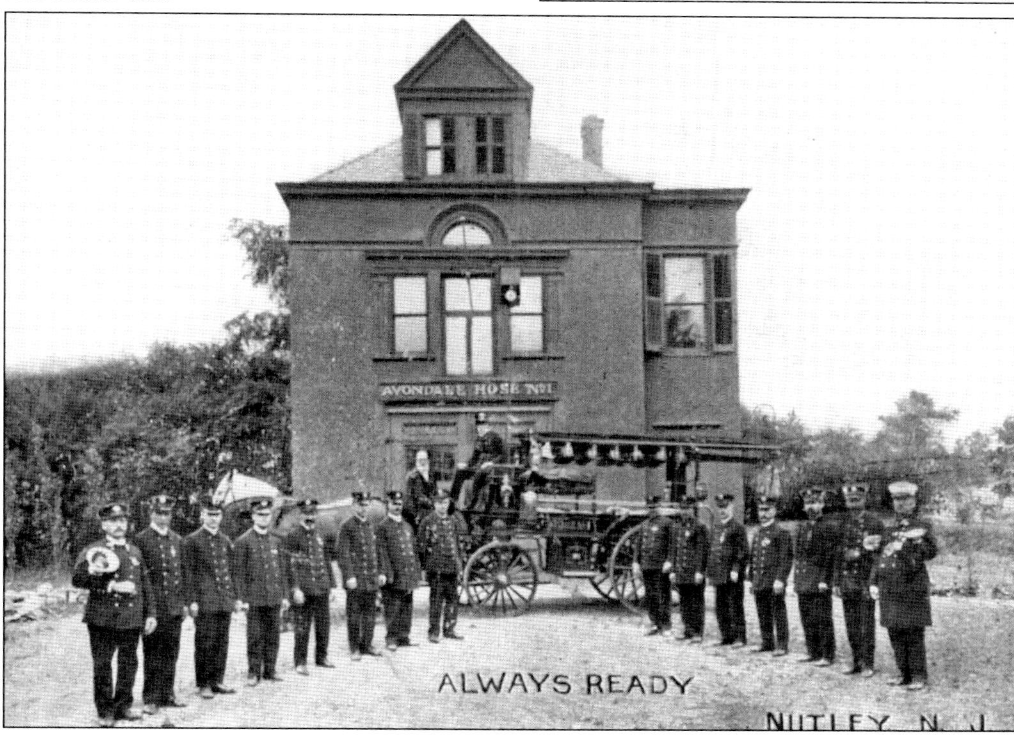

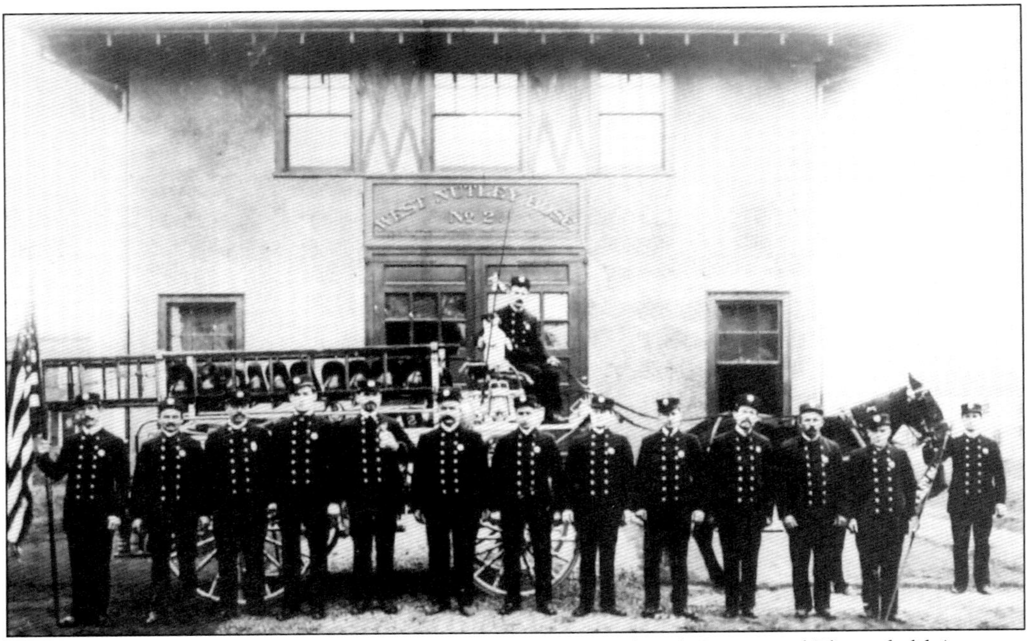

West Nutley Hose #2 was formed in 1909, near the corner of High Street and Bloomfield Avenue, the year before Nutley would order its first motorized fire engine. In 1912, the company's name was changed to Hose #2.

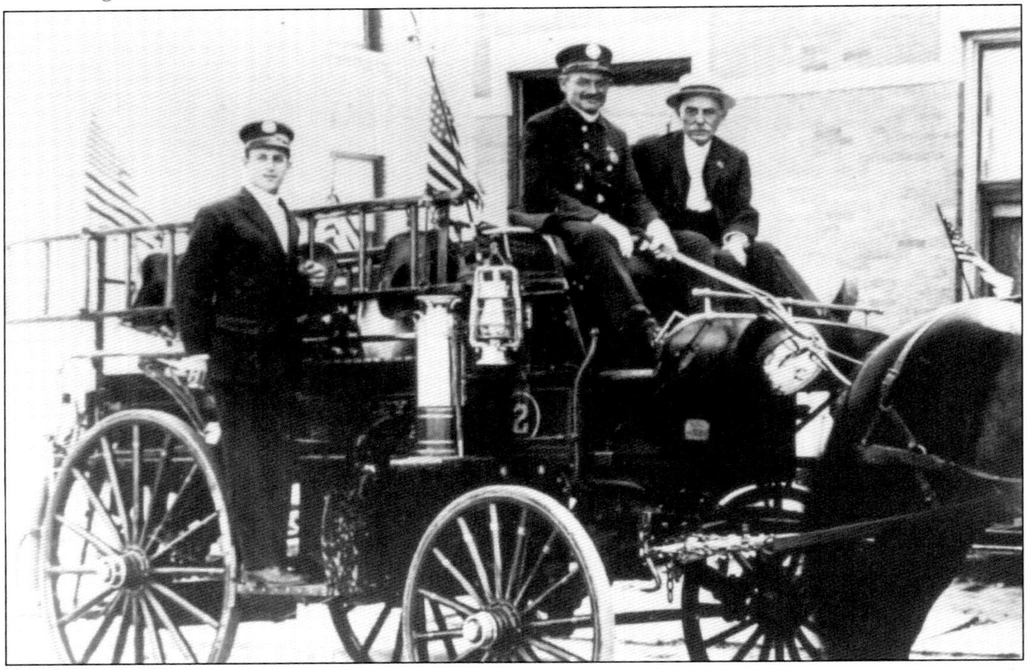

In 1912, the town changed to the commission form of government. In this *c.* 1912 photograph are, from left to right, Ellsworth Post, Abram Paxton, and Abram Blum (the first mayor under the new town government). Mr. Blum was also a charter member of Yantacaw Hose and Truck in 1894. The cart in this picture belonged to Hose #2.

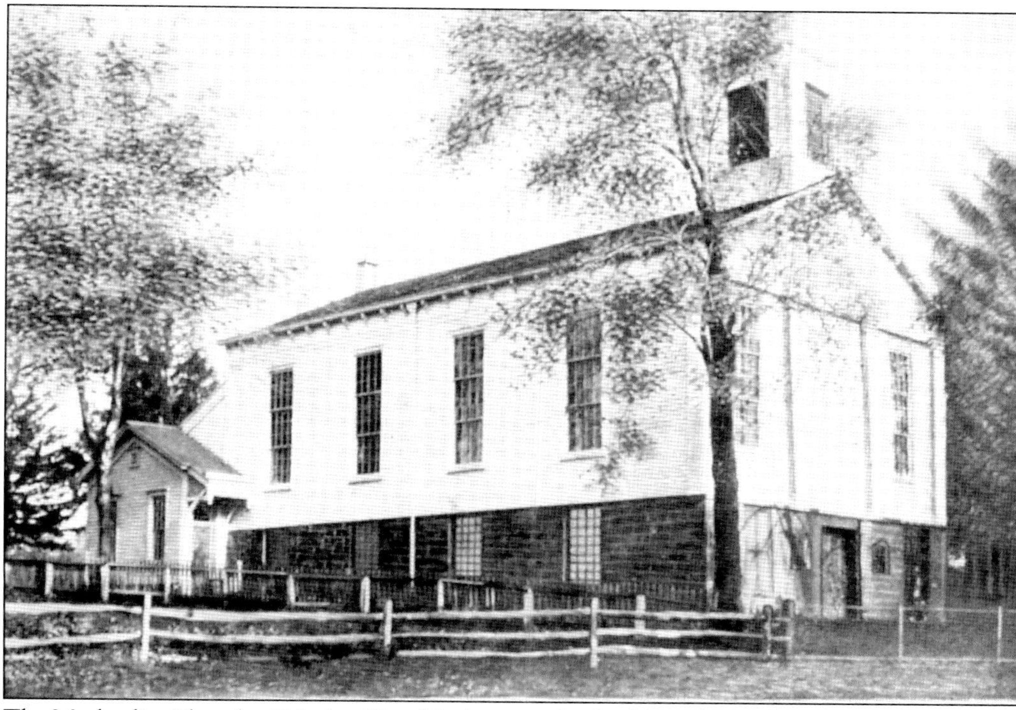

The Methodist Church of Nutley (Franklin) was in this building, located at Passaic Avenue near Oakridge Avenue, c. 1853. In 1910, services were held in the newly built Vincent Methodist Church, on Vincent Place. This building was sold to Reilly's Dairy and was used as a barn for his cows.

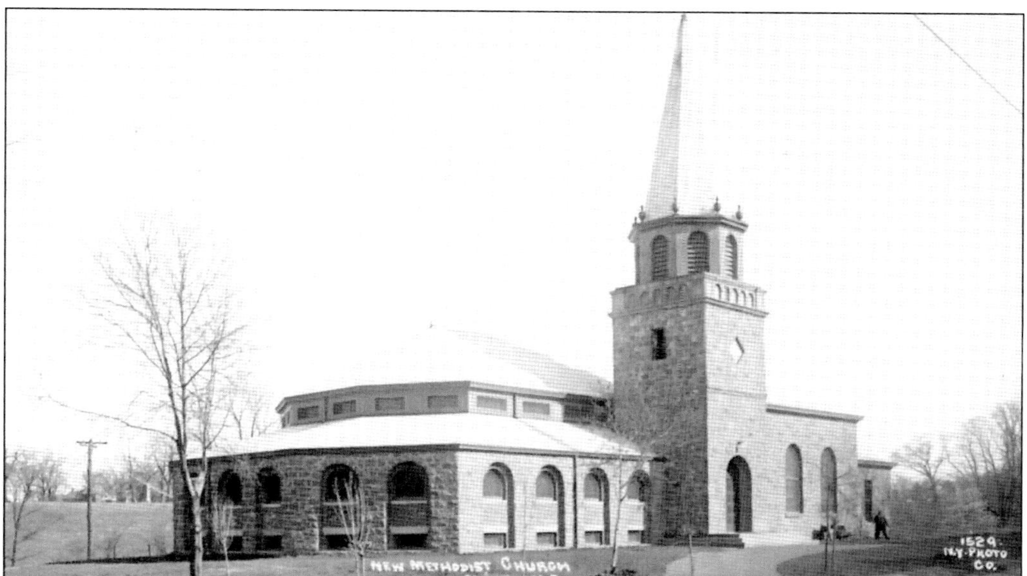

The ground-breaking for the new Vincent Methodist Church took place on January 6, 1909. The church replaced the old Stitts (Yantico) Mill building. In 1930, work was completed on the three-story educational building in the rear.

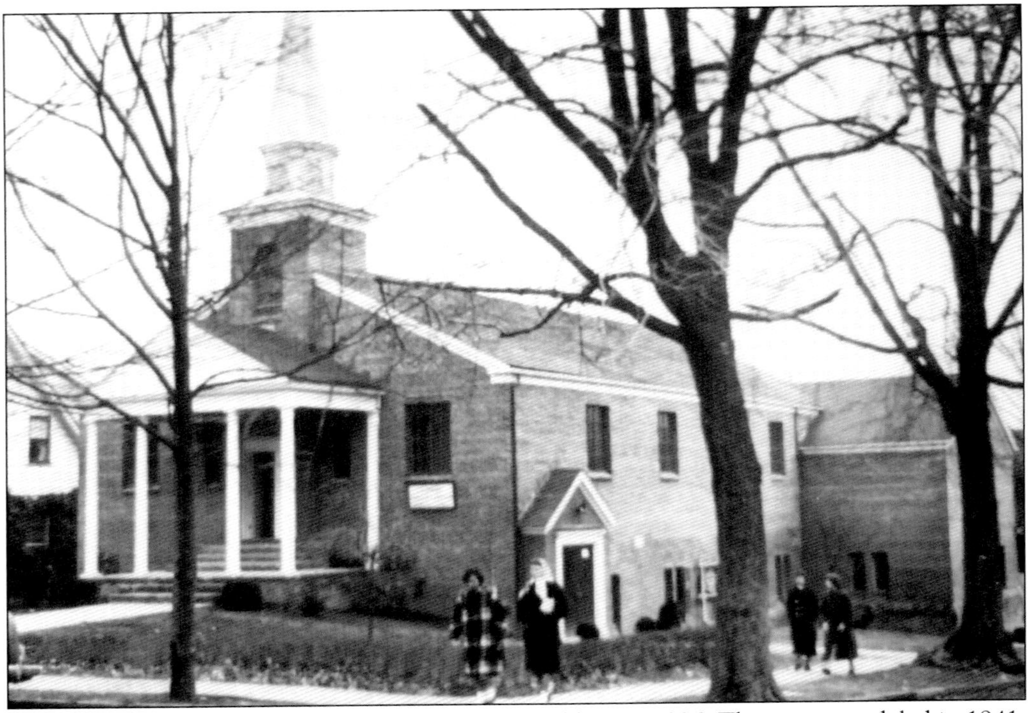

Holy Trinity Lutheran Church built a basement building in 1926. This was remodeled in 1941, but for the most part it still remained a "basement" church. In 1949, funds were obtained, and the roof of the church was jacked up high enough to complete a main floor in between the basement and roof.

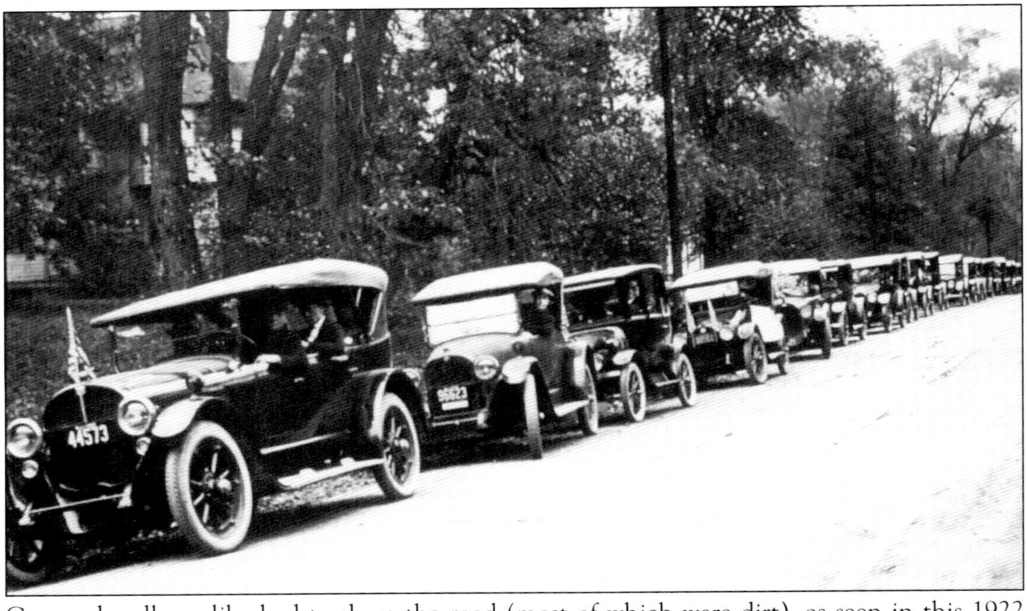

Cars and trolleys alike had to share the road (most of which were dirt), as seen in this 1922 photograph of Auto Sunday by members of Saint Paul's Congregational Church. It was the automobile and bus that would soon lead to the demise of the trolley line.

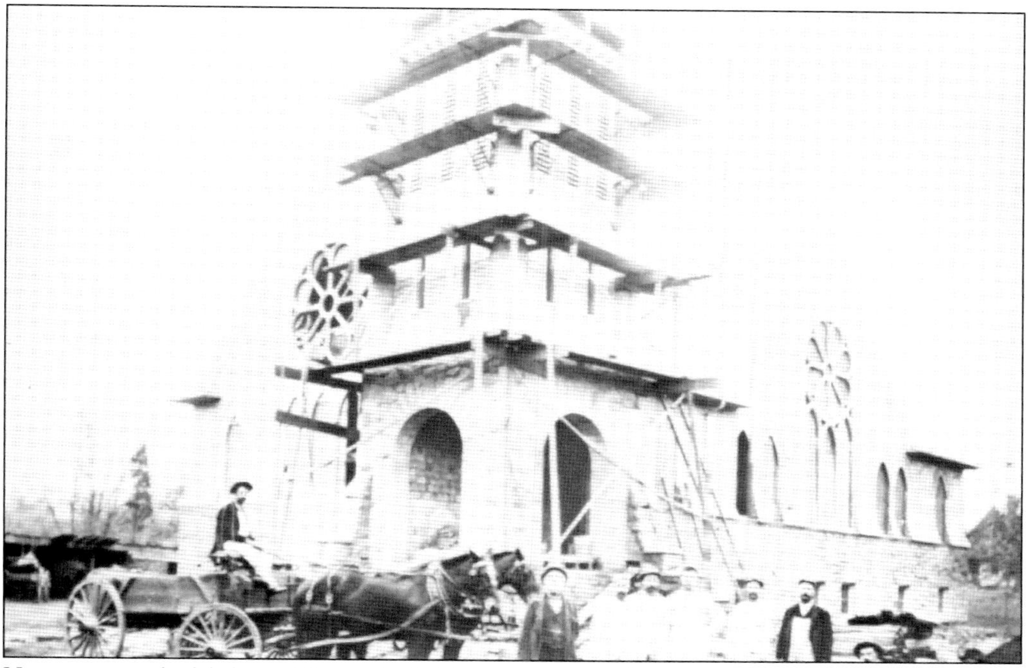

Here is a wonderful shot of Saint Paul's Congregational Church just prior to its completion in 1898. Designed by William Lambert when he was just twenty-seven years old, Saint Paul's filled the need for a church to serve the people on the northwest side of town.

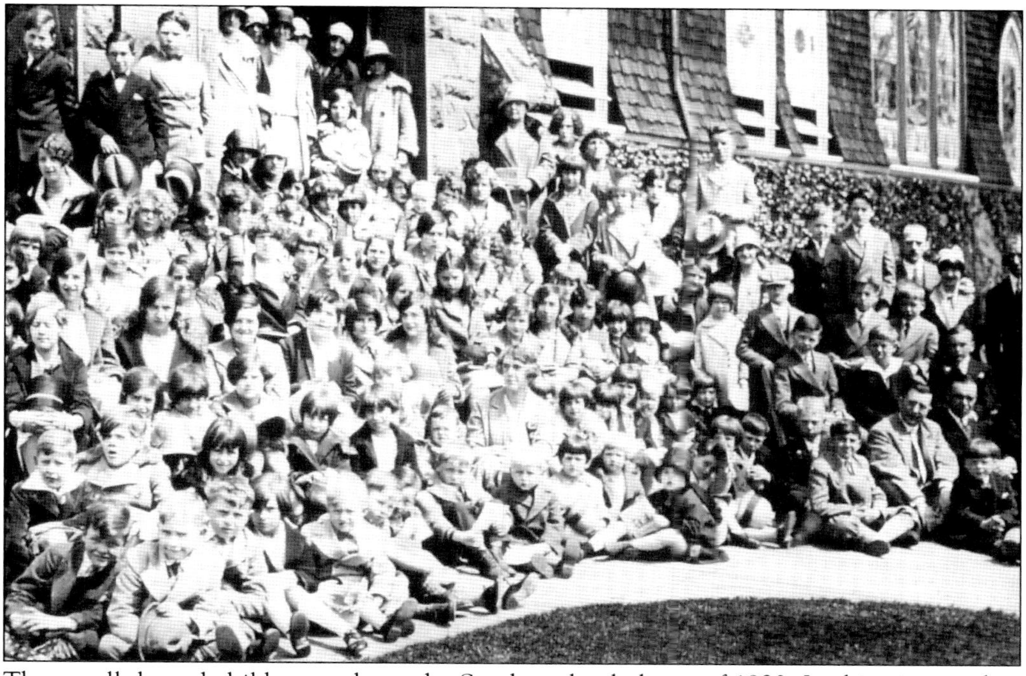

These well-dressed children made up the Sunday school classes of 1930. In this picture, they are seated outside of Saint Paul's Church. There were tough times ahead for the country and for little towns like Nutley during the Great Depression, which was just beginning.

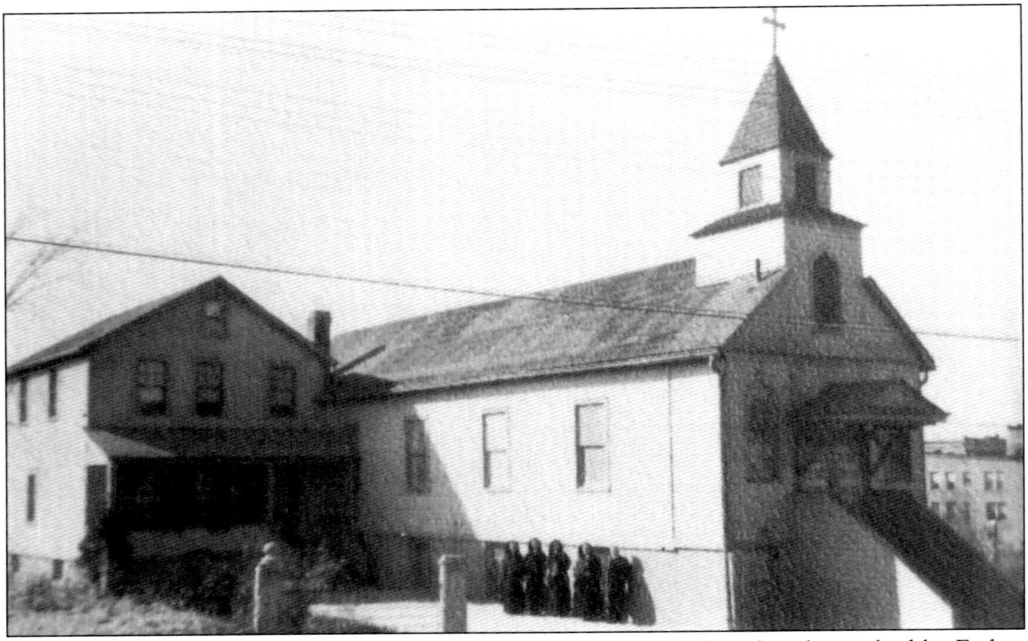

In 1911, the cornerstone of the first Holy Family Roman Catholic Church was laid by Father James P. Smith of Belleville. The building, still standing at 115 Harrison Street, could only hold 140 people. The church moved to its next location on Brookline Avenue in 1938. Its current church was built in 1965.

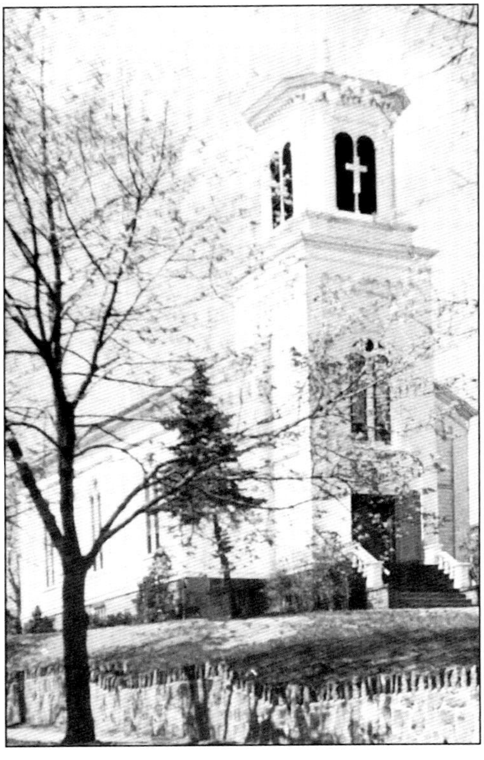

The Franklin Reformed Church was built in 1861, on land donated by Henry Stager in 1859. Prior to this, Sunday school and church services were held on the second floor of the wooden School #5, across the street. The school was burned down and rebuilt in brick in 1875. The new brick school eventually became what is now the town museum.

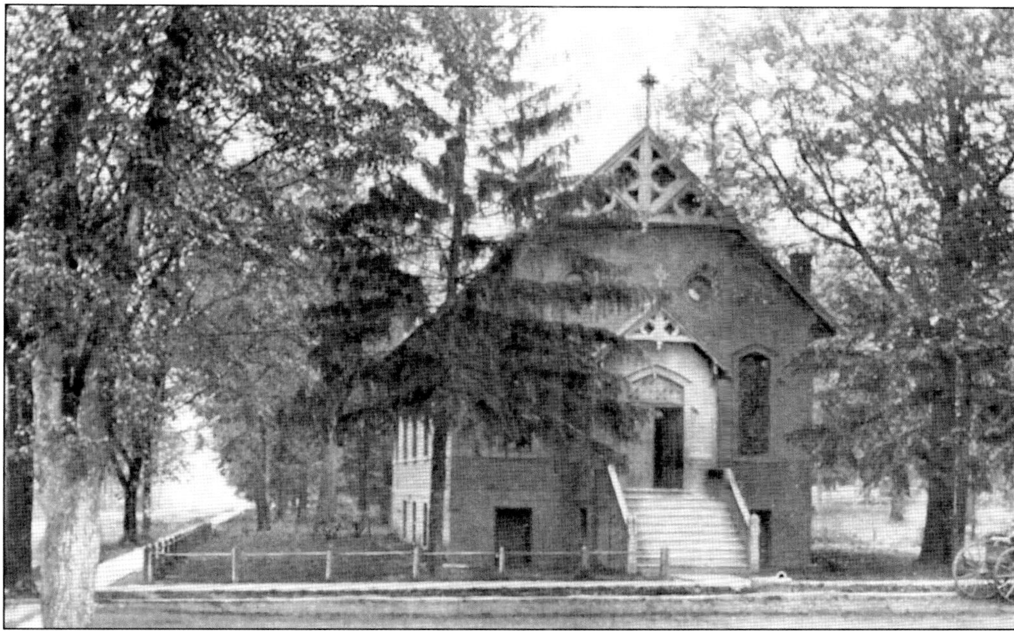

The original Grace Church was a small wooden building built on the northeast corner of Grant and Whitford Avenues, *c.* 1873. In 1908, plans were made to erect a new, larger stone church at the corner of Highfield Lane and North Road.

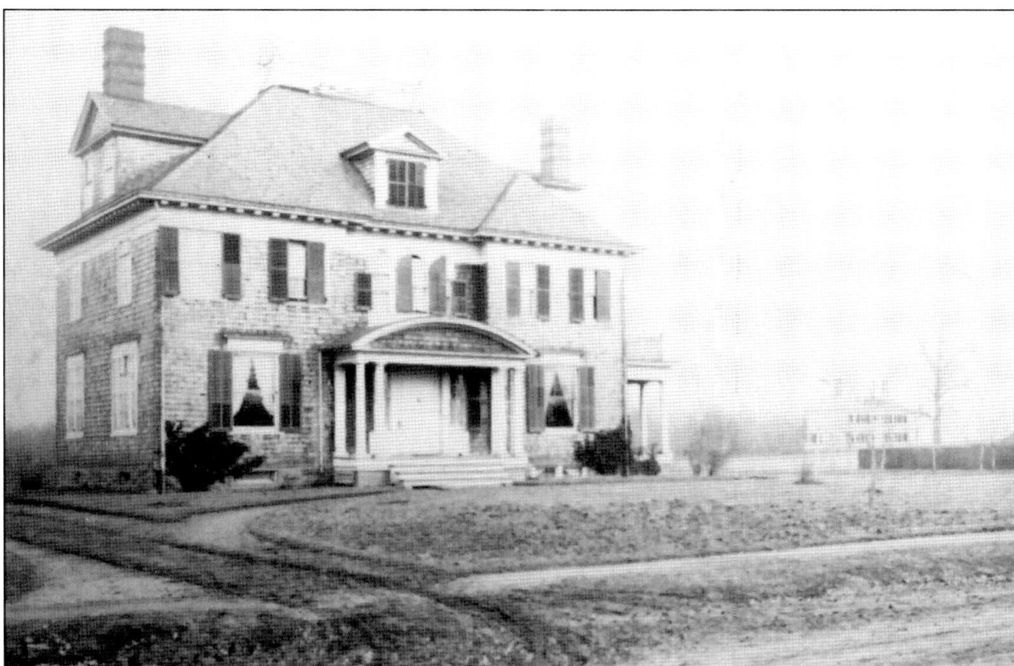

This is an early view of 204 Highfield Lane looking northeast, toward North Road. When Grace Episcopal Church decided to build a new church building, the spot to the right of this house was chosen. The house was purchased with the land and became the rectory.

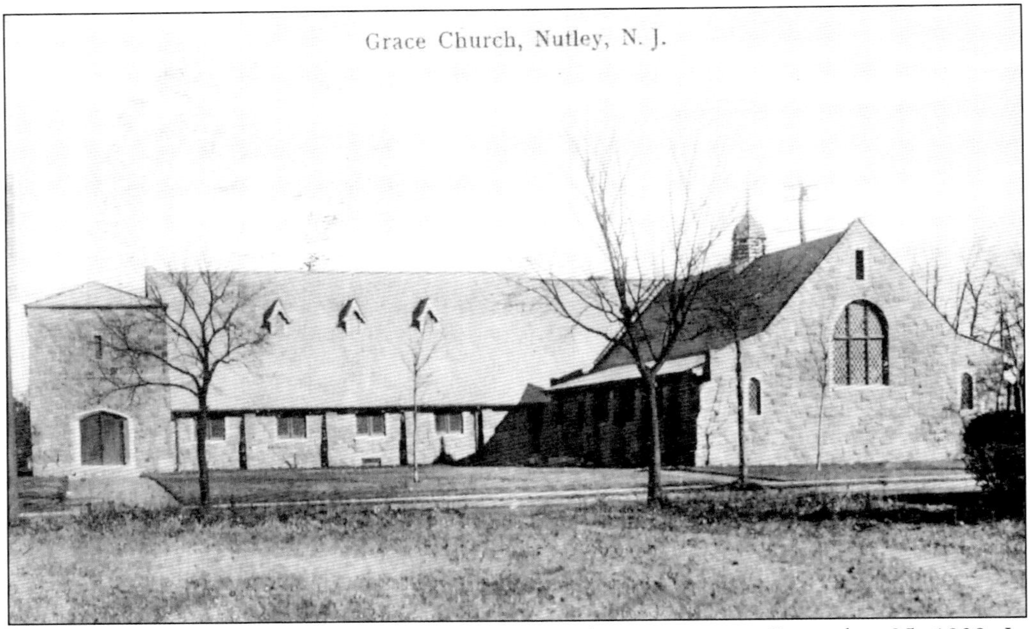

Grace Church, which is still in use today, held its first services on December 25, 1908. In 1923, enough money was acquired to add the spire and tower, giving the church its current appearance. A fire in 1925 damaged a good portion of the church building and roof; fortunately, everything was covered by insurance.

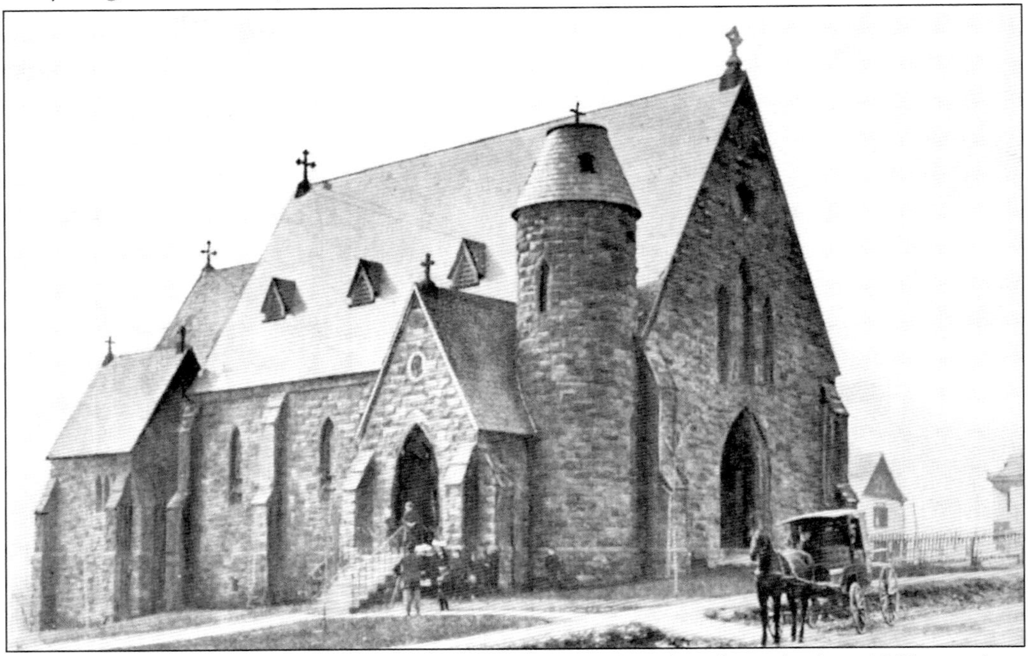

The first Saint Mary's (Our Lady of Grace) Roman Catholic Church was built in 1872 as a place of worship for the Irish and Italian quarry workers. The land and brownstone were donated by Mr. and Mrs. William Joyce, whose quarries were on the east side of Washington Avenue near Park Avenue.

Four

Street Views; Around Town

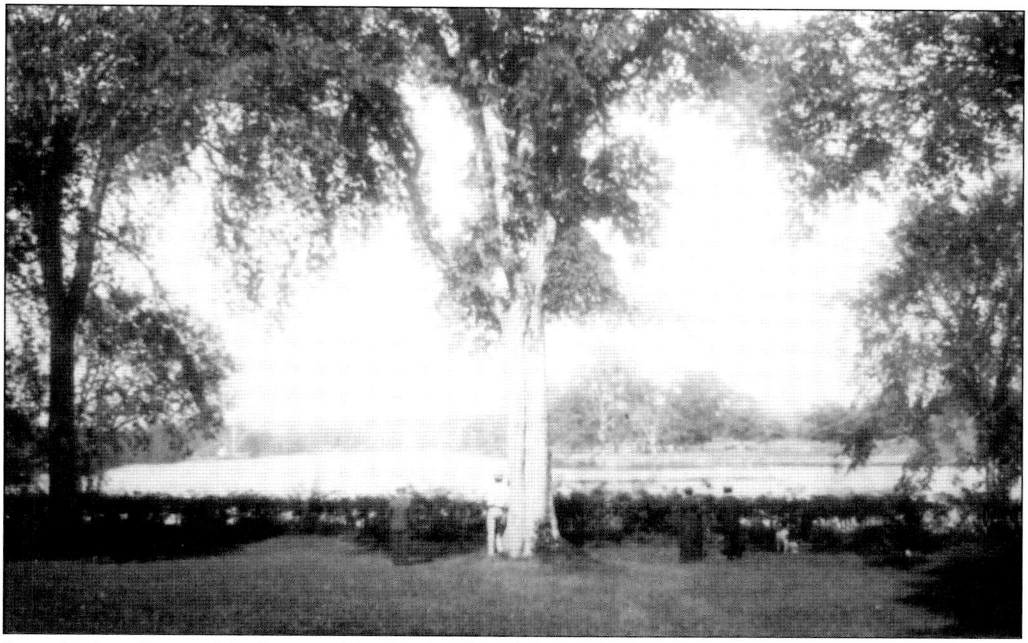

Long before Route 21, this is what the banks of the Passaic River looked like in Nutley. It was not uncommon to go for a walk or picnic along the lush green areas near the river. Boating on the river was also a relaxing way to spend the day.

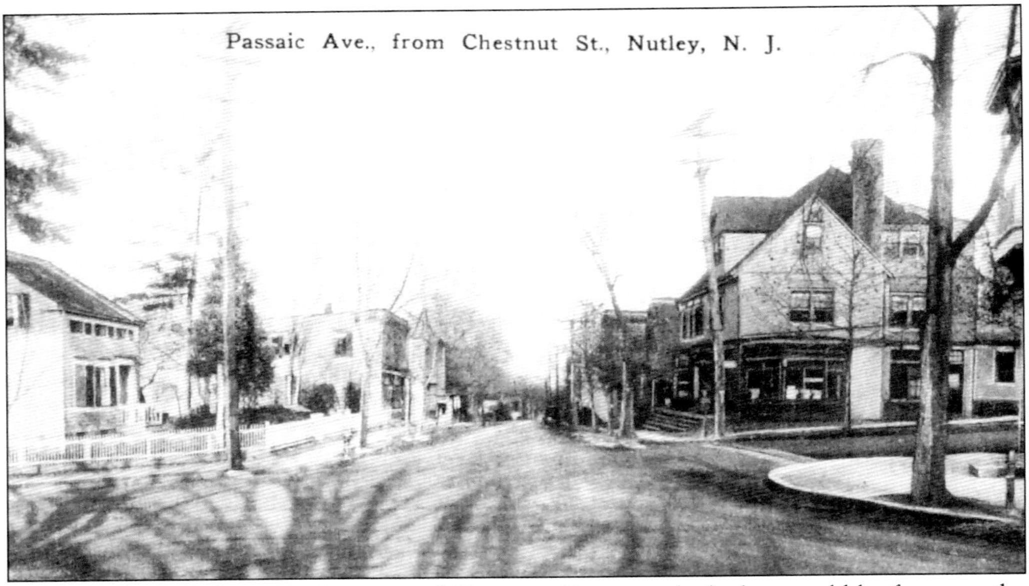

The four corners of Passaic Avenue and Chestnut Street marked what would be for years the business center of town. Stores and businesses congregated in this area, which was within walking distance of the Nutley (Stitts) Train Station. It was the coming of the trolley and the decision not to let it pass on Passaic Avenue that led to the relocation of the commercial district to Franklin Avenue.

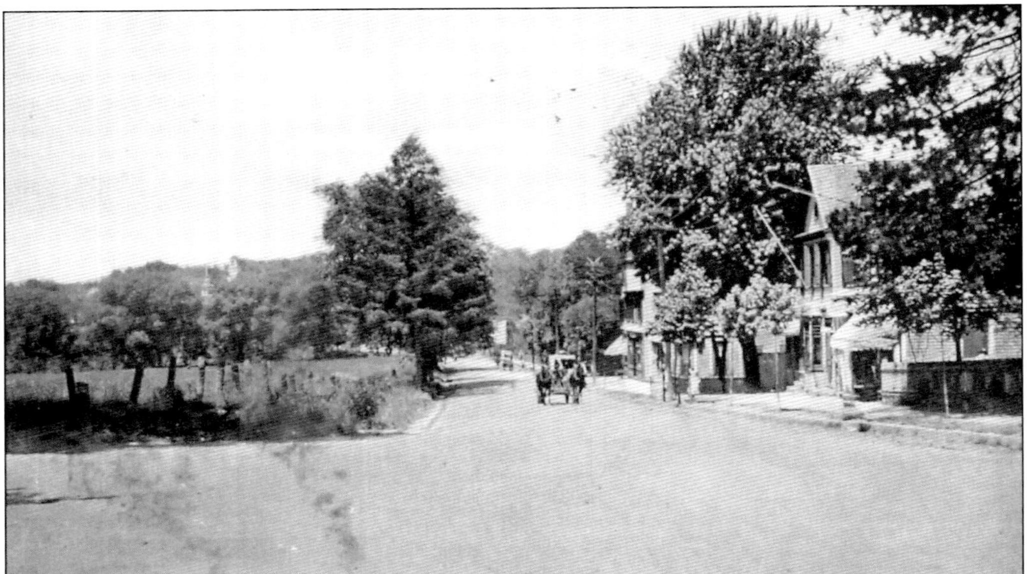

This c. 1915 view looks west onto Chestnut Street from Passaic Avenue. The whole southwest corner was empty and was occasionally visited by Mr. Stirratt's cow to graze. The cupola of the town hall and the Franklin Reformed Church can be seen faintly in the background.

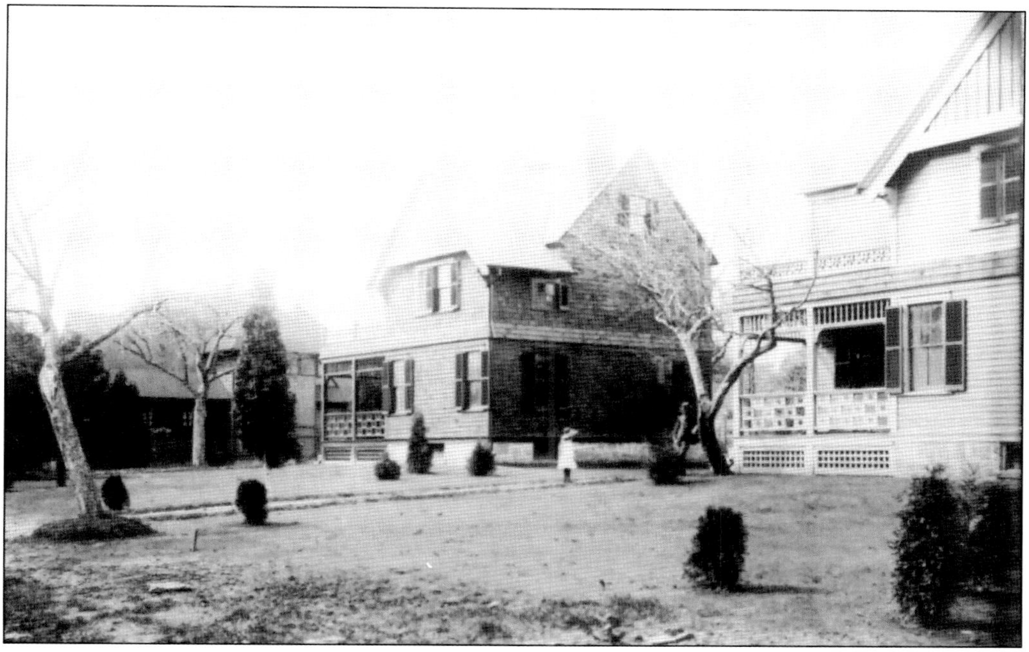

Before Franklin Avenue was a thriving business center, it was a quiet residential area, especially north of the Franklin Avenue trestle where this *c.* 1895 shot was taken. The houses shown, from left to right, are numbers 653, 661, and 665; all of them are being used as commercial properties today.

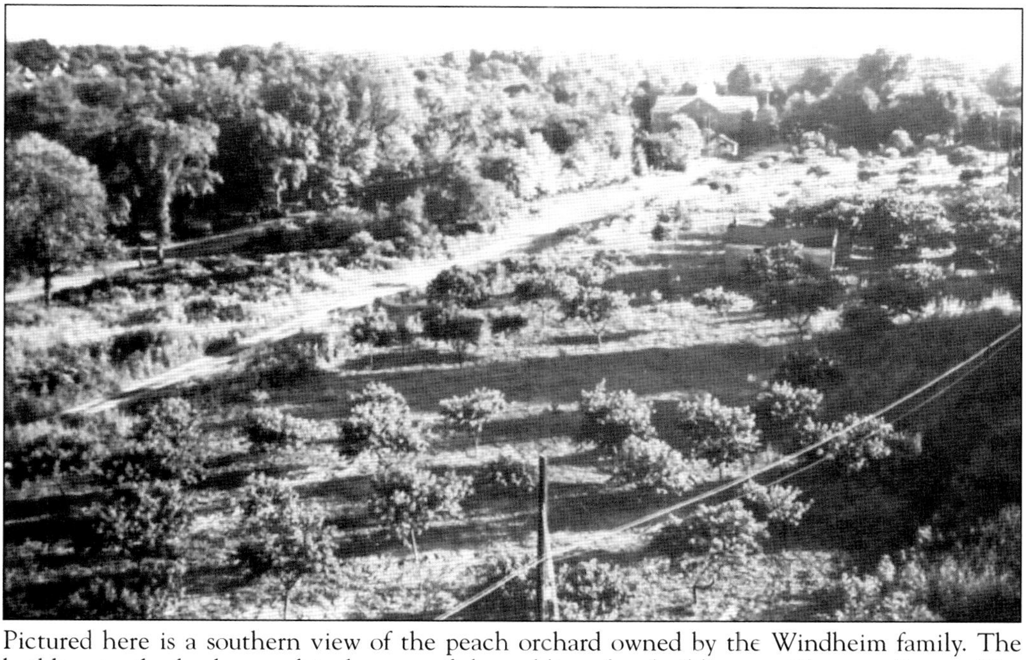

Pictured here is a southern view of the peach orchard owned by the Windheim family. The building in the background is the rear of the public safety building on Chestnut Street. The road leading up to the building is Warren Street. The land has since been developed with a large apartment complex covering most of this area.

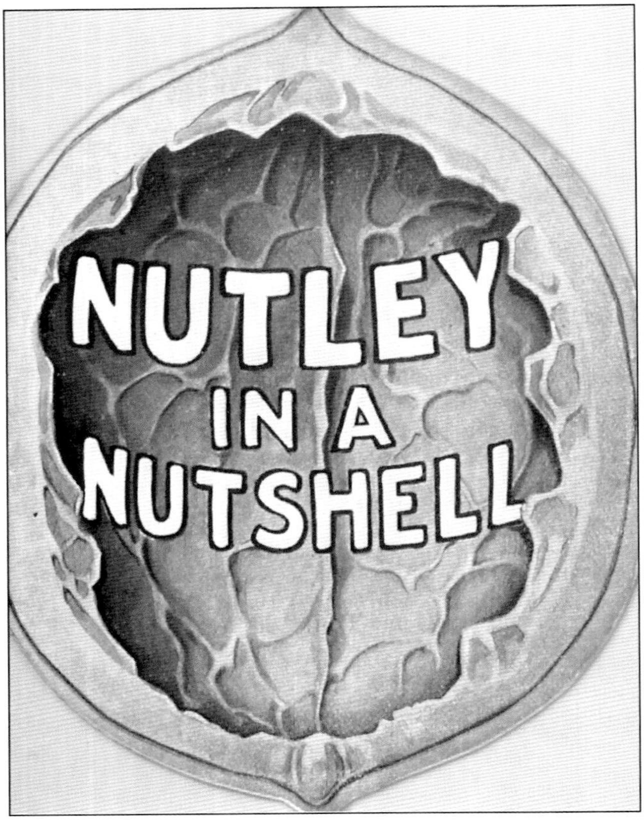

This was one of the more interesting sales techniques used by the Nutley Realty Company. "Nutley in a nutshell" was a sales brochure distributed at the realty company's sales offices at Nutley and New York. This large version is from 1916, when the population was around 8,500.

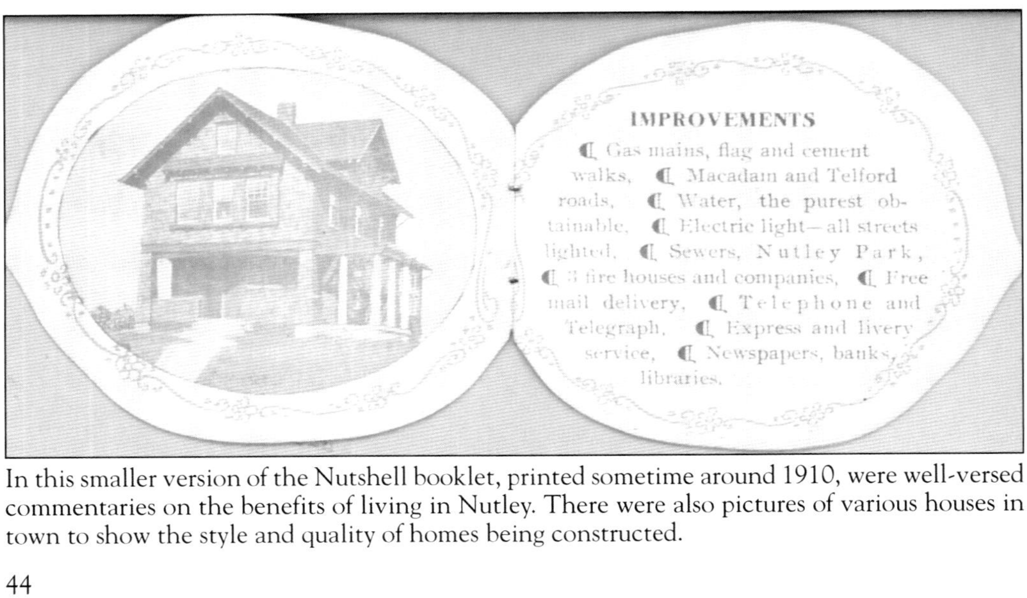

In this smaller version of the Nutshell booklet, printed sometime around 1910, were well-versed commentaries on the benefits of living in Nutley. There were also pictures of various houses in town to show the style and quality of homes being constructed.

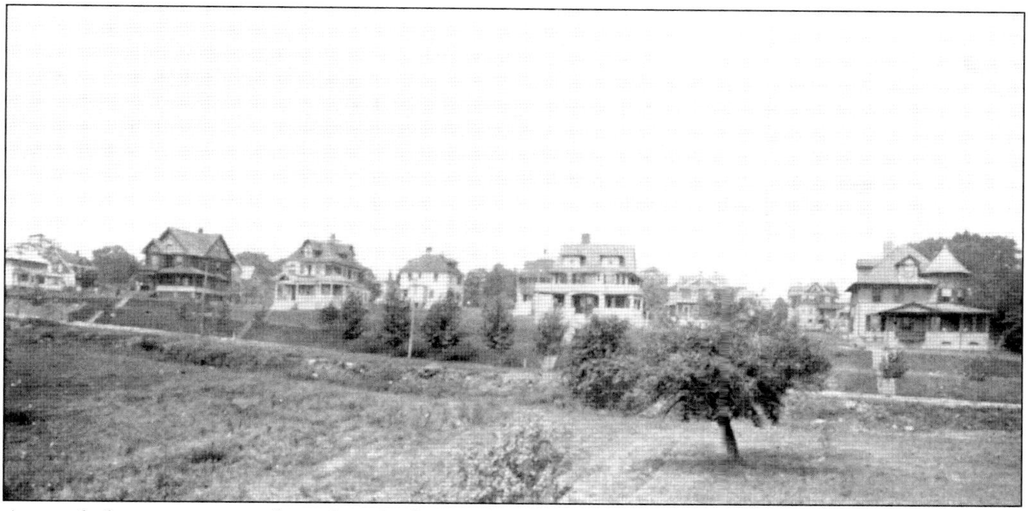

Around the same time that the Nutley Park section was being developed, the west side of Franklin Avenue had its own development called Prospect Heights. The houses in the foreground are in Hillside Avenue, viewed westward from High Street, c. 1906.

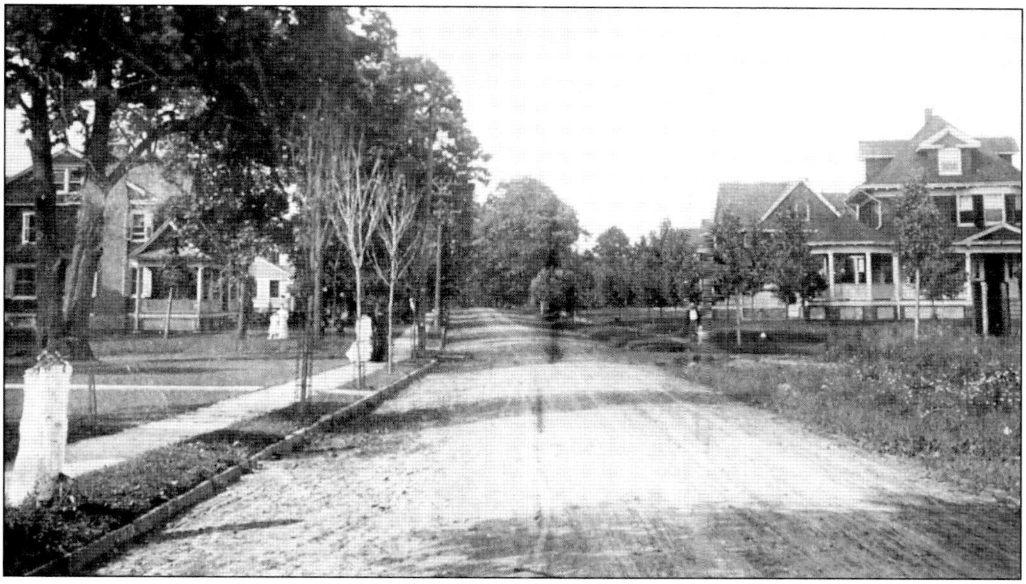

It seems that everybody came out to be photographed on the day when a photographer from Crammond and Snyder took this image of Prospect Street. James Crammond had a store in the Masonic building at Franklin Avenue and High Street. He was responsible for many of the postcard views of Nutley we have today.

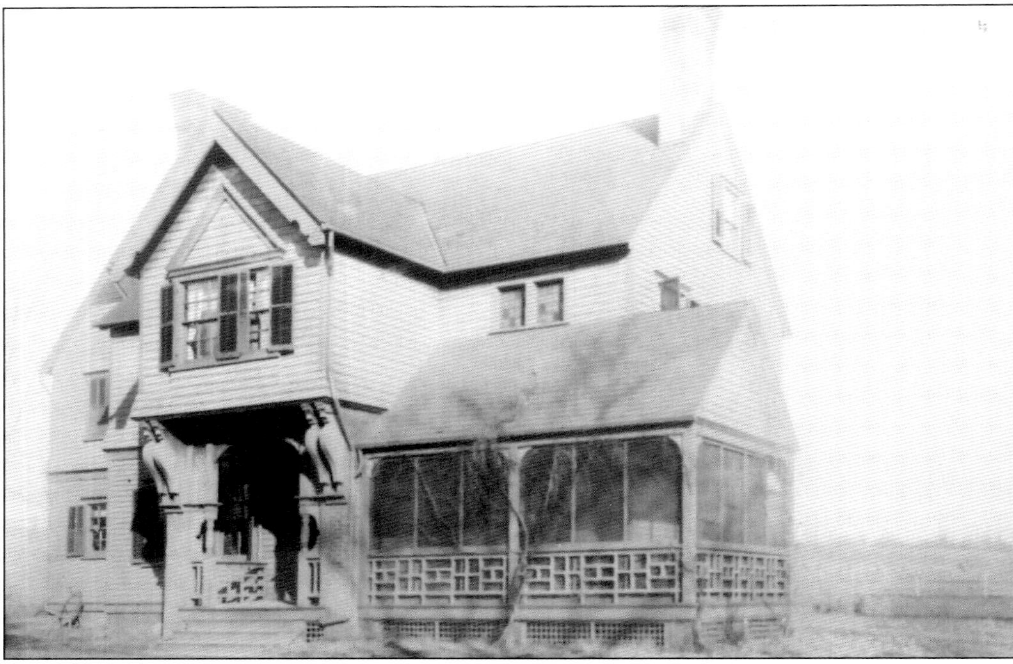

The charm and elegance of the homes from the late 1800s is evident in this modest, but finely designed, house. It is one of several buildings using these features, with its heavy front brackets and stick-style front rails, and is located at 152 Nutley Avenue; a similar one can be found at 192 Nutley Avenue.

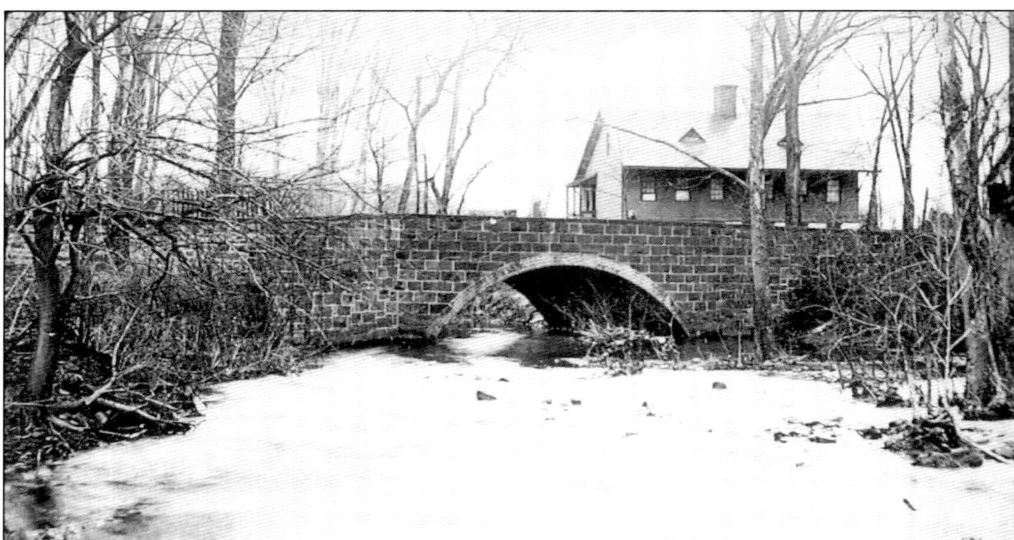

This scene below the Kingsland Falls, looking north at the Kingsland Avenue Bridge, was photographed *c.* 1906. There is no longer a house on the other side of the bridge, but you can still find the precision-cut brownstone arch serving its purpose.

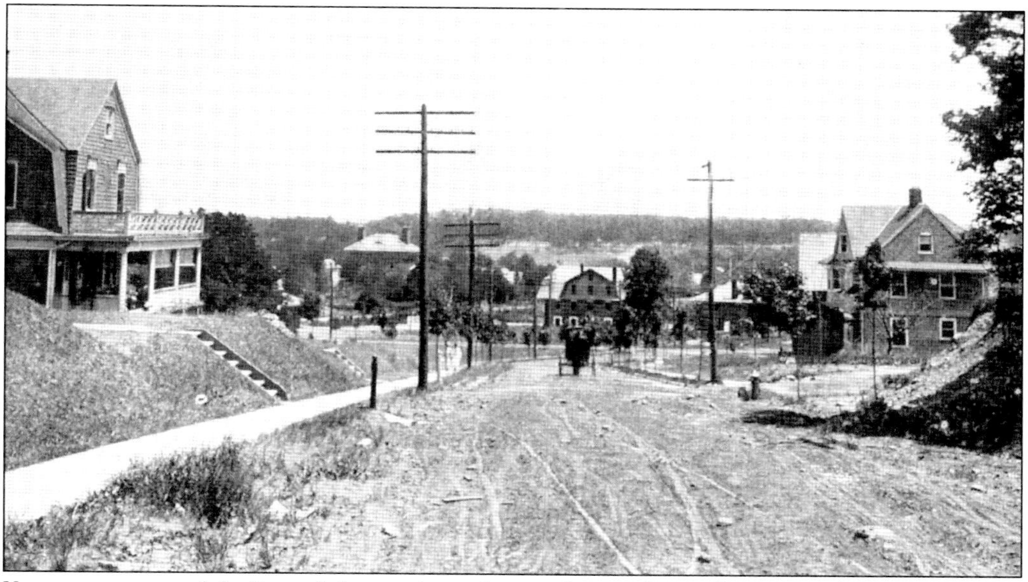

You can get a real feeling of the road conditions during the early twentieth century as you view Hawthorn Avenue, looking east from Prospect Street. Dust, mud, rocks, and debris were common annoyances for the early traveler. Note the early version of Yantacaw School in the background.

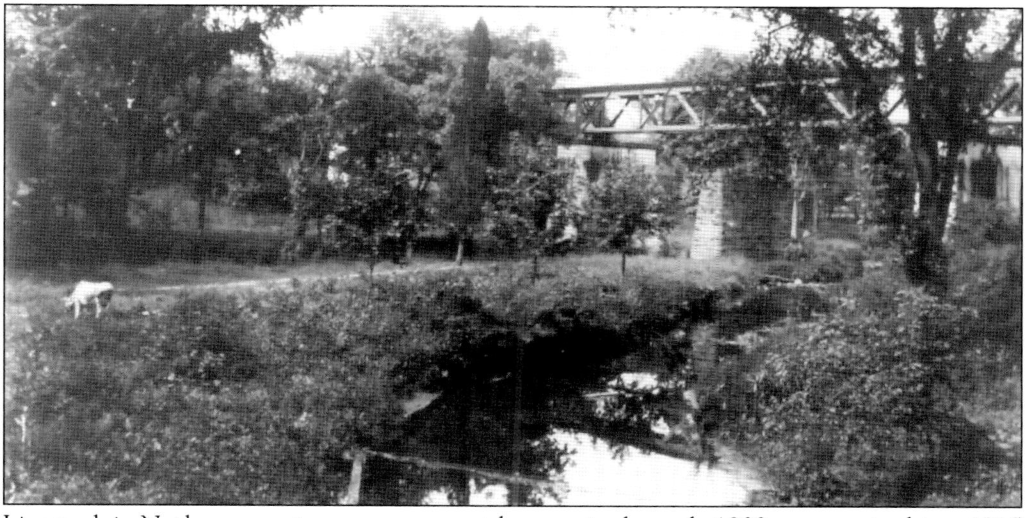

Livestock in Nutley was not an uncommon sight even in the early 1900s, as seen in this *c.* 1915 view of the Third River. The railroad trestle shown is the one that crosses over Passaic Avenue near Satterthwaite Avenue; the cow is unidentified.

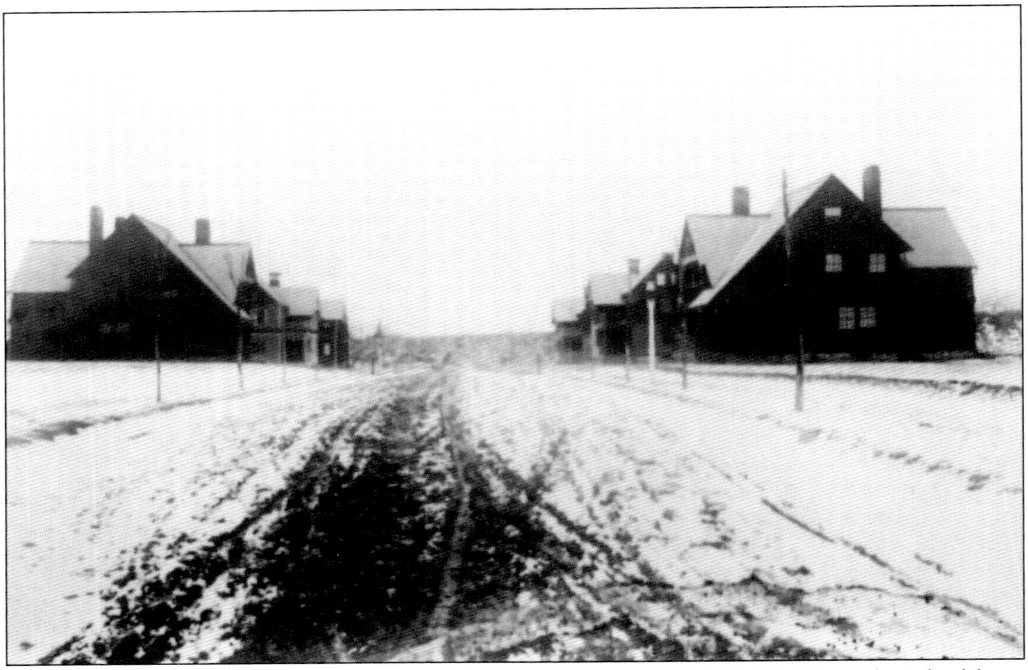

This is a view of Maple Place, looking north from Vreeland Avenue. The heavy sloped saltbox-style roof line is very common throughout the town, especially in the northeast section of town developed by J.R. Hay and A.T. Barney. The rise in the background is the Erie railroad tracks.

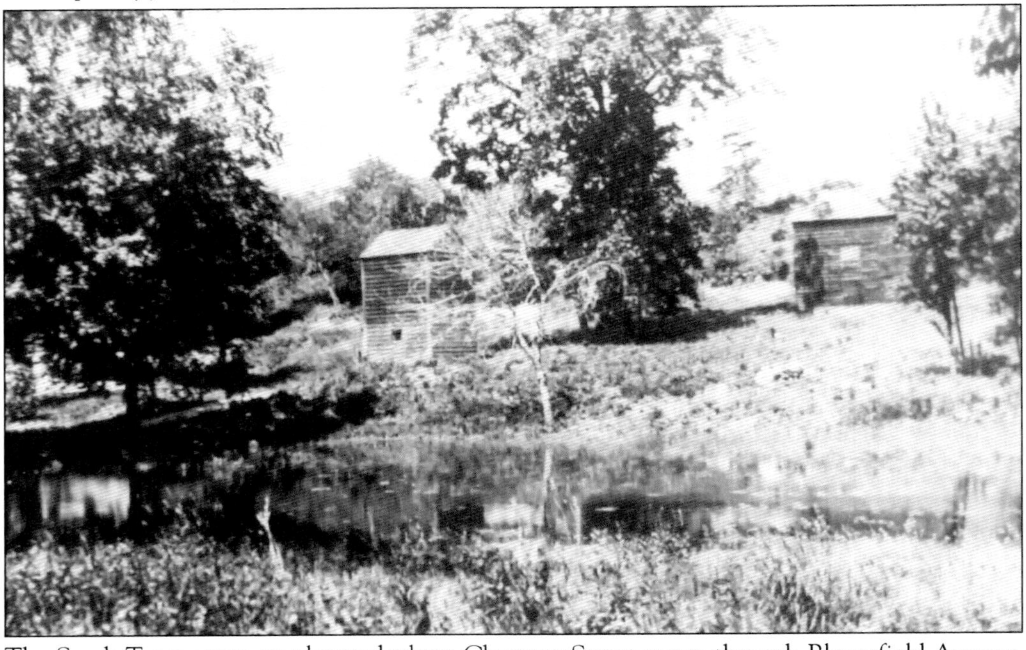

The Sarah Tuers estate was located where Chestnut Street passes through Bloomfield Avenue. This view is looking west from that intersection toward the Tuers pond. The pond was eventually drained, and Chestnut Street was brought up from where it ended at Prospect Street, to run through and past Bloomfield Avenue.

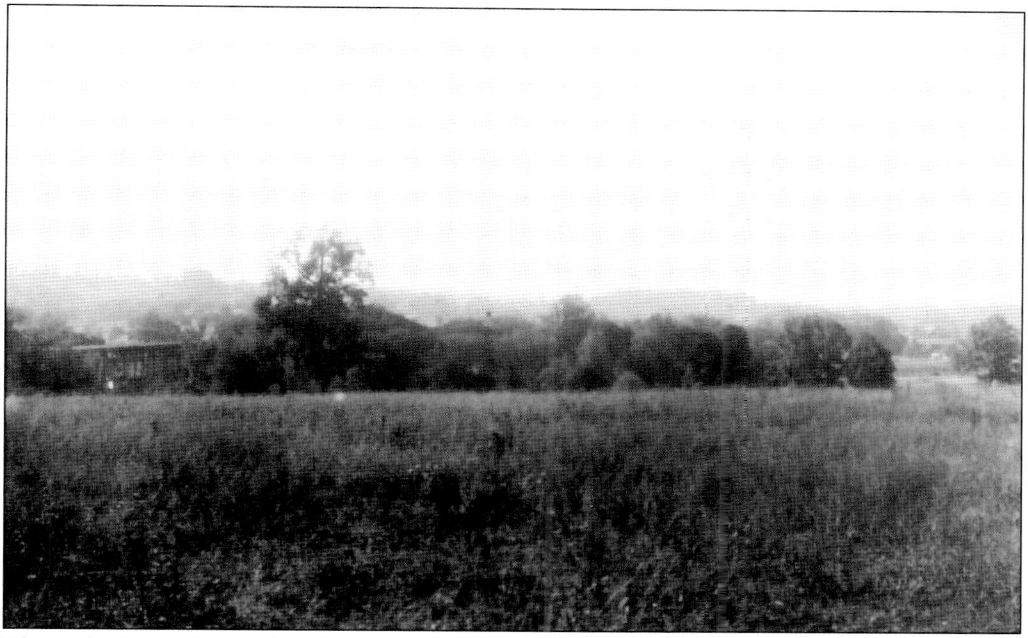

The only thing that makes this early 1900s view of interest is its lack of interesting things to see! In fact, the only clue that this is a southwestern view of Nutley is the railroad trestle crossing Passaic Avenue on the left.

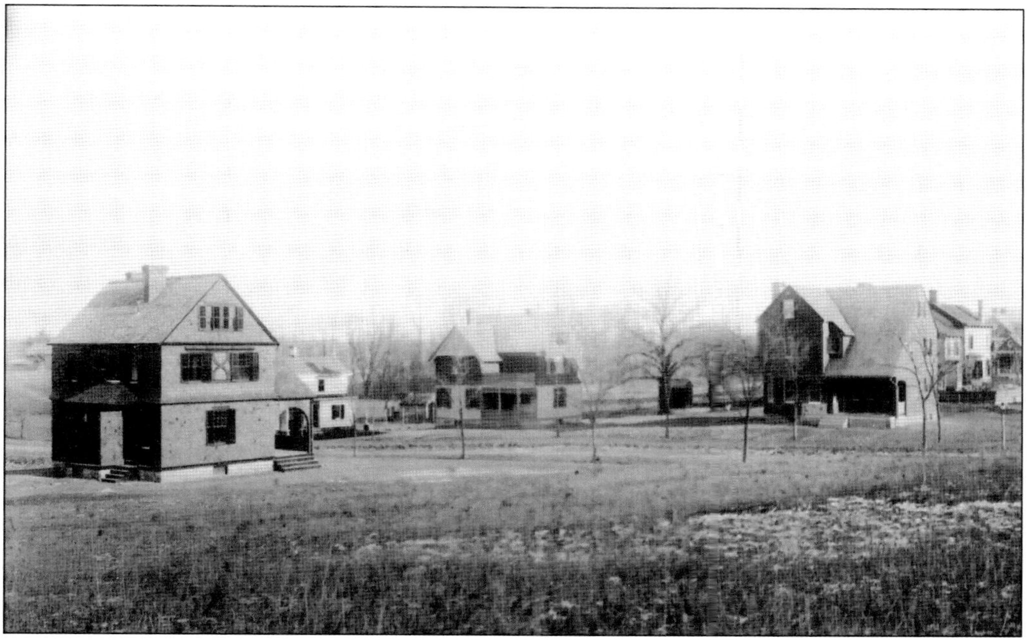

It is hard to believe that this is Franklin Avenue in its infancy. The two prominent houses in the center and right are numbers 602 and 590 respectively. The house to the left is number 599 on the west side of the avenue. This picture was taken sometime in the 1890s when land was still plentiful and Franklin Avenue was mostly residential.

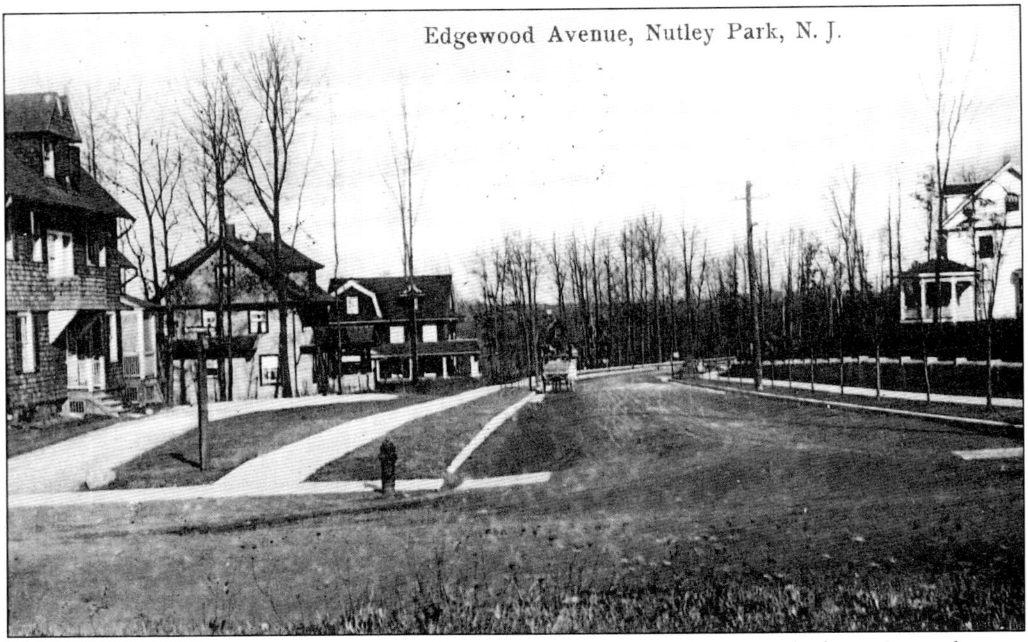

The old horse cart in this picture of Edgewood Avenue, looking north from Satterthwaite Avenue, is what really makes this view different from today. The Nutley Park area, due to the efforts of the Nutley Realty Company, was one of the fastest growing sections of town in the early 1900s.

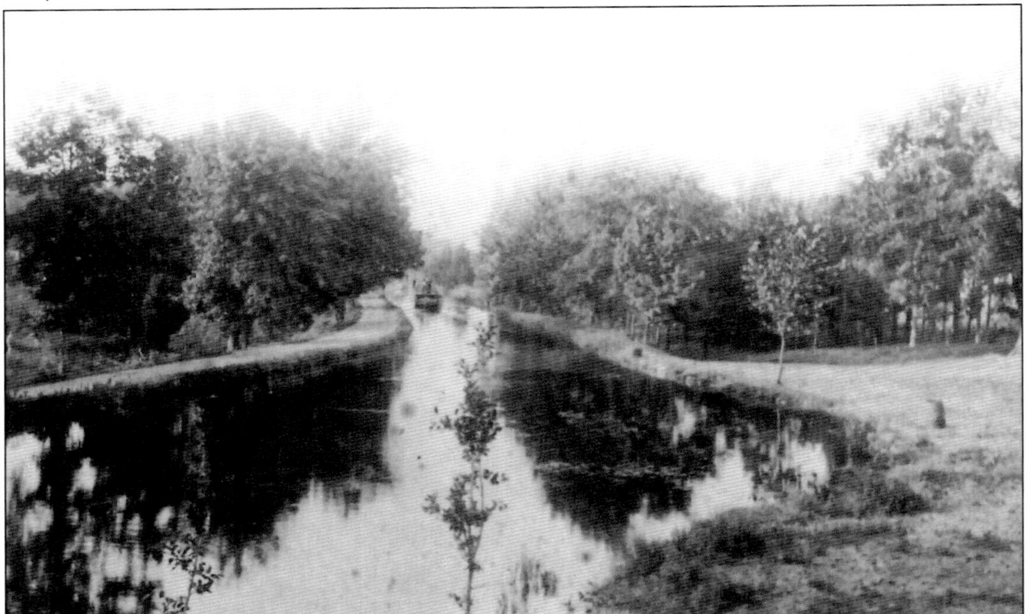

In the days before the railroad was king, the Morris Canal was the best way to ship freight and coal across New Jersey. With its inclined planes and locks, the canal was a man-made wonder which only brushed up against the Nutley border at East Passaic Avenue where the parkway runs.

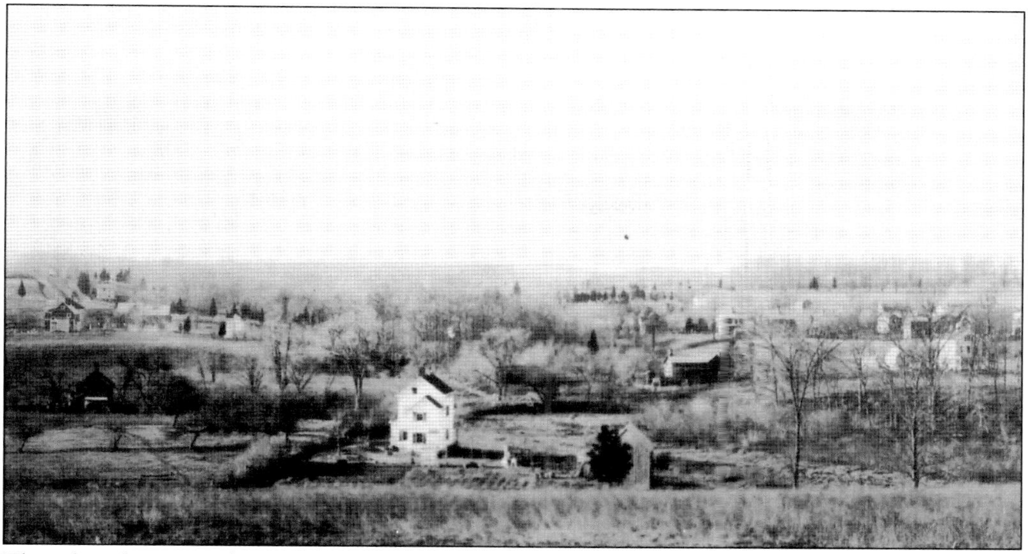

The white house in the center of this photograph is located at 302 Whitford Avenue. The two houses in the right foreground are, respectively, 575 and 591 Passaic Avenue. Around 1890, farmland was still available, and every home had a garden.

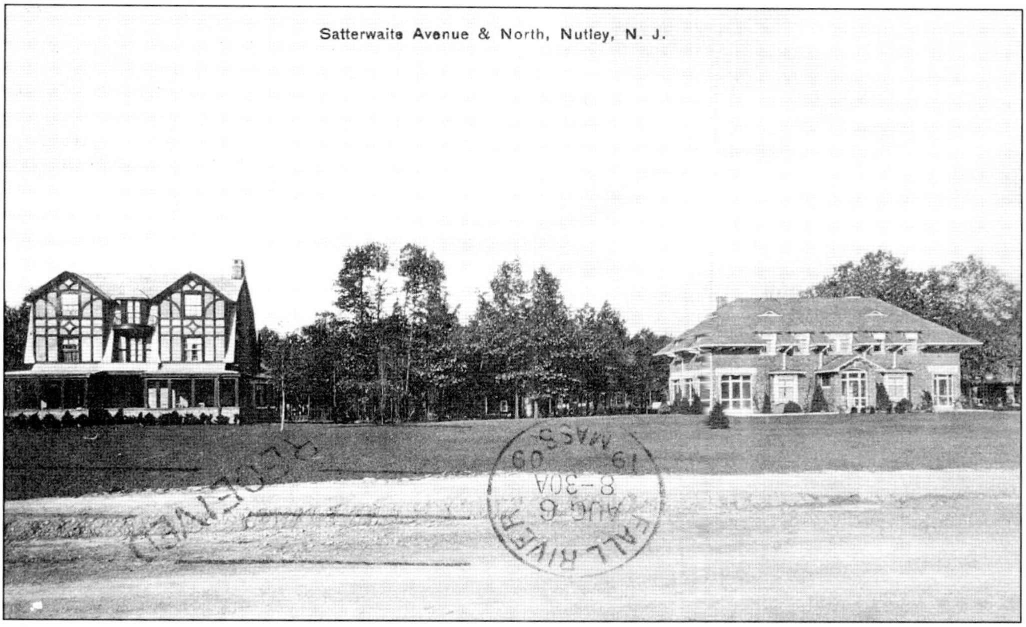

This postcard view shows one of the rare occasions where the view today looks better. The postmark dates this card to August 6, 1909. Both of these homes are still around today on Satterthwaite (note misspelling) Avenue, between North Road and Edgewood Avenue. The trees have all matured, and there is a very settled look to this block today.

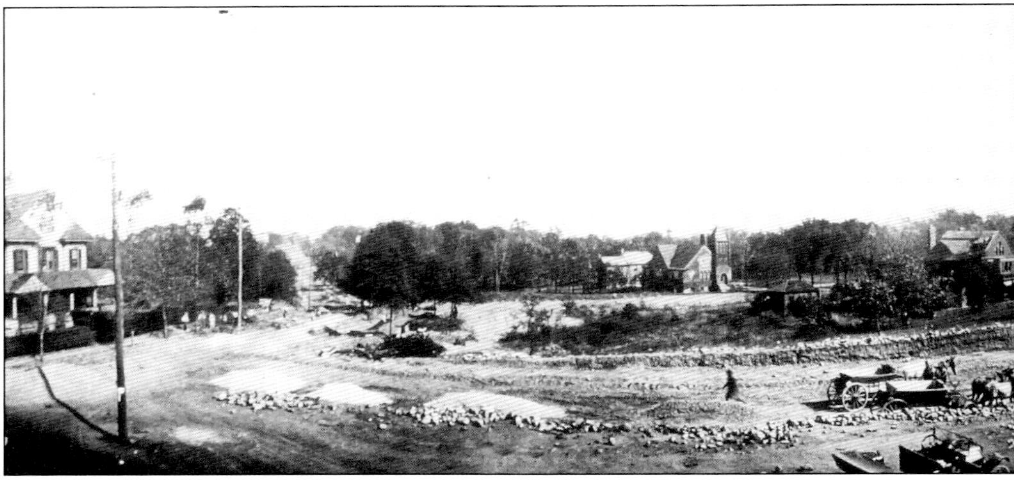

This vintage image of early Nutley was taken from the Franklin Avenue Train Station at High Street, looking north. The clearing in the trees slightly left of center is Hillside Avenue. Saint Paul's Church can also be seen toward the right. The work crew in the picture was grading what is East Plaza today.

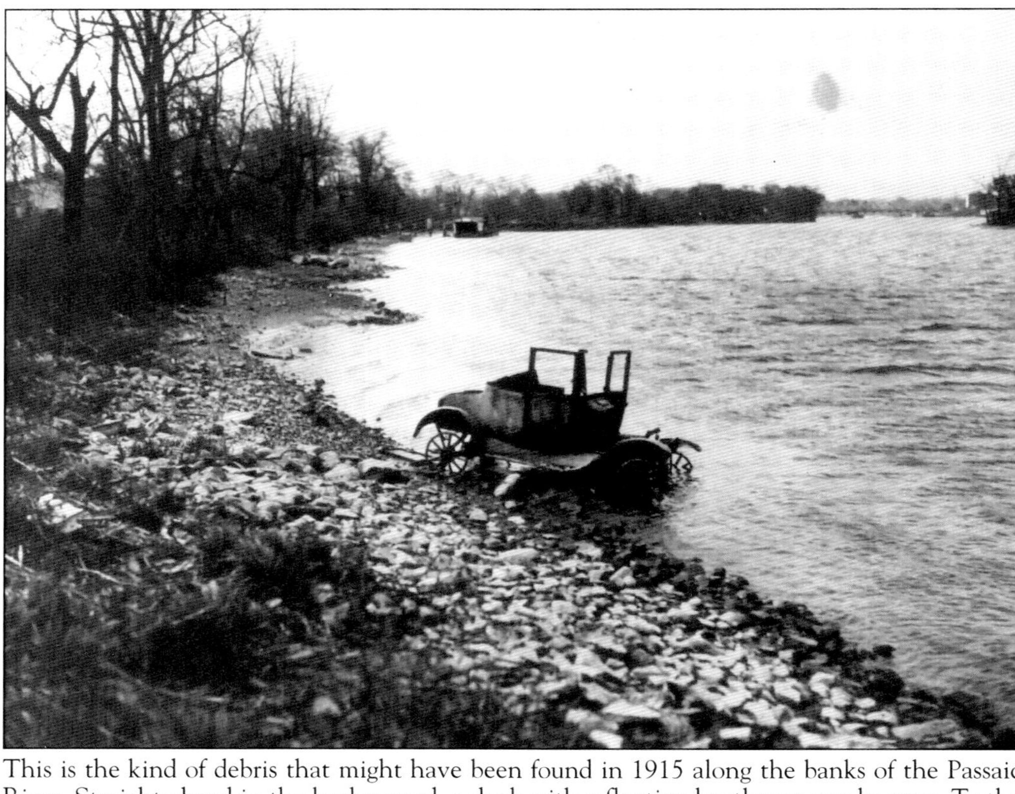

This is the kind of debris that might have been found in 1915 along the banks of the Passaic River. Straight ahead in the background, a dock with a floating boathouse can be seen. To the right, beyond the bend of the river, the bridge can be seen crossing over the Passaic.

Five

Parks

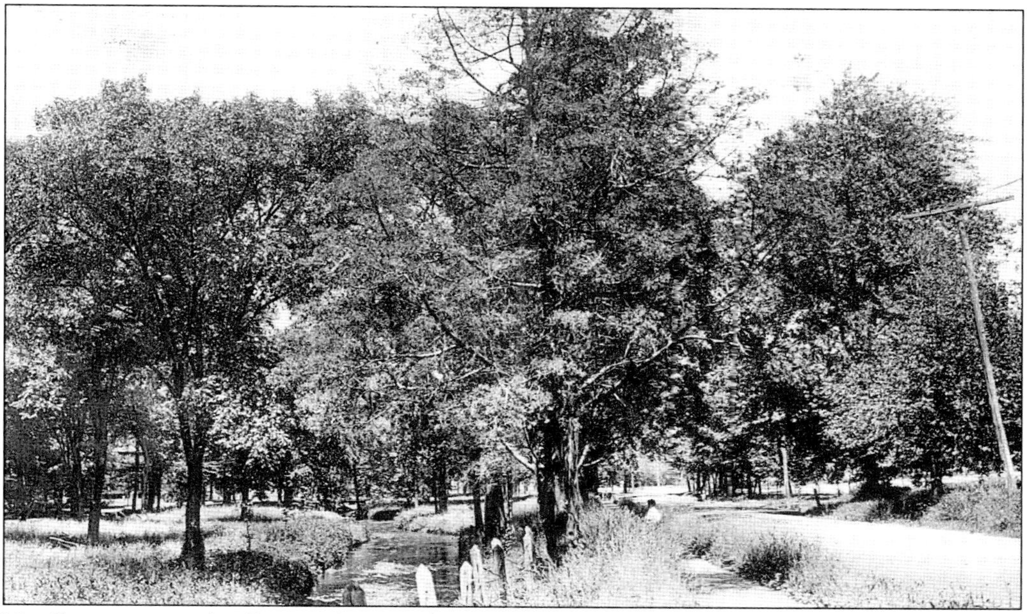

Needless to say, today Passaic Avenue does not look much like this *c.* 1909 view; the road has been widened and the trees are not as clustered. The old leaning telephone pole carrying one wire has given way to poles bringing strings of electric, phone, and cable TV service.

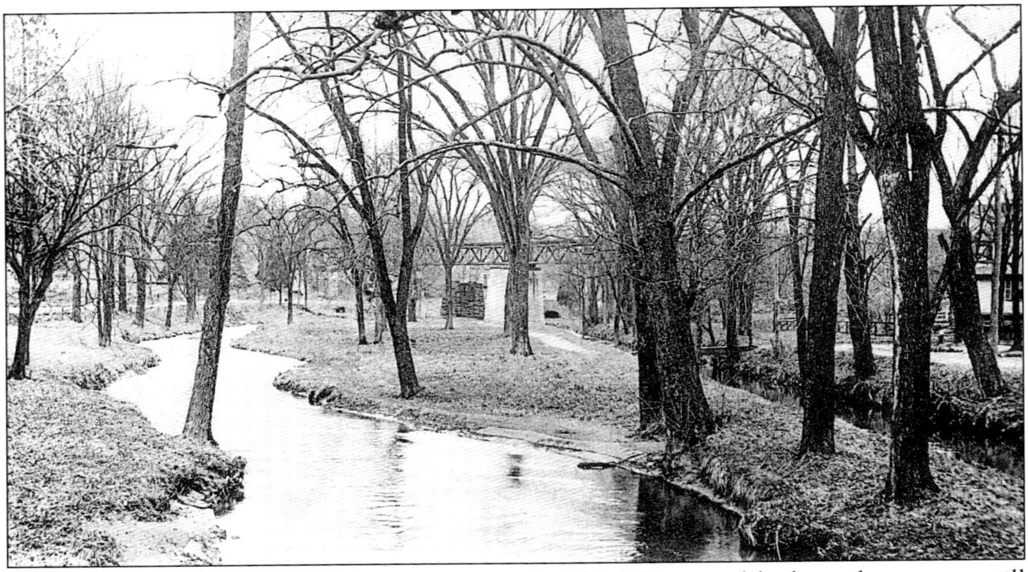

If you stand where Brookfield Avenue crosses the Third River and look south, you can still catch this view of the park. In this image, the trestle in the background is resting on its new concrete piers, but the old brownstone ones remain below; a house on Brookway can be seen on the right.

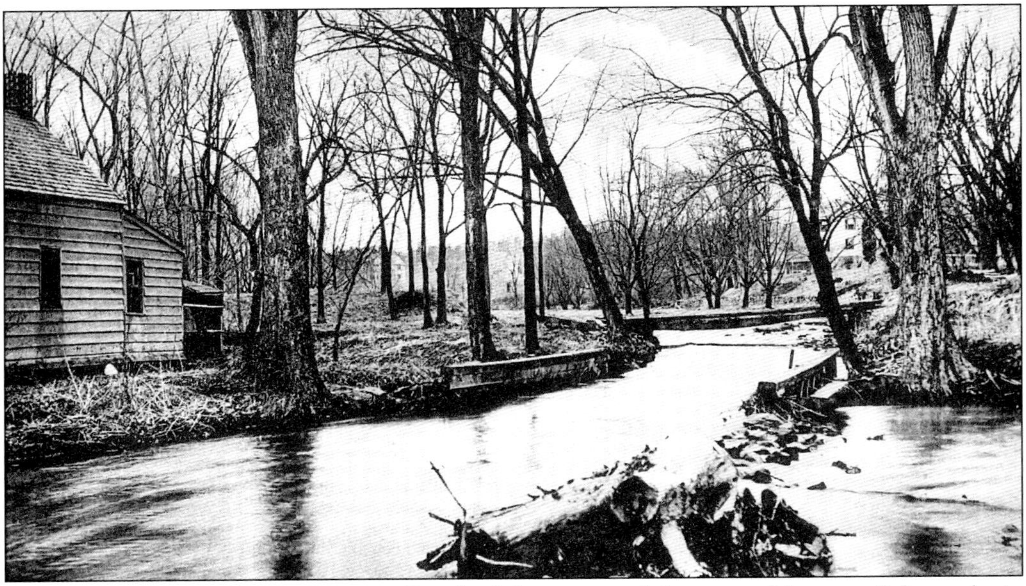

This *c.* 1906 image shows Yantacaw Brook. A large part of the natural beauty of the parks in Nutley is due to fact that the Third River runs through most of them. The first proposal for a park was in 1909 under a county park appropriation bill. Due to severe inaction by the town and county, Yantacaw Park was not started until 1911. It was finished in 1914.

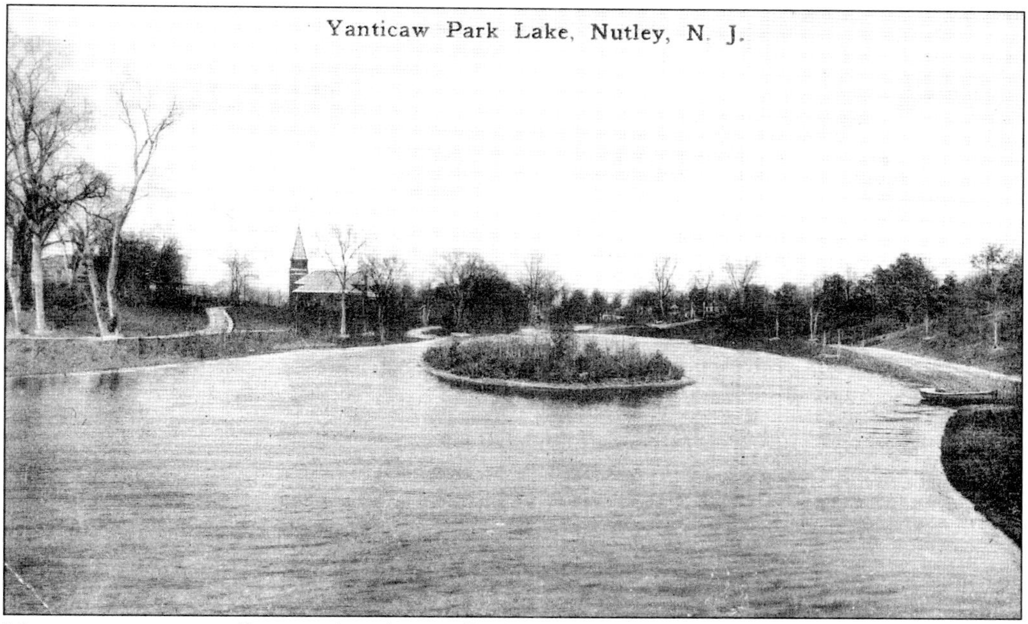

Many in town can still remember the small island which sat in the middle of Yantacaw Lake, behind the Methodist church. The younger schoolchildren of the day spread tales of wild alligators living out on the island. The lake was eventually channeled, and the island was lost forever.

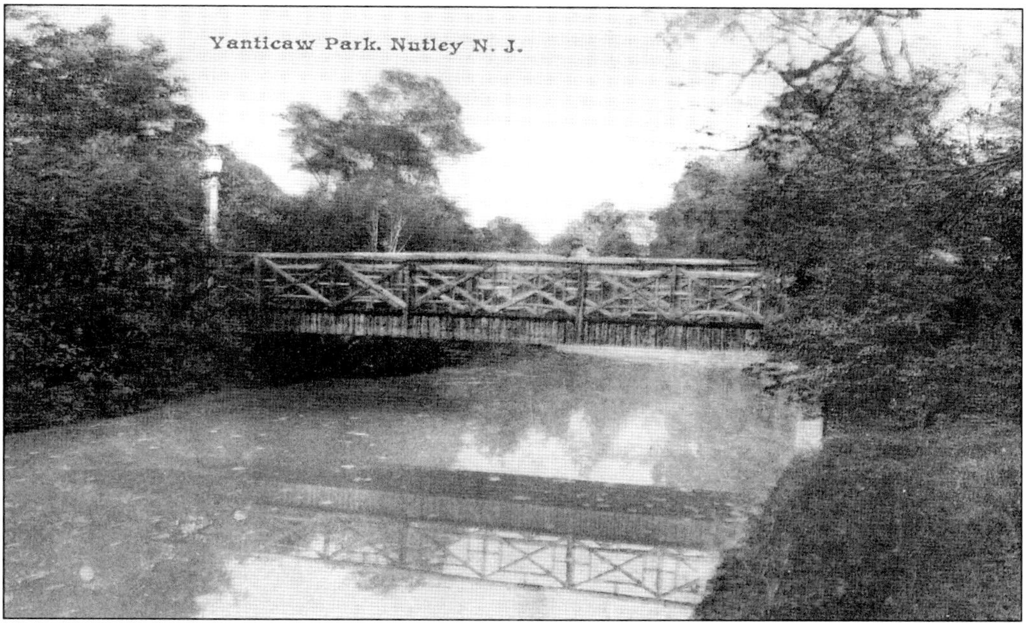

Yantacaw Park was originally designed to be three times larger than what the county finally agreed upon; $40,000 was allotted for land appropriation and $200,000 was set aside for development. Plans included walking paths, a lake, a field house, playgrounds, sports fields, and bridges like this wooden one, all on 29 acres of land.

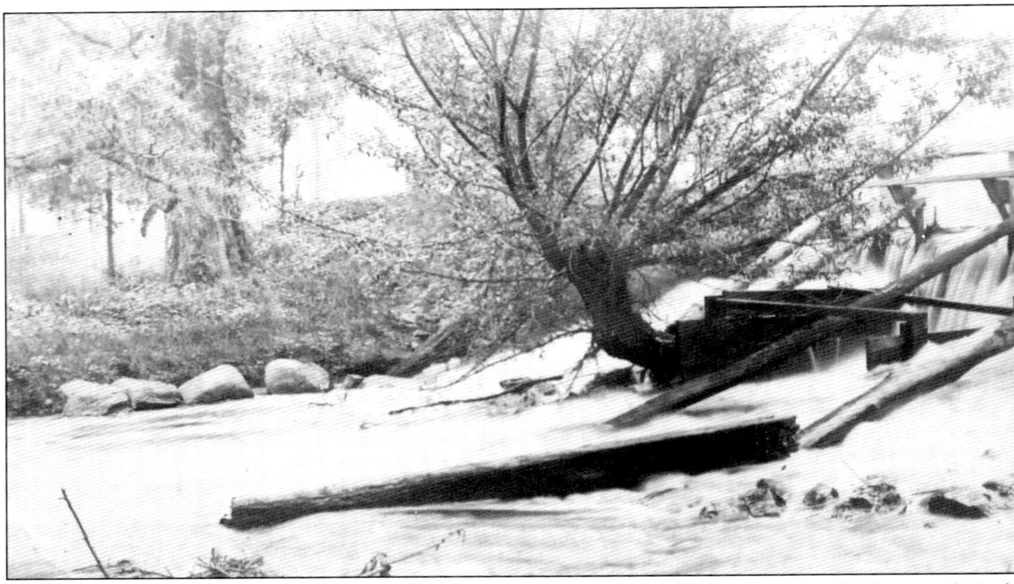

This is a view of the dam that once was at the present Mudhole section of Memorial Park. The dammed water was used to power various mill operations in this area, including Duncan's Cotton Goods Mill. The dam is shown here during some flooding, which still occurs when the river breaks over its channeled path and floods the park.

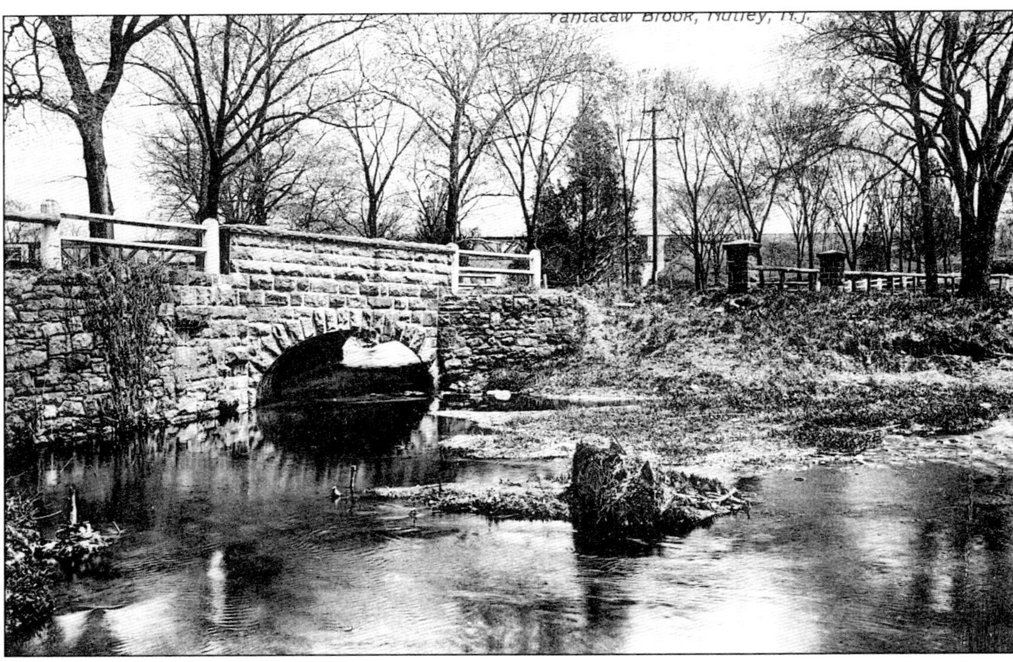

This is Vreeland Avenue, where the Third River divides to pass under the street via two brownstone bridges. The bridge shown here spans the water that was the raceway for a mill previously located nearby. The second bridge is closer to Passaic Avenue and is not seen in this 1907 view.

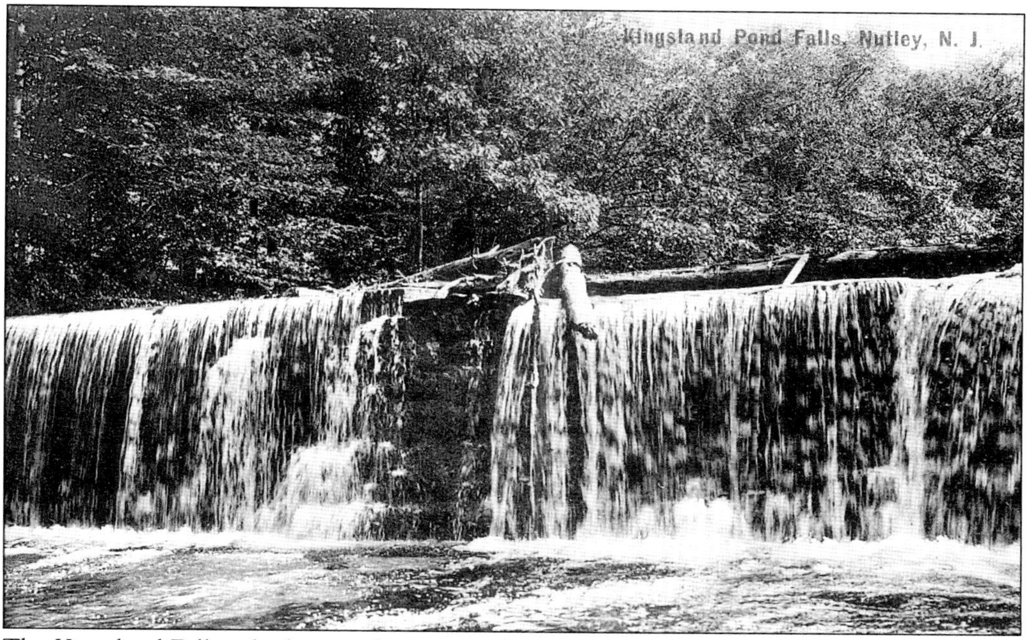

The Kingsland Falls, which were the source of power for the early Kingsland Mills, were once slightly higher than they are today. They were lowered to alleviate flooding problems that would occur at several streets along the Third River.

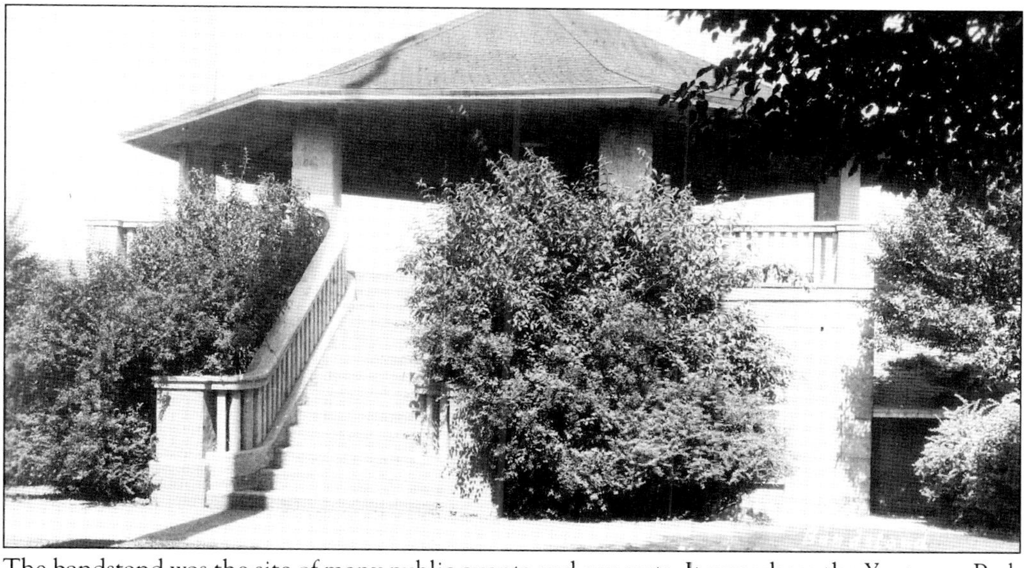

The bandstand was the site of many public events and concerts. It was where the Yantacaw Park storage building is now, at the end of the tree-lined path heading west from the Park Avenue steps. This photograph was taken *c.* 1906.

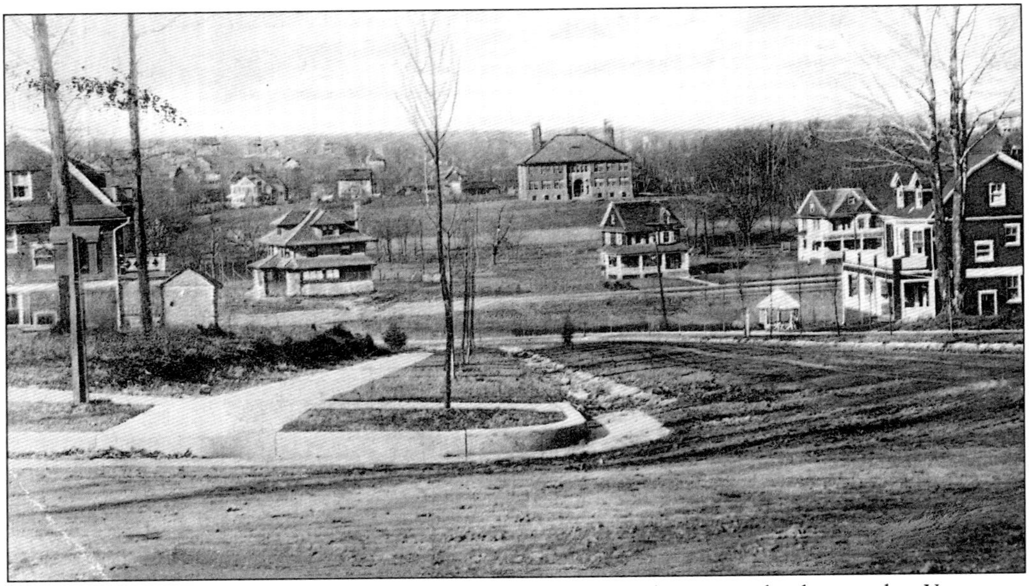

This *c*. 1910 view looks west from Brookfield Avenue. In the center background is Yantacaw School, which was only eight years old at the time this picture was taken. The land shown between the school and Passaic Avenue, next to the Third River, was eventually purchased *c*. 1920 by the town to be used as a park.

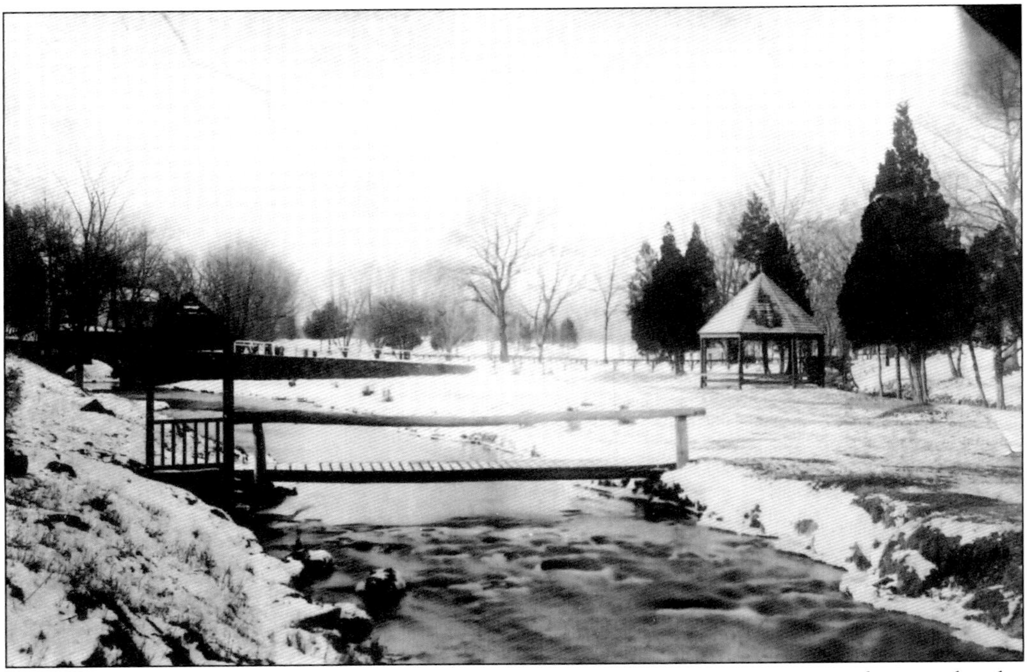

This view is looking southward at the point where the Third River comes out from under the Vreeland Avenue bridges (background). The mill race can just barely be seen behind the gazebo. This area is now part of Nutley's Memorial Park.

In 1911, the town decided to start acquiring land north of Chestnut Street, along the river, for park land. Once acquired, the land was turned into Memorial Park during the years of 1919–22. New trees for the park were sponsored, and the 427 planted represented the men from Nutley who fought in World War I.

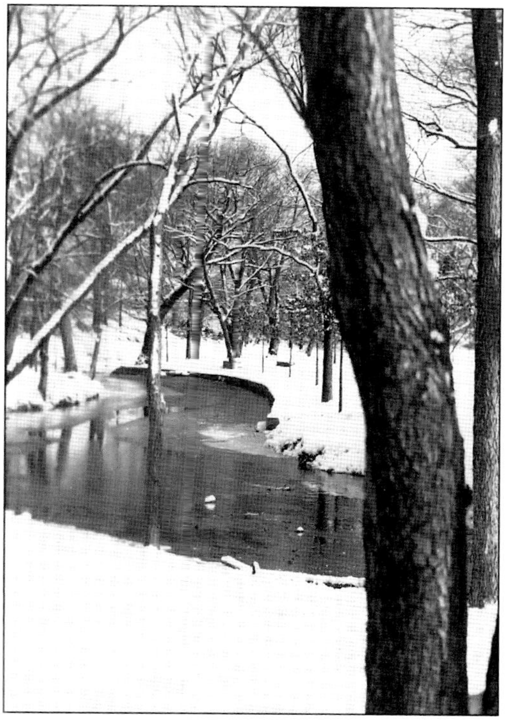

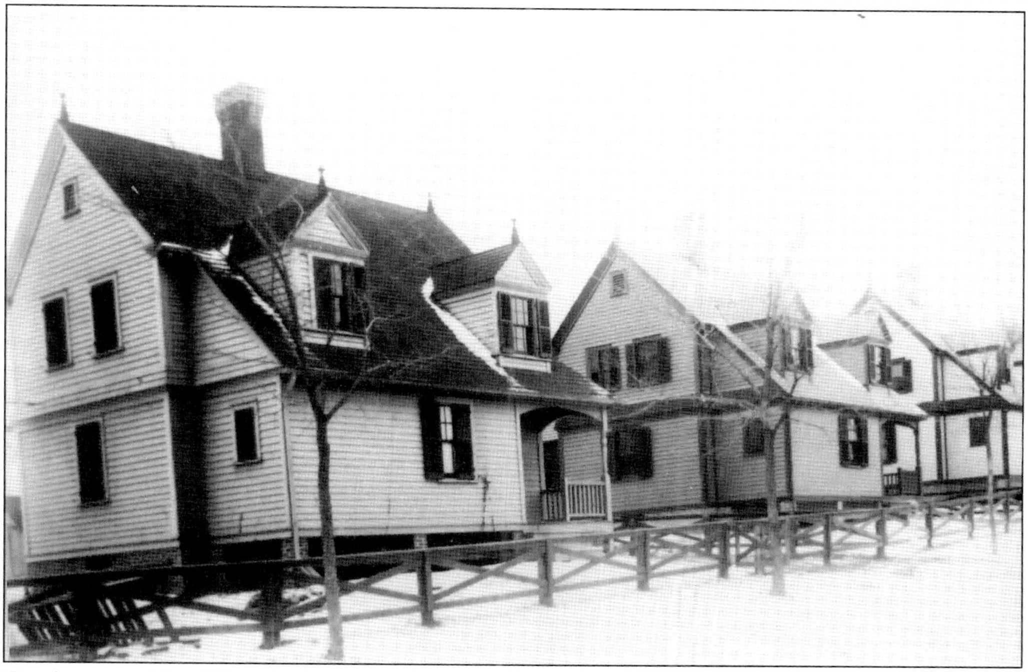

On the west side of Passaic Avenue, adjoining the park, are the houses of the Erie Place district. They were built *c.* 1873 for the employees of the U.S. Express company, which carried goods to and from railroad stations under a lease/purchase agreement unique in this area. Also unique was the early use of the "reverse saltbox" roof design.

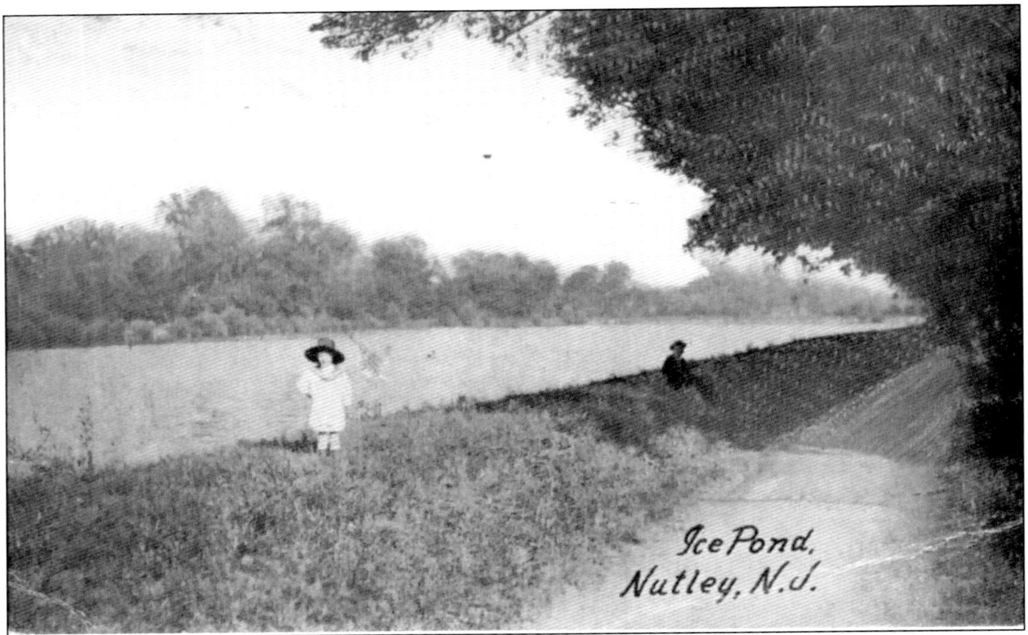

This postcard of an ice pond in Nutley has been postmarked 1912, but it is difficult to identify its location. Nutley had several ice cutters in its day prior to having ice brought in from up north. One dealer was William Banta, who cut his ice from Nichols Pond before the water was considered too dirty.

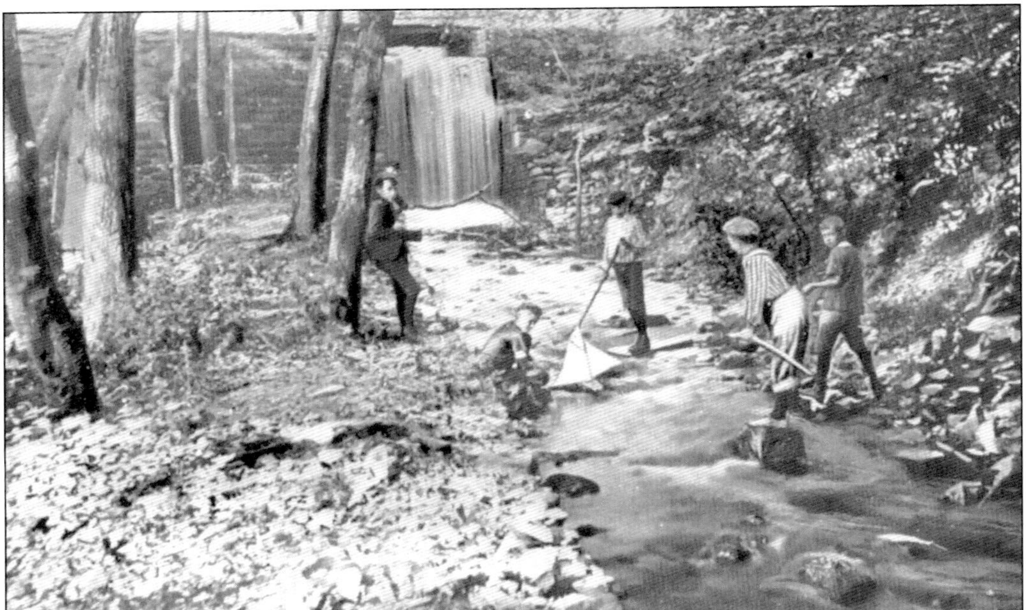

Although the falls are real, the boys are not. The postcard publishers of this shot of the falls at Nichols Park would add or delete these "cut and paste" kids during various printings of this card. Around the year 1906, the falls were right behind the site of the former Nichols Hat Factory, later the Black Prince Distillery, and the *Nutley Sun*'s offices at 800 Bloomfield Avenue.

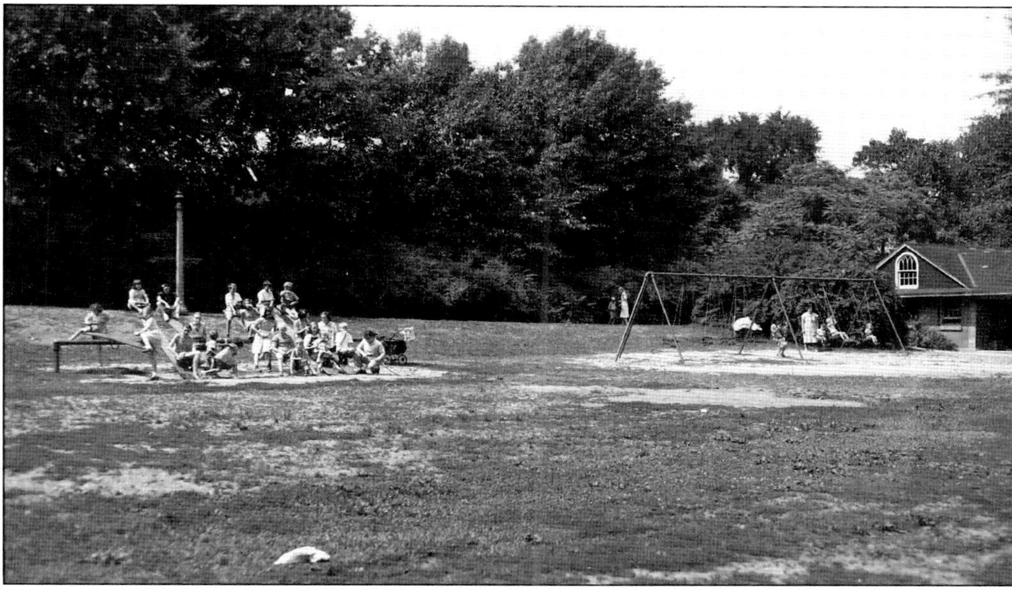

Known in town as Girls Park, this playground had a recreation house, play sets, and a shallow in-ground wading pool that children could enjoy during the warmer months. The park is located on the north side of the Centre Street Bridge.

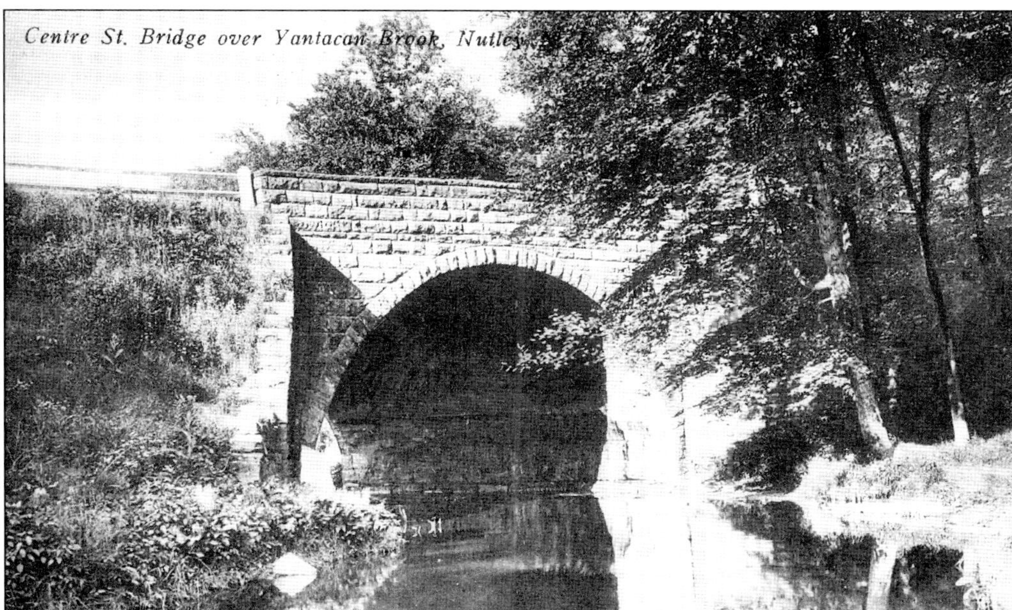

This is a 1913 view of the Centre Street Bridge. An 1896 report stated that the wooden bridge that was used to cross the water was not suitable for the trolley line that was to be laid down Centre Street. The county approved and paid $7,100 for the brownstone bridge, with the $3,500 filling and grading work being paid for by the Passaic Newark Rail Company.

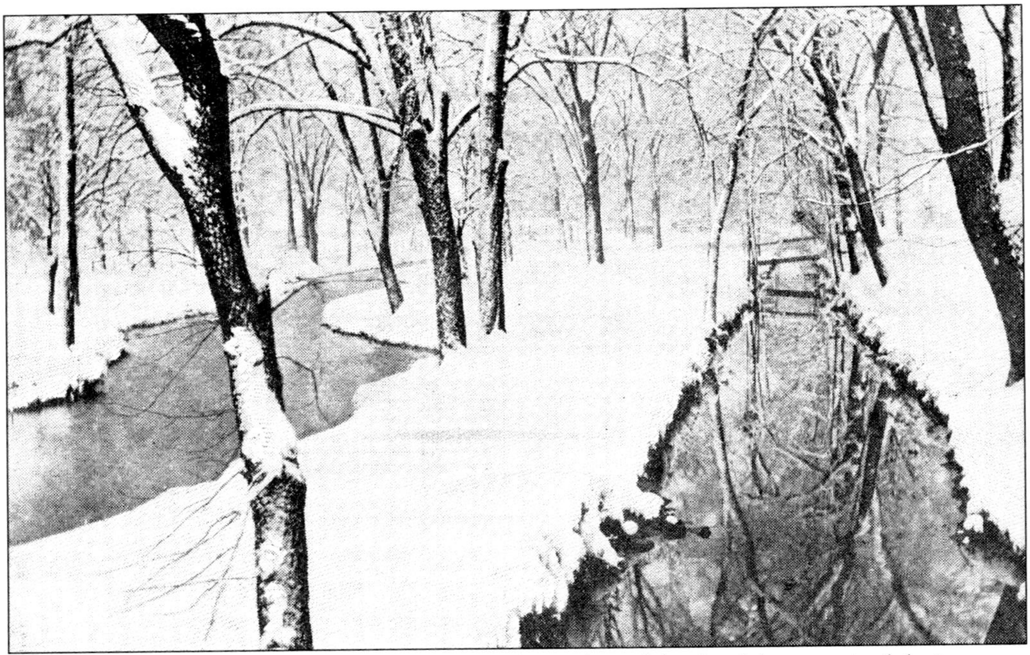

This is one of the oldest picture postcards that the author of this book has acquired during years of collecting. It is postmarked 1904, only two years after Nutley became the official town name. This date is the beginning point of the popularity of picture postcards in the United States.

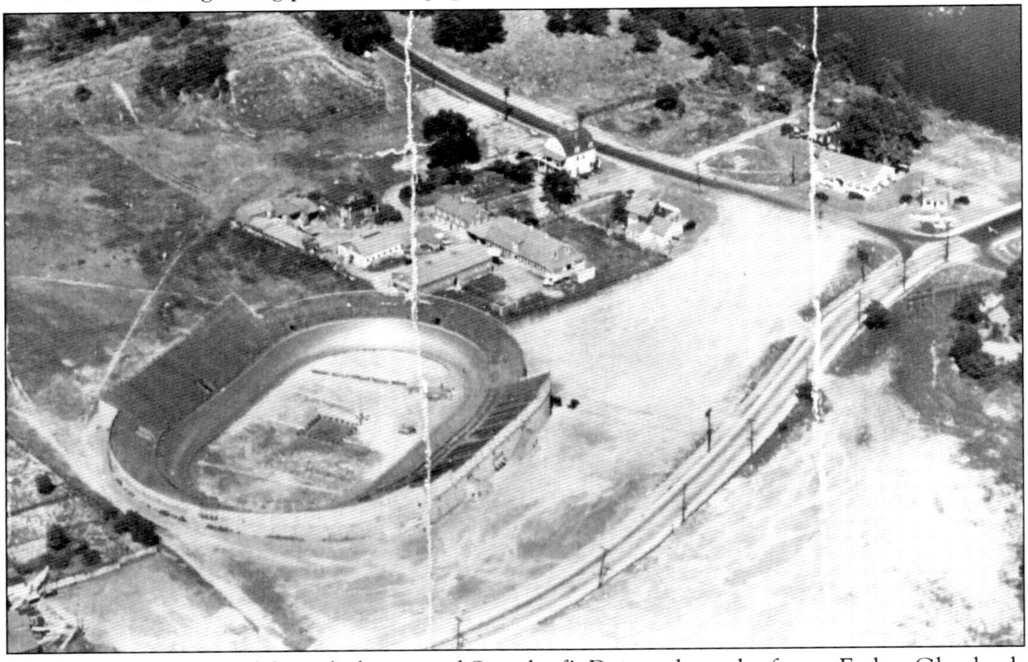

This is an aerial view of the velodrome and Steinlauf's Dairy, where the future Father Glotzbach Park would be located. It was once the site of a quarry (note the large mound of grass-covered rubble stone), but ended up as commercial property with the creation of the park in 1949–54. In this *c.* 1930s photograph, the elevated Route 21 has not yet been constructed.

Six

War and Peace

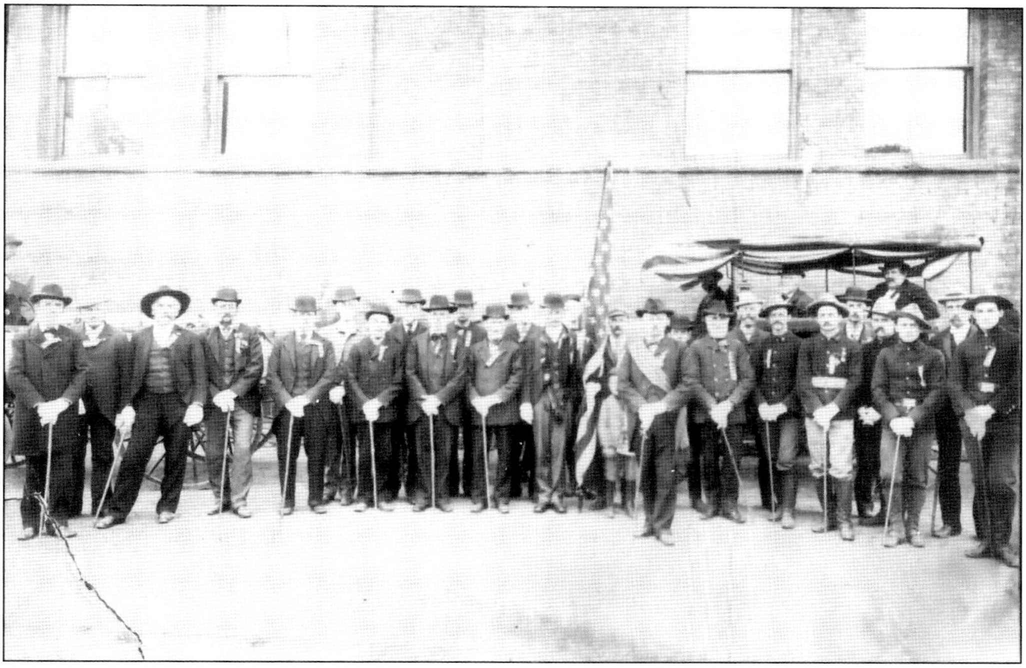

GAR members and other veterans are shown in this 1899 Memorial Day photograph. The GAR was established for Union veterans of the Civil War in 1866. Most of the older veterans shown here are GAR members, but there are also men from the Spanish-American War of 1898. These men marched in many of Nutley's parades until their numbers became too small.

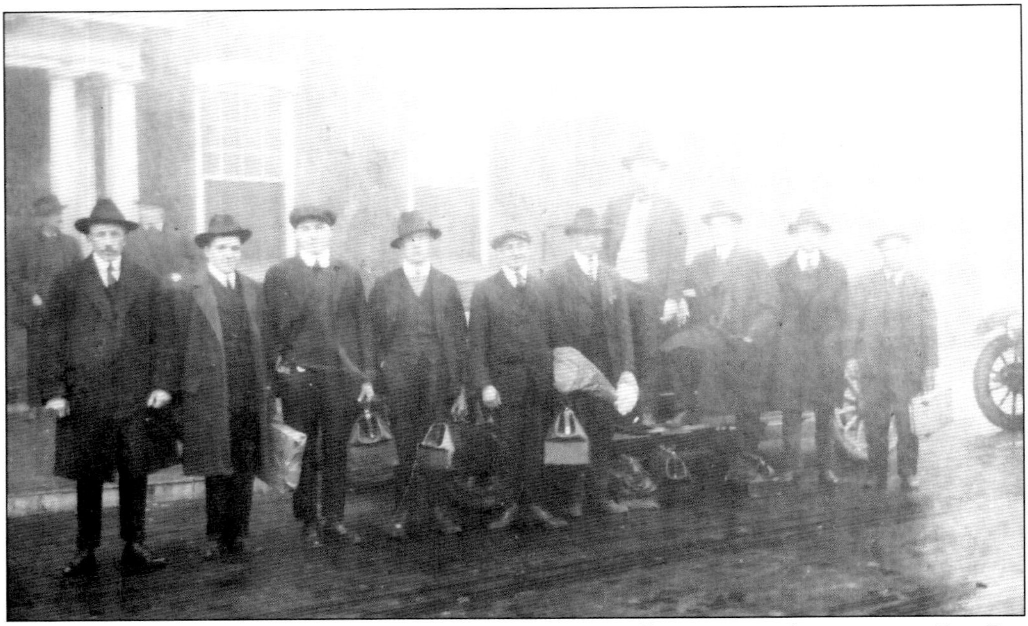

These men were photographed in front of Nutley Town Hall just prior to being sent to Fort Dix for training. They were the latest recruits for entry into World War I. The photograph, taken in March 1918, shows the ten men waiting to be driven to the Newark Courthouse, where they would meet up with recruits from Belleville. The Red Cross had presented the men with woolen sets earlier that day.

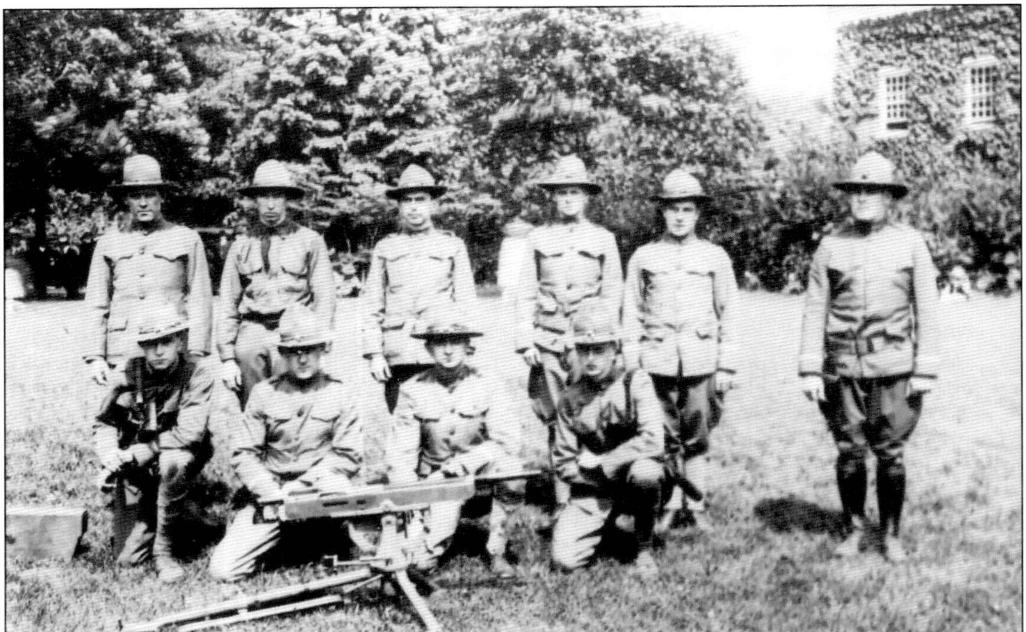

This image shows Nutley's Home Guard, *c.* 1917. The Home Guard was a volunteer organization that trained men to help and protect their local community. This was particularly important during wartime, when many of the available men were shipped out to the front.

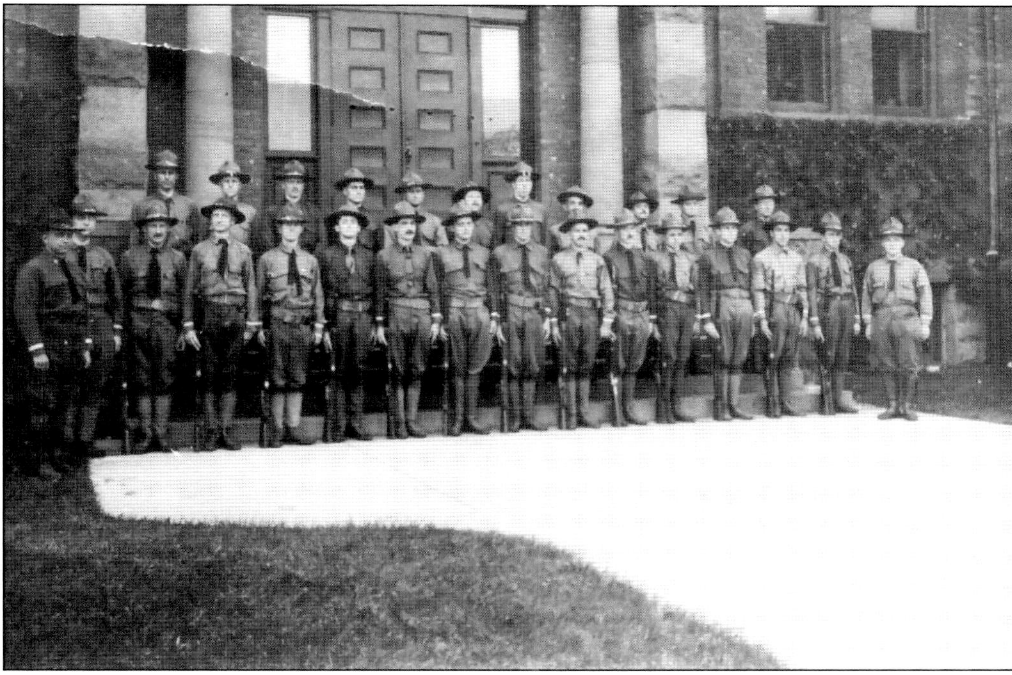

Pictured above is another group of Nutley's Home Guard Defense. During the harrowing years of World War I, the United States lost over 50,000 men, with another 205,000 wounded. The small town of Nutley would lose seventeen men to the war, one of whom was Raymond Blum. There is currently a small memorial bridge dedicated to him in the park between Mudhole and Vreeland Avenues.

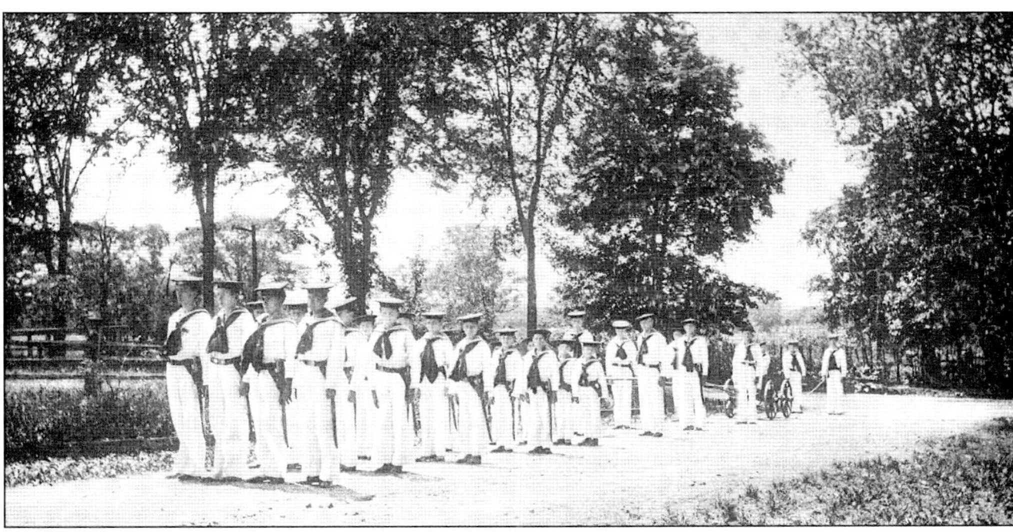

During World War I, patriotic organizations such as the Home Guard and American Legion were established in town. These young men were part of a group called the Nutley Naval Brigade. They would frequently march in parades or drill on public grounds, occasionally firing their miniature cannon.

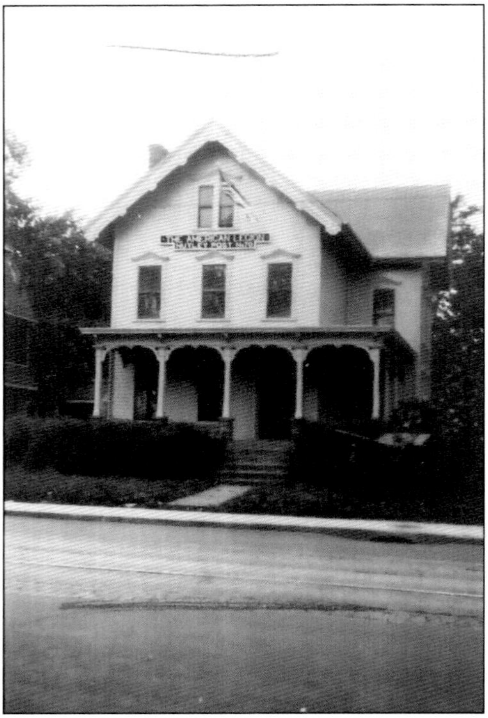

In 1919, the American Legion was born. The first meeting place of the Nutley post was in the town hall. J.C. Buxton was the first leader of Post #70, and in 1929, the group purchased the building shown here for its headquarters. The house stood at 507 Franklin Avenue.

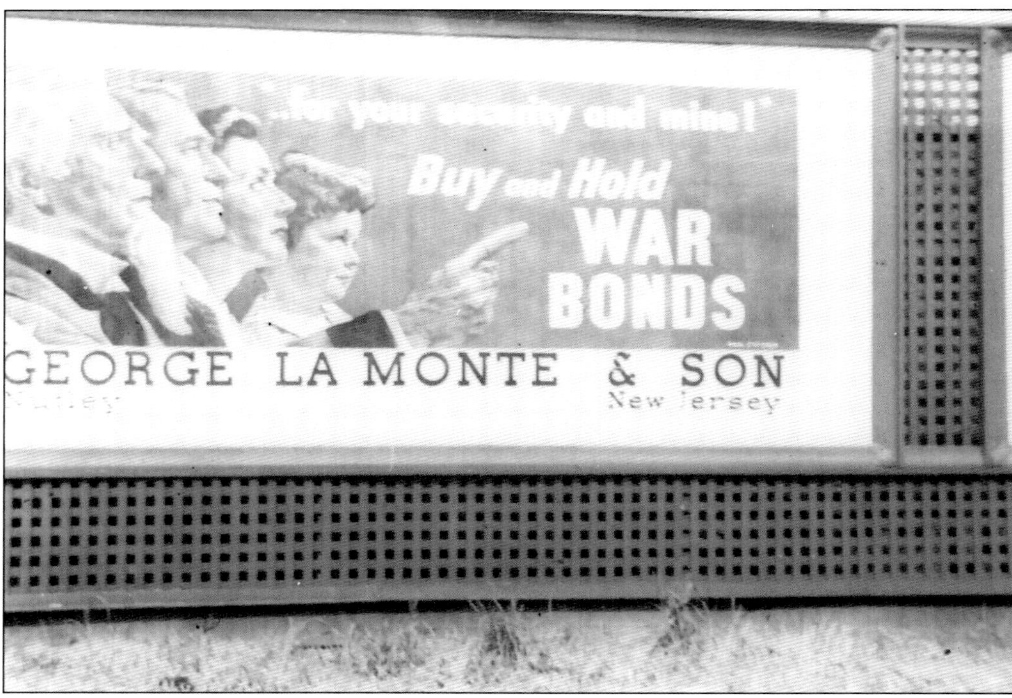

Patriotism during wartime materialized again in Nutley during World War II. Advertisements like this one for war bonds were very common around town. Scrap metal drives were also an important community activity involving adults and schoolchildren alike.

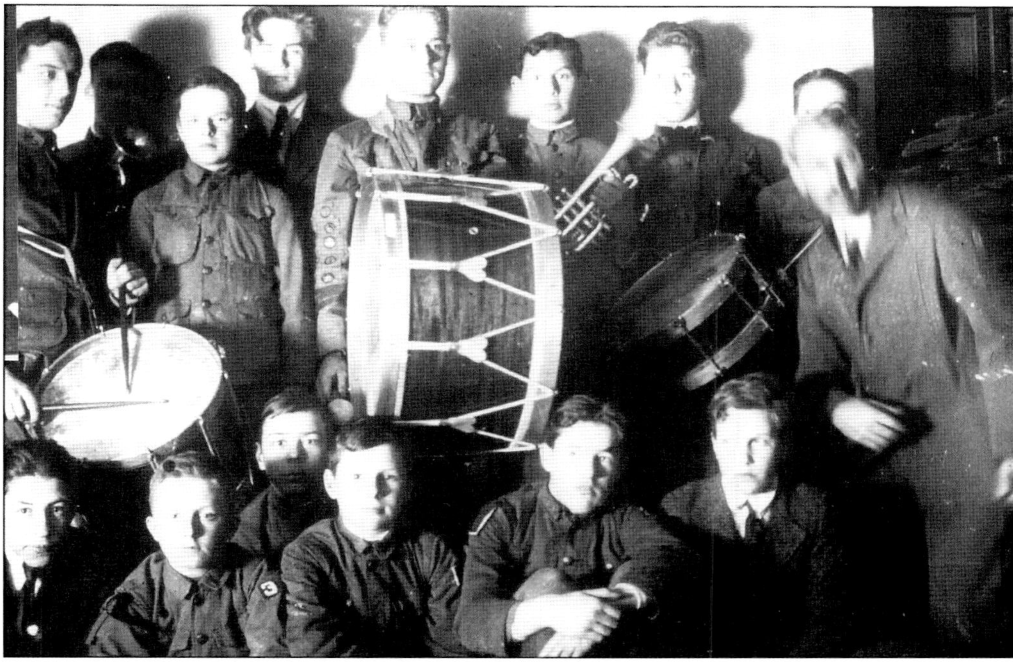

Nutley has the distinction of having one of the oldest Boy Scout troops in New Jersey. Troop #3 was organized under the leadership of Edgar Bellows. These boys are part of the 1919 troop. During a reorganization of numbers, Nutley lost the designation of the #3 troop, but the troop still remains in town.

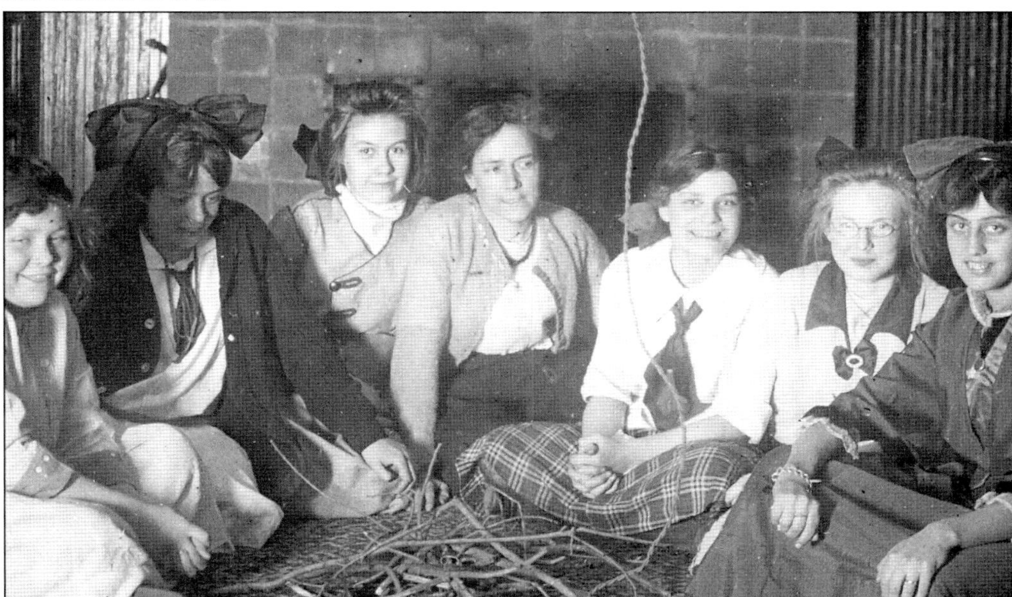

Agnes Baden-Powell, the sister of the man who founded the Boy Scouts in England, founded one of the earliest groups for girls, called the Girl Guides. In America, Juliette Gordon Low started the Girl Scouts in 1912. These young ladies are part of another group known as the Camp Fire Girls, who were under the leadership of Mrs. Erler, who was guardian of the fire.

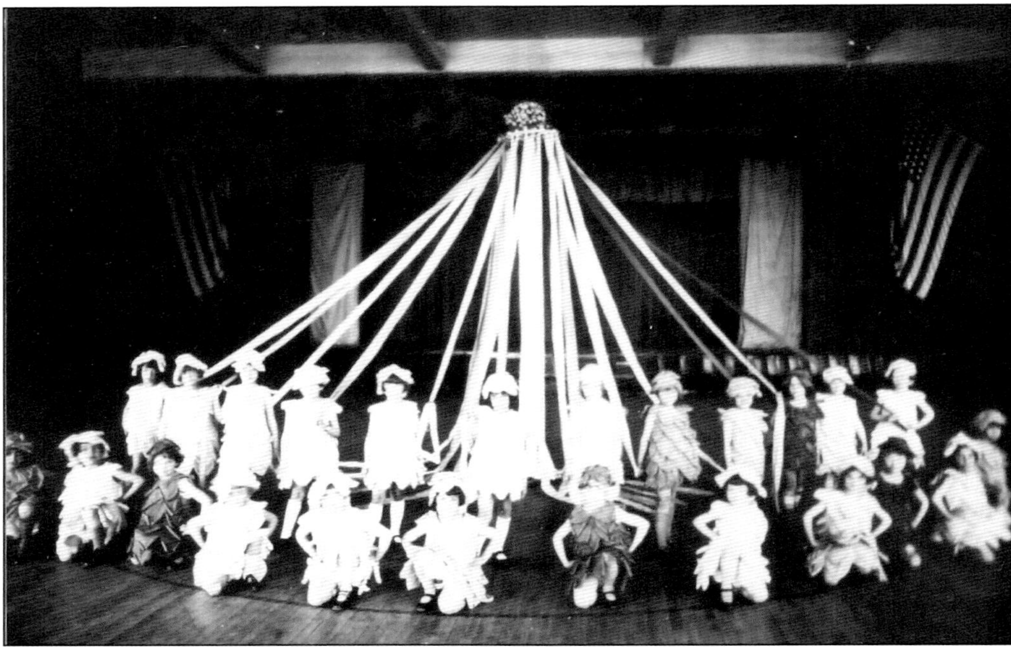

On May 1st you could celebrate the splendor of spring as these Nutley children did with a maypole dance. The idea of celebrating nature's rebirth in May dates back to ancient Rome around 258 B.C. The Romans would pay homage to Flora, the goddess of flowers and spring. The streamers in the dance are thought to represent the sun's rays.

This is a scene of an 1890s picnic. During those days, the town, of course, had many varieties of nut trees. It was not uncommon for residents, when outside, to have a "nutting party" or to go "nutting." A blight in the early 1900s led to a large loss of Nutley's trees.

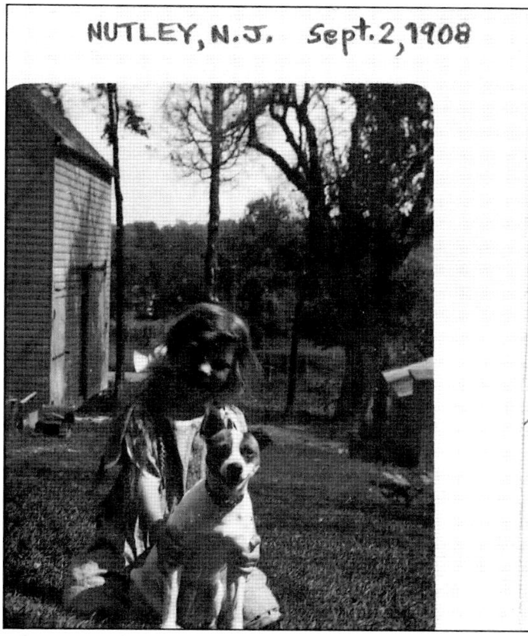

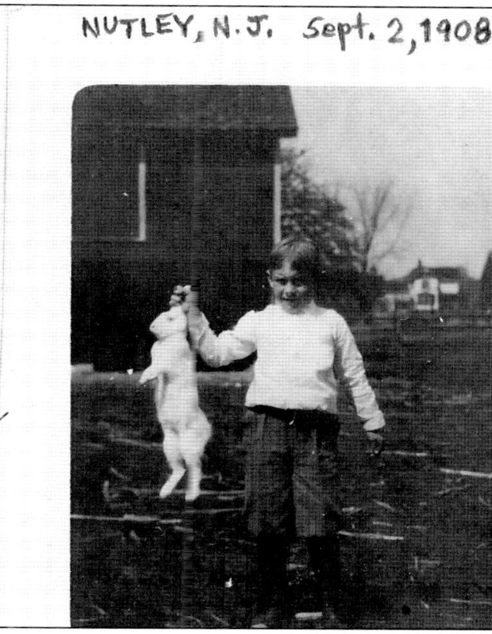

These are the Parke kids from Nutley, who had their pictures made into postcards that were sent to their aunt on September 2, 1908. The author was never able to find any information about Helen and Russel Parke but likes to believe that their childhood days in Nutley were happy ones.

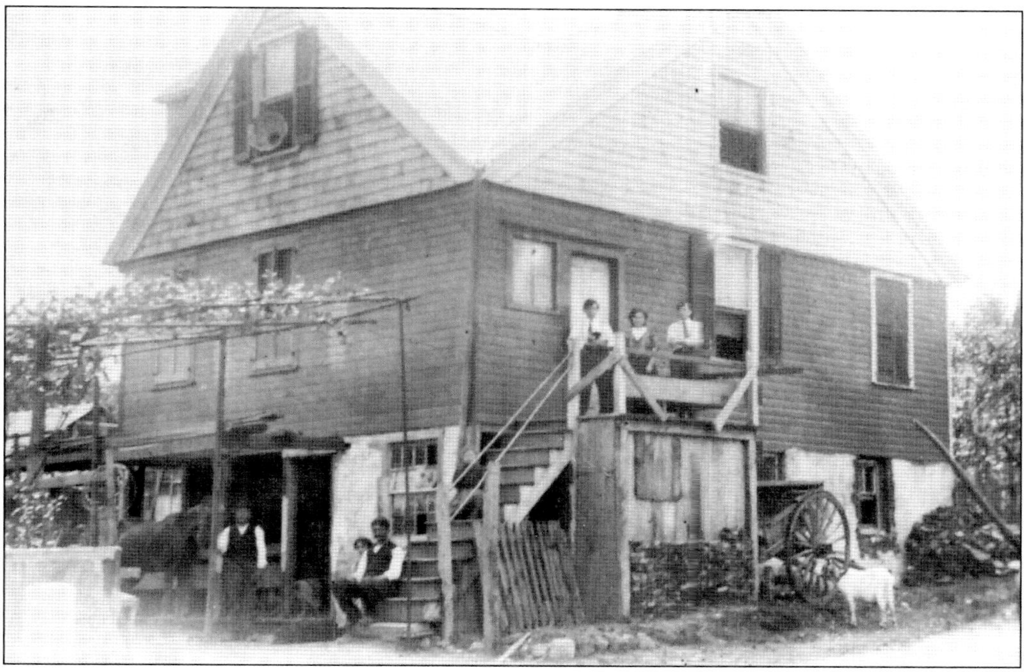

The Andriola family home, located at 15 Wilson Street, is shown here c. 1905. Mr. Anthony Andriola stands near the family horse while his son William stands at the top of the stairs. You can also see a goat, horse cart, and victrola horn (hanging out of the top-floor window).

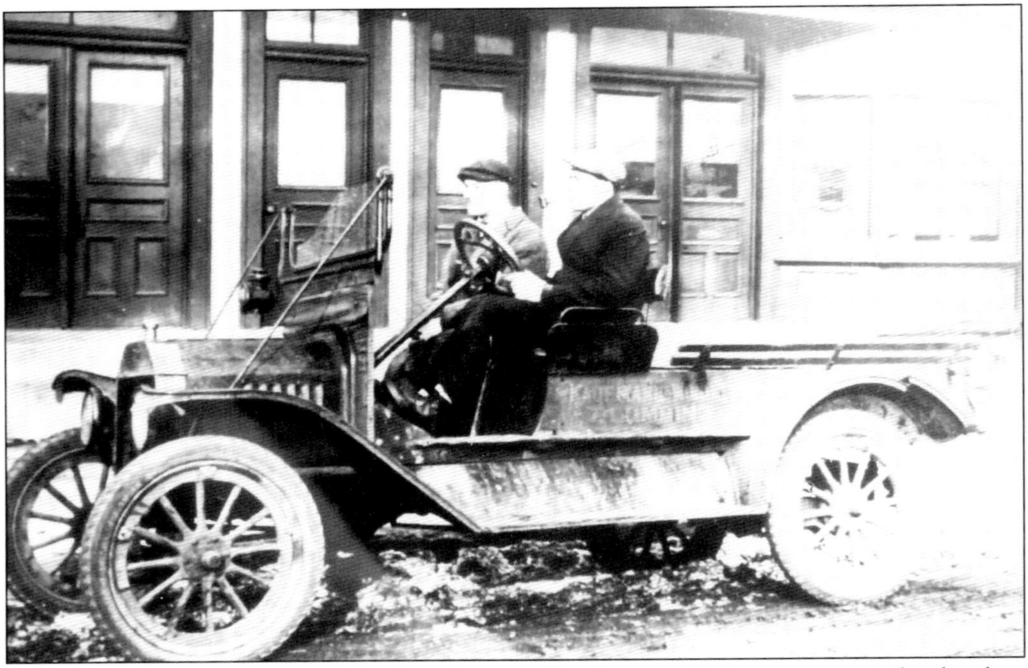

The driver of this early model truck is Conrad Windheim and the passenger is his brother, Fred Windheim Sr. This photograph was taken around 1911 when the two men started their plumbing business, then known as Kaufmann-Windheim Plumbing. The truck is parked outside of the shop at 309 Franklin Avenue, just left of the Franklin Middle School.

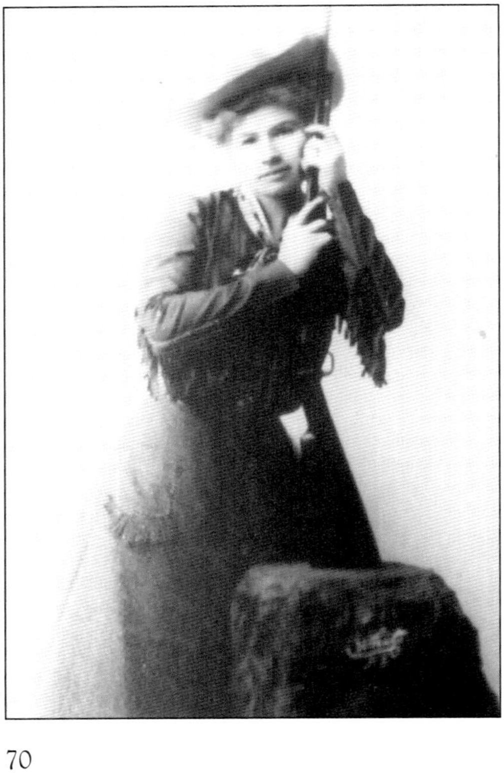

This is one of Nutley's more famous residents, Annie Oakley (Phoebe Anne Moses). She and her husband, Frank Butler, purchased a plot of land at 304 Grant Avenue and had a house built there. Even though they owned the house for about ten years, they were rarely in it due to their busy work schedules. The house was taken down in 1937, and two new brick ones were built on the site.

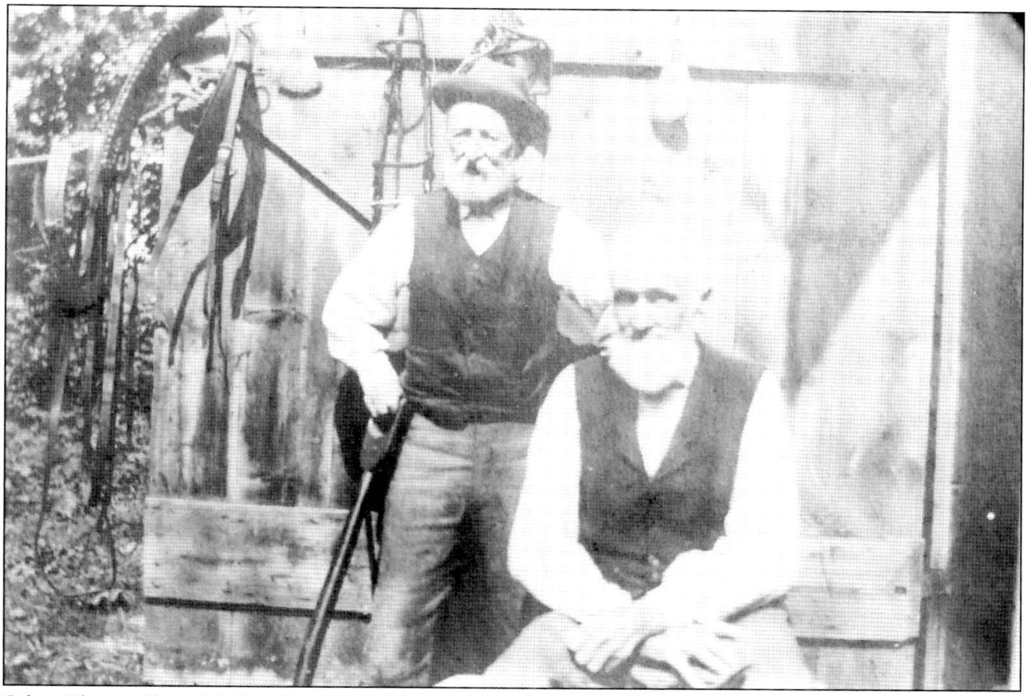

Silas Chappell and John Stager are shown here later on in their lives. The Stagers are a well-known Nutley family whose ancestors came to this area c. 1780. It was a Stager family member that donated land for the Reformed Church; the land where the museum is today was purchased for school use from Henry Stager in 1857 for $220. Four Stagers fought in the Civil War.

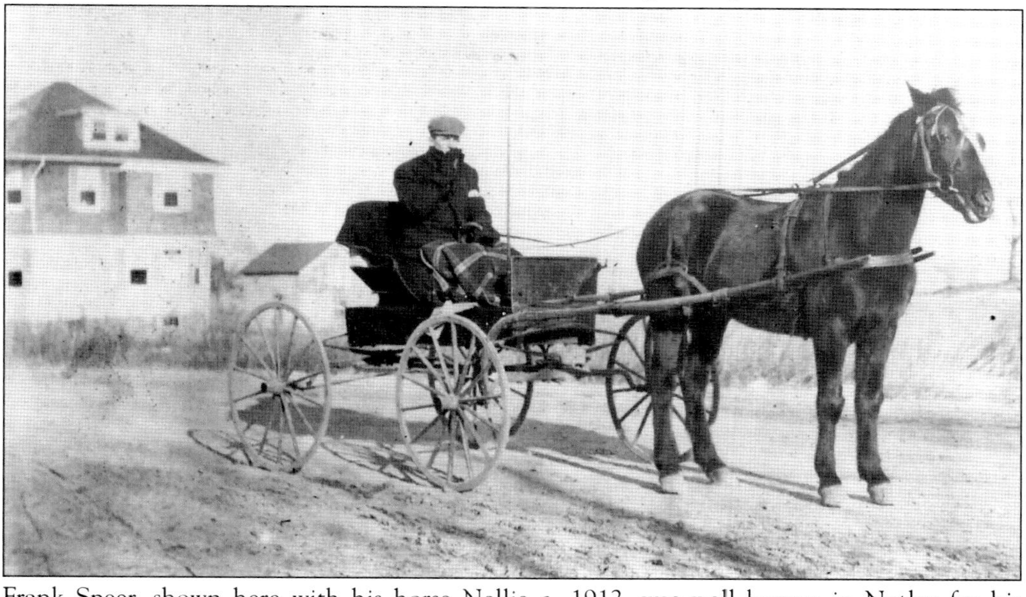

Frank Speer, shown here with his horse Nellie c. 1912, was well known in Nutley for his memories and recitals of early town history. Born in 1882, he lived during a time when there was tremendous growth and change in the town. It is from his recollections that many of the things that we know about early Nutley were obtained.

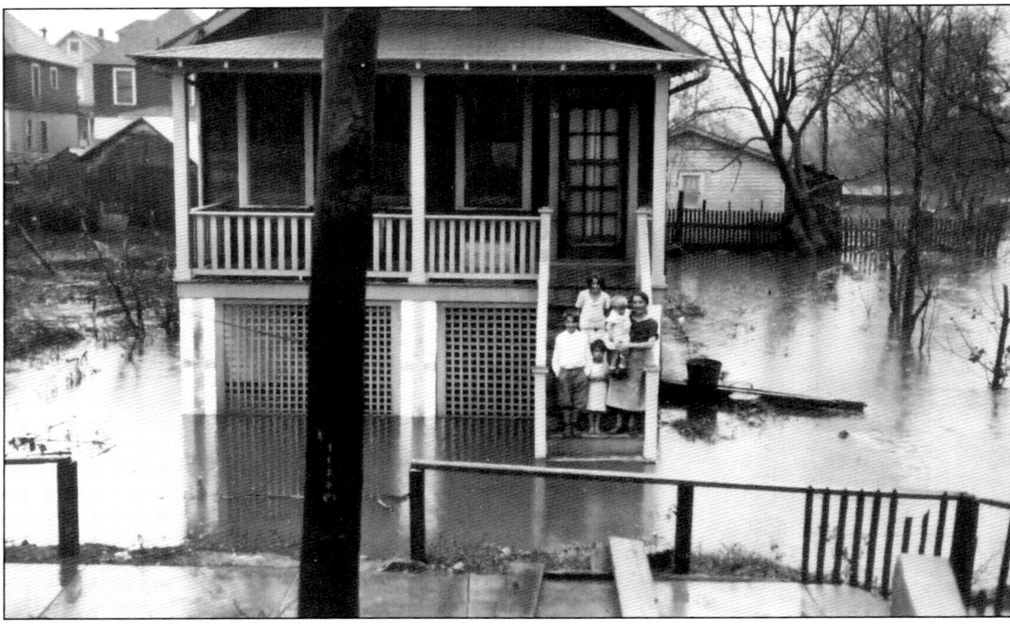

The usually quiet Third River can rage at times. In 1932, after some heavy rains, the river broke over its banks and flooded many nearby homes. The Gennaro family, shown here, had to use planks provided by the town to get to the sidewalk. The house is at 51 Albany Avenue.

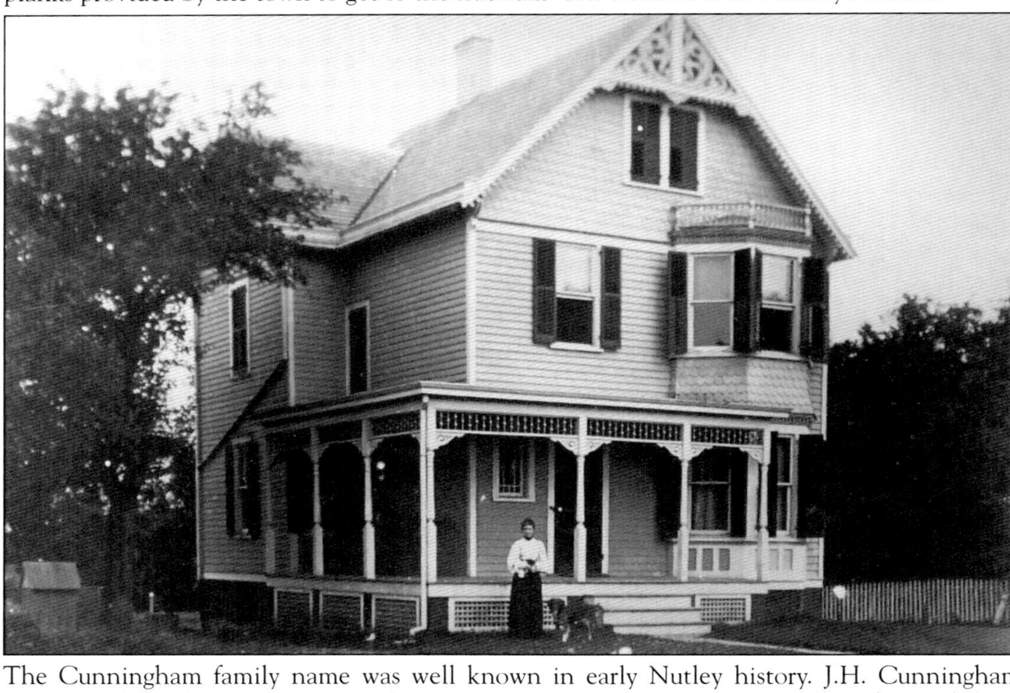

The Cunningham family name was well known in early Nutley history. J.H. Cunningham was one of the fifty-eight men to leave Nutley and fight in the Civil War. Three of those men, including Cunningham, were killed in battle. R.S. Cunningham was the collector of taxes during the early 1890s. This is the Cunningham home at 382 Prospect Street, near Chestnut Street.

These children are part of another well-known Nutley family. Carmen would become a town commissioner and mayor, while his brother Frank would come to own the town newspaper. The photograph was taken in front of the east Nutley Garage at 55 Washington Avenue; the children are, from left to right, Mary, Carmen, and Frank Orechio.

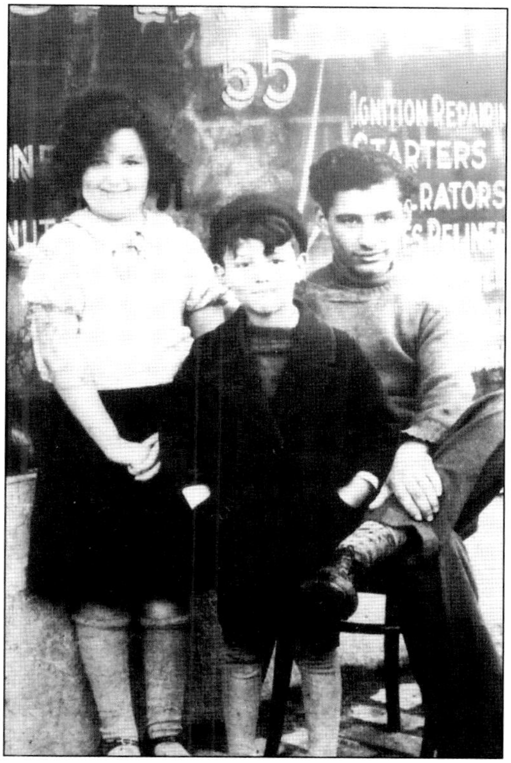

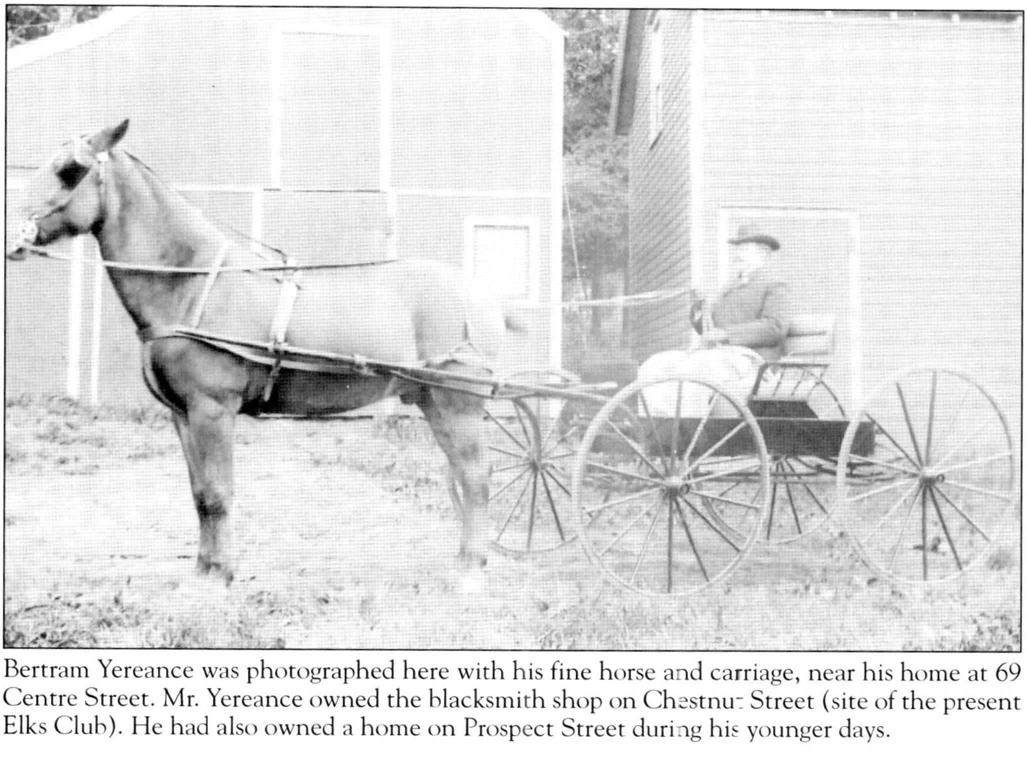

Bertram Yereance was photographed here with his fine horse and carriage, near his home at 69 Centre Street. Mr. Yereance owned the blacksmith shop on Chestnut Street (site of the present Elks Club). He had also owned a home on Prospect Street during his younger days.

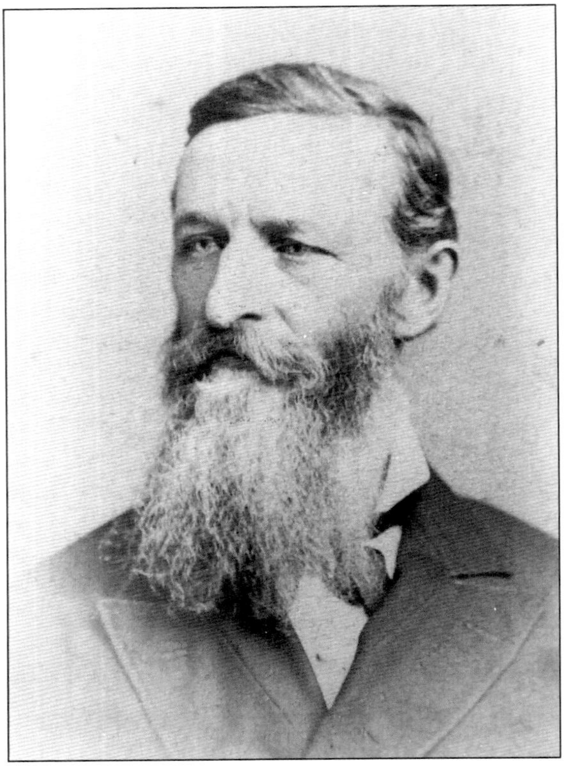

Silas Chappell was part of a family that would merge with the Stagers and Speers through marriage. Silas was born in the late 1820s and worked, at age eight, for the Duncan Mill along the Passaic River. This mill produced block-printed handkerchiefs and scarves. It was another Chappell, Albert, that donated land for one of Nutley's earliest public schools, built *c.* 1825.

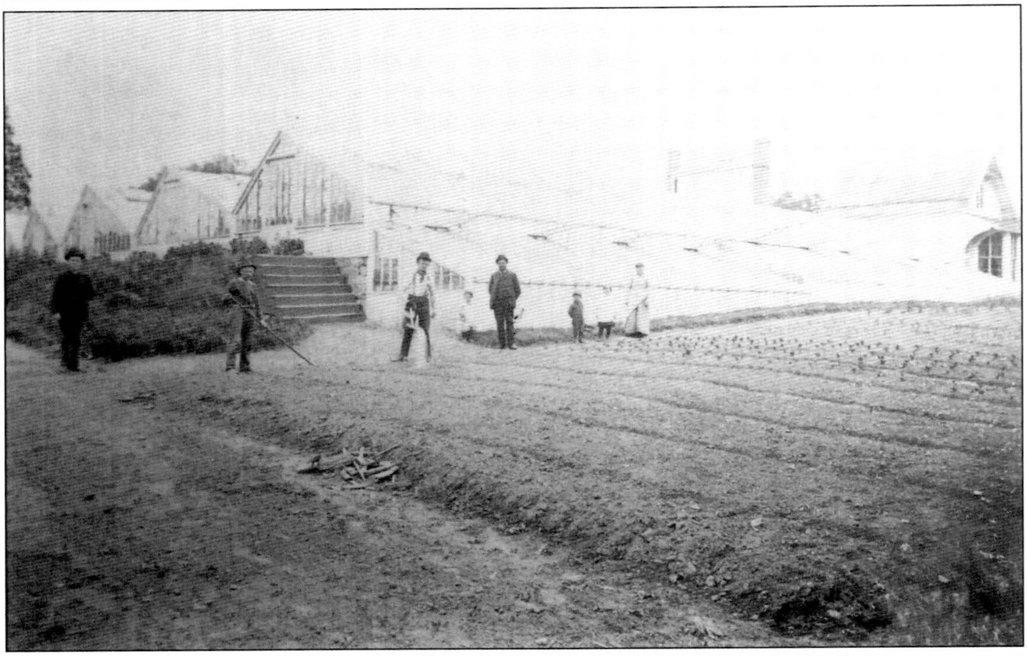

The greenhouses of Windheim Florists were located on the west side of Walnut Street, near Park Avenue. The Windheims were well known for their flowers, which they sold commercially around the area. The family also owned a peach orchard on the east side of Franklin Avenue.

Seven

School Days

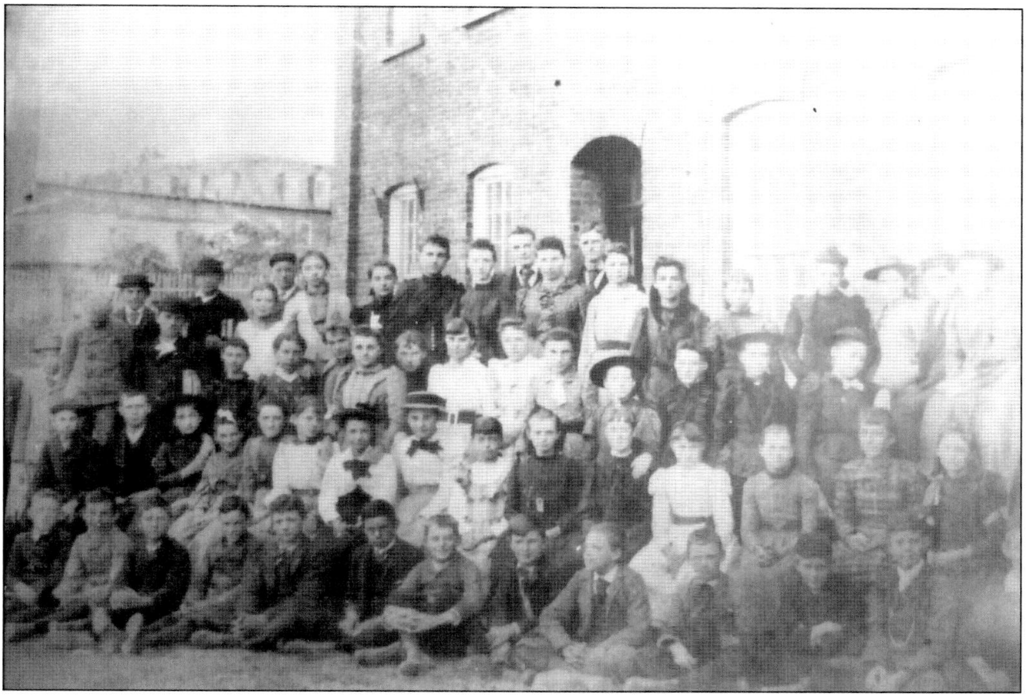

These students were taught at Park Hall in 1892. Park Hall was one of the mill buildings on the old Duncan Mill site. The mill property was obtained for school use because school space was needed for the growing town. In 1894, Park School was built (where the present high school is), and Park Hall eventually became Nutley Town Hall.

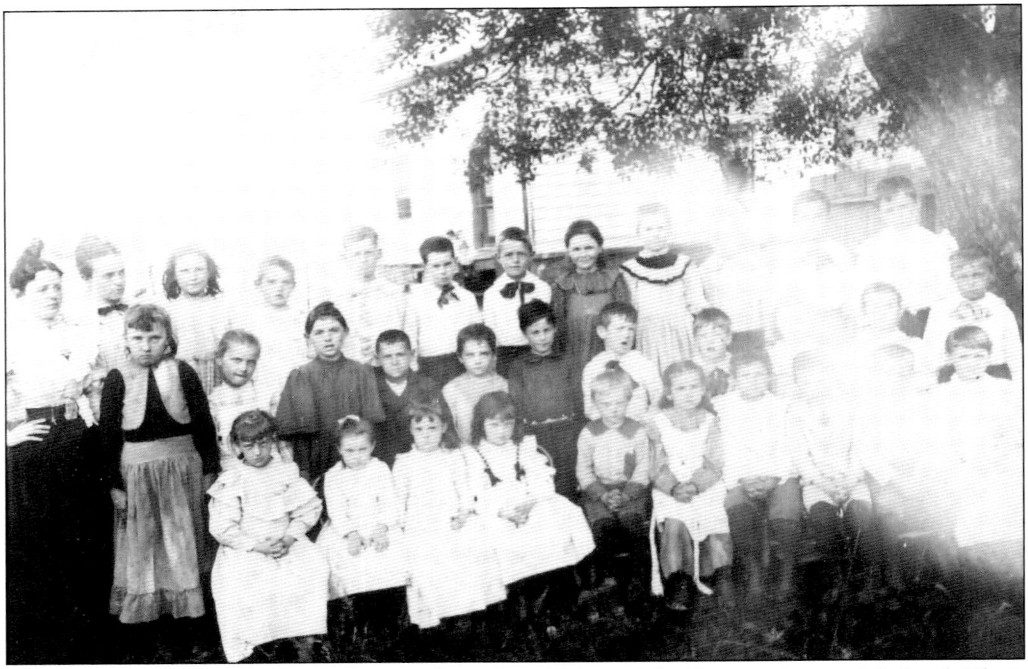

These youngsters on May 31, 1895, are from the old Avondale (Passaic Avenue) School. Their teacher was Miss Ackley, and the children seem to vary in age quite a bit. The unhappy little girl standing up front next to the teacher is Addie Austin, who seems to be having a really bad day.

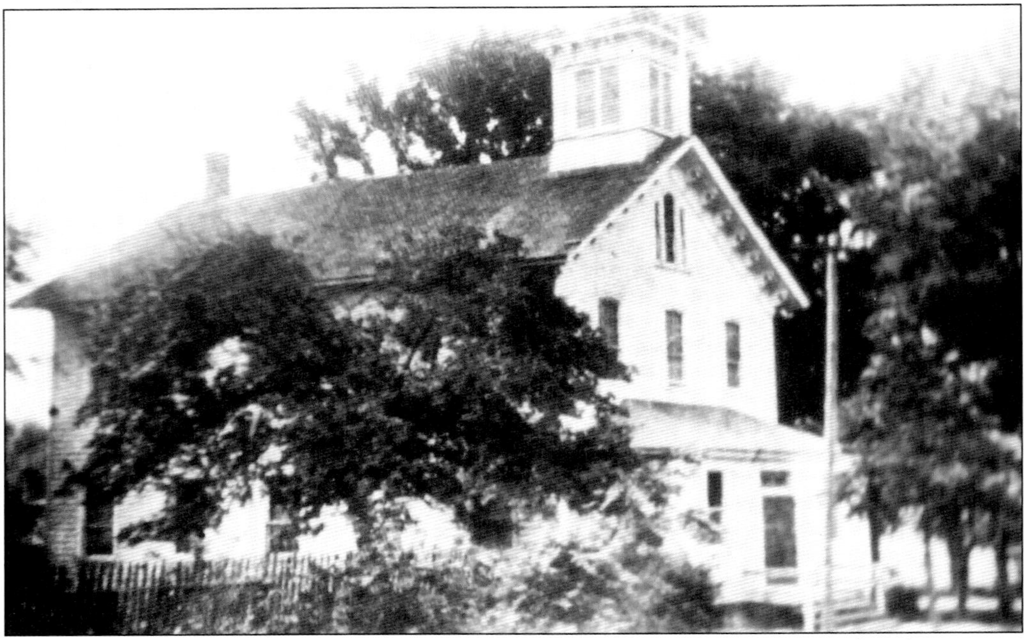

The Passaic Avenue School, which stood on the northeast corner of Passaic and Park Avenues, was one of Nutley's earliest schools. Built around 1850, this school had the first graduating high school class in town in 1892.

The Church Street School, which replaced a fire-damaged frame building on the same site, was built in 1875. It was used as a public school for many years before it became a vocational school and VFW headquarters. Today it is home to the Nutley Historical Society and is on the National Register of Historic Places.

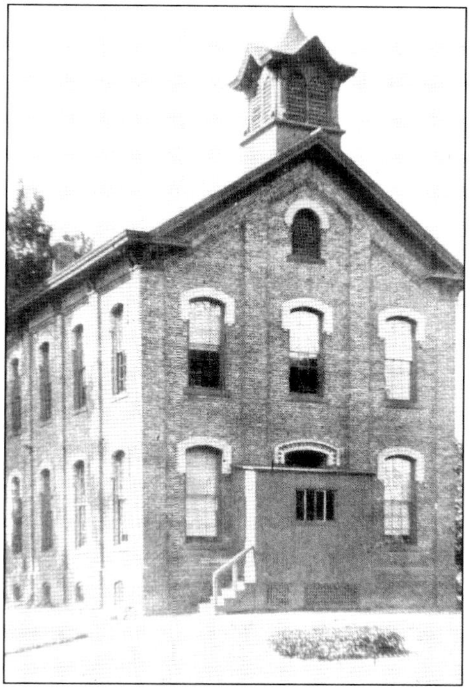

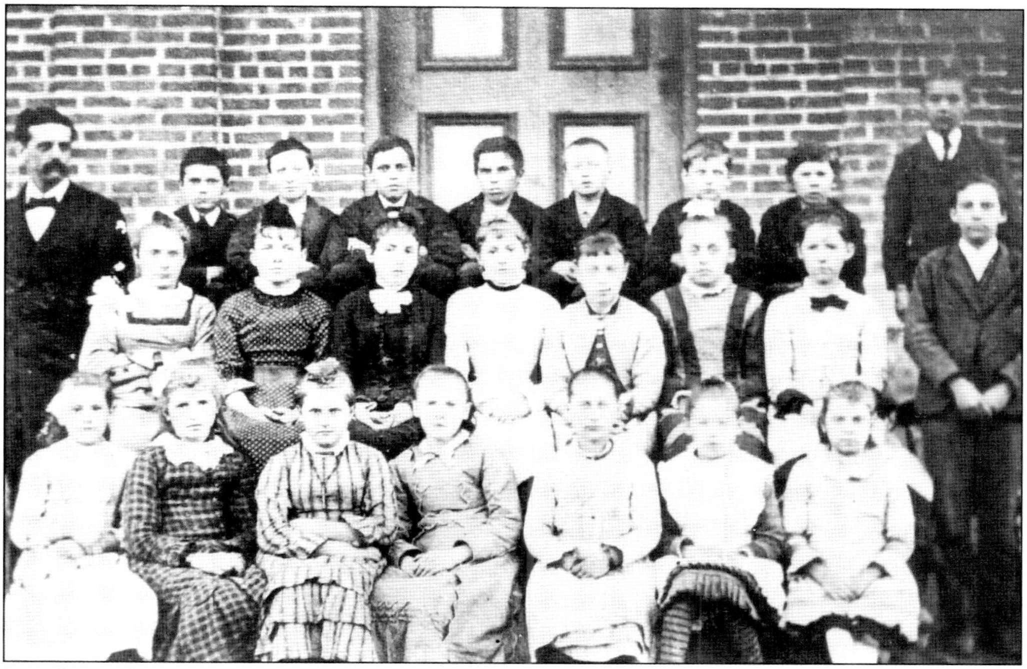

It is the author's unconfirmed suspicion that a heavy fine would befall your family if your child smiled during a school photograph! Actually, their stoic faces can probably be attributed to the fact that shutter speeds were a lot slower in 1879, when this photograph was taken, and trying to hold a smile could result in a blurred photograph. The kids are under the watchful eye of their teacher, Mr. Applegate.

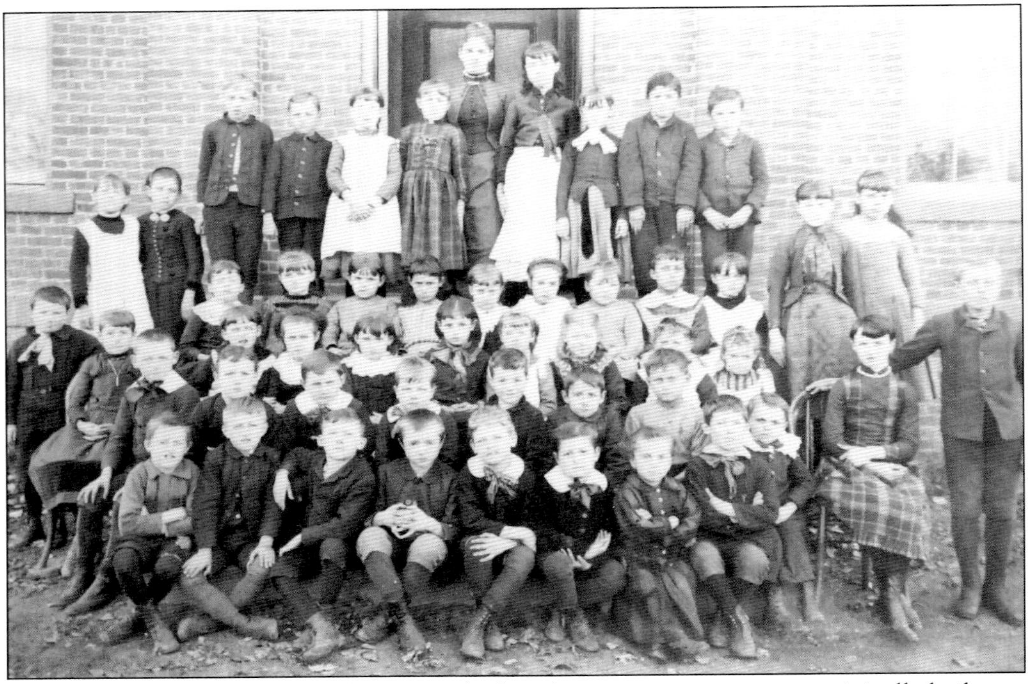

The brick building at 65 Church Street, which is the current museum, was originally built as a school. Technically, it was designated as School #5, but most people called it the Church Street School. In this photograph, it is spoken of as "Hill School," whose 1887 class is shown here with their teacher, Miss Gertrude Broadbent.

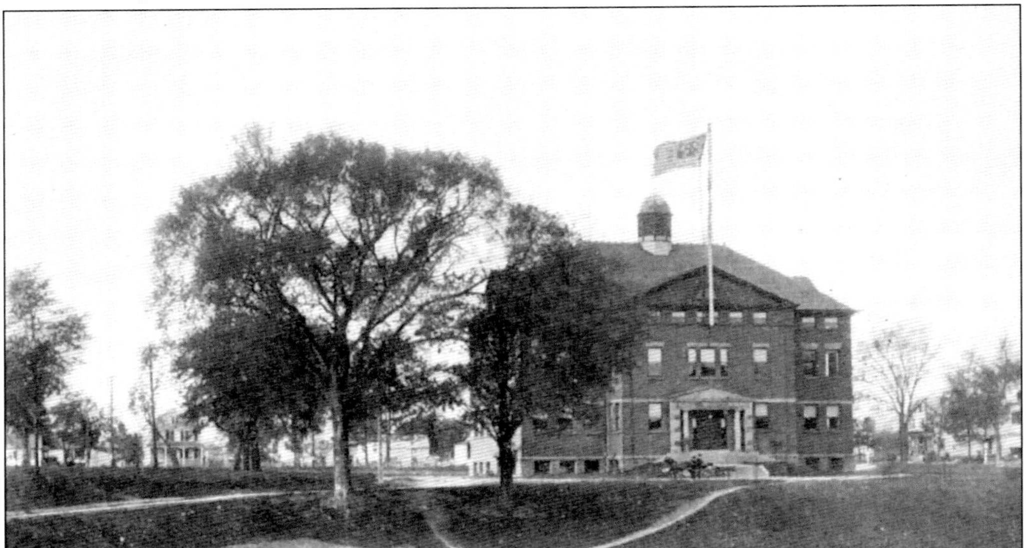

In 1894, the original section of what was to be known as Park School was built to accommodate the growing number of school age children. Prior to this, time there were only the Passaic Avenue School and the Church Street School. Classes were also held at various locations around town, such as the Duncan homestead (site of the present library) and Park Hall (today's town hall).

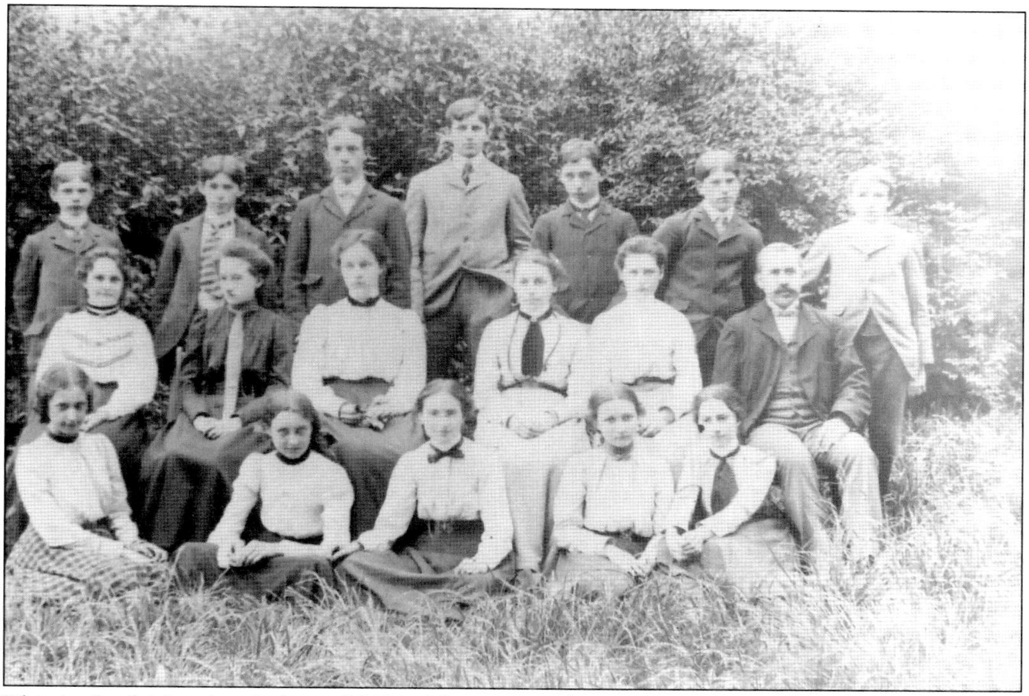

This is the high school class of 1901. The principal, Mr. Wright, is seated at the end of the second row. Listings of the graduating class of 1901 show that there were thirteen students, but for some reason seventeen young adults are shown in this photograph.

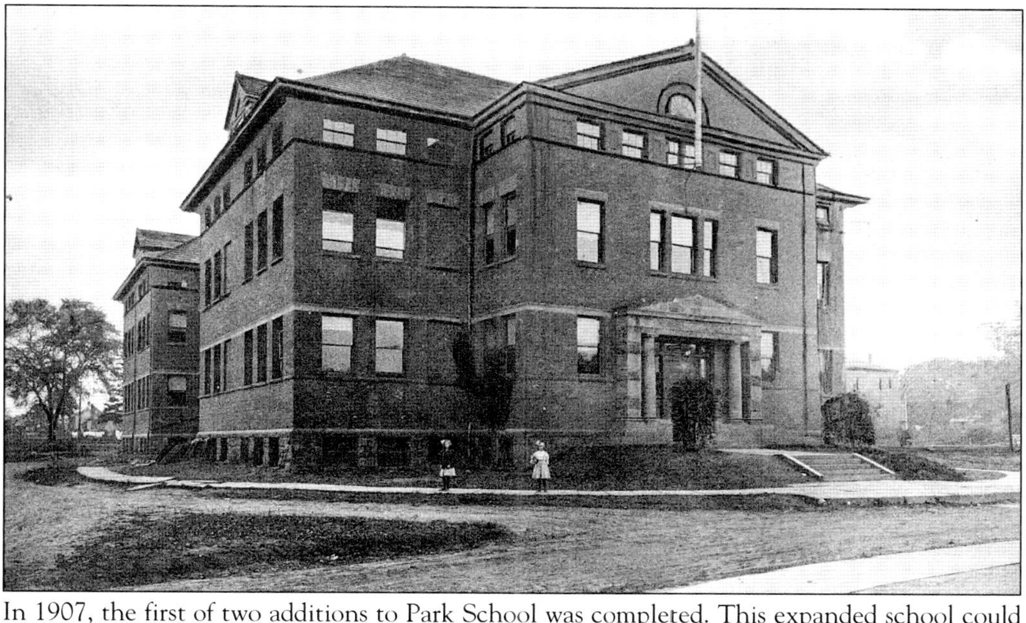

In 1907, the first of two additions to Park School was completed. This expanded school could now house all grades of schoolchildren and would be sufficient in size for the next fifteen years, when once again the expanding population of Nutley would strain the school's limits.

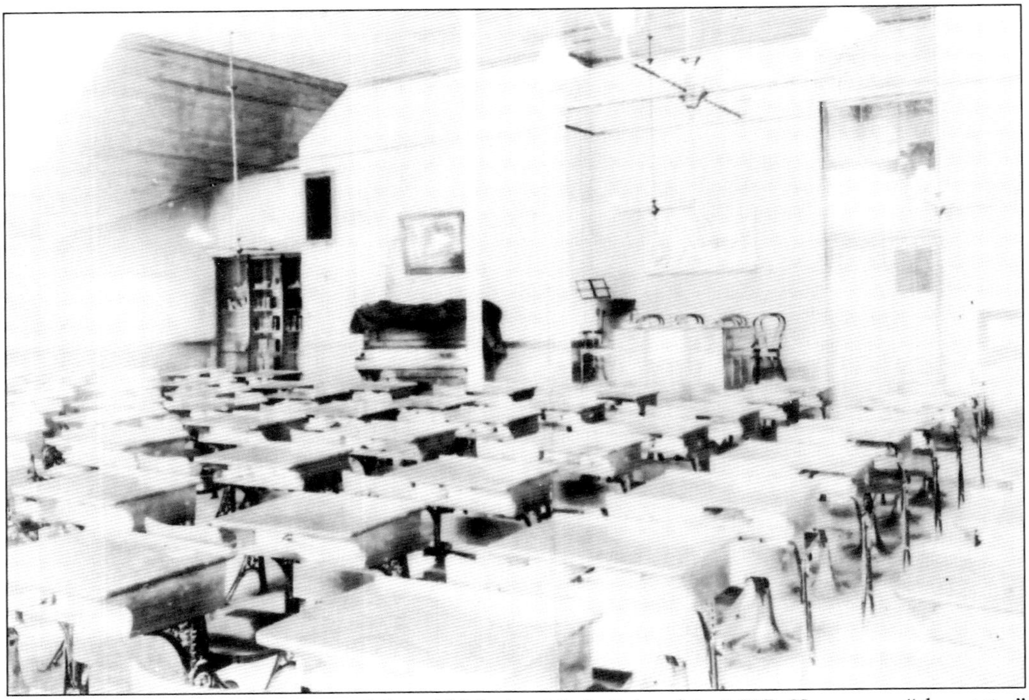

This is the top-floor classroom of the old Nutley High School in 1897. Known as "the attic," this and other rooms of the Park School (as it was called then) were used until 1956, when the building became too old and dangerous to renovate.

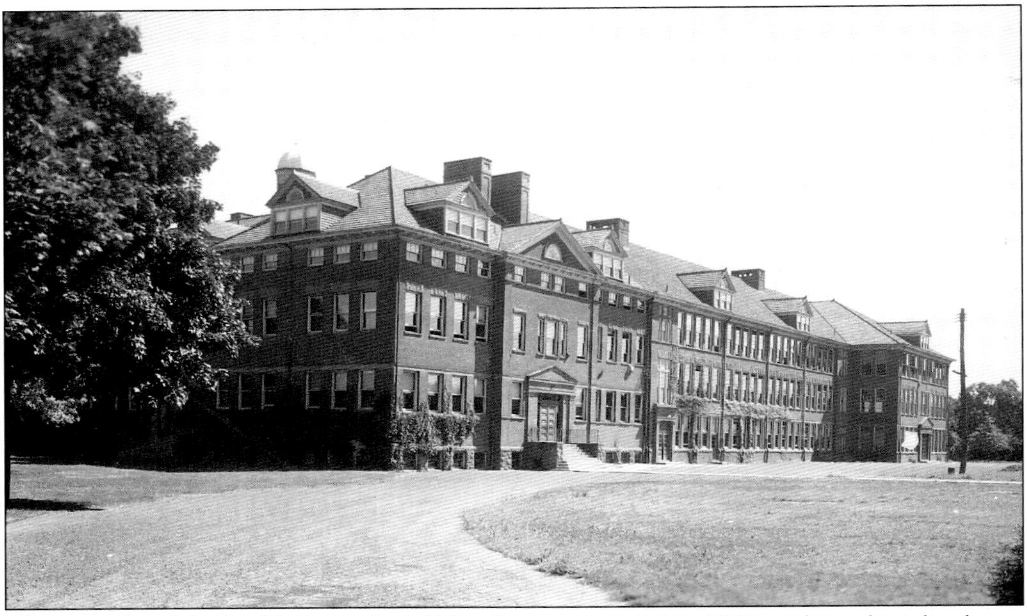

The second and final addition to Park School was completed in 1923, making the school very formidable indeed. In 1956, the original 1894 school and its 1907 addition were taken down. Now only the 1923 addition can still be seen attached to the back of the present high school.

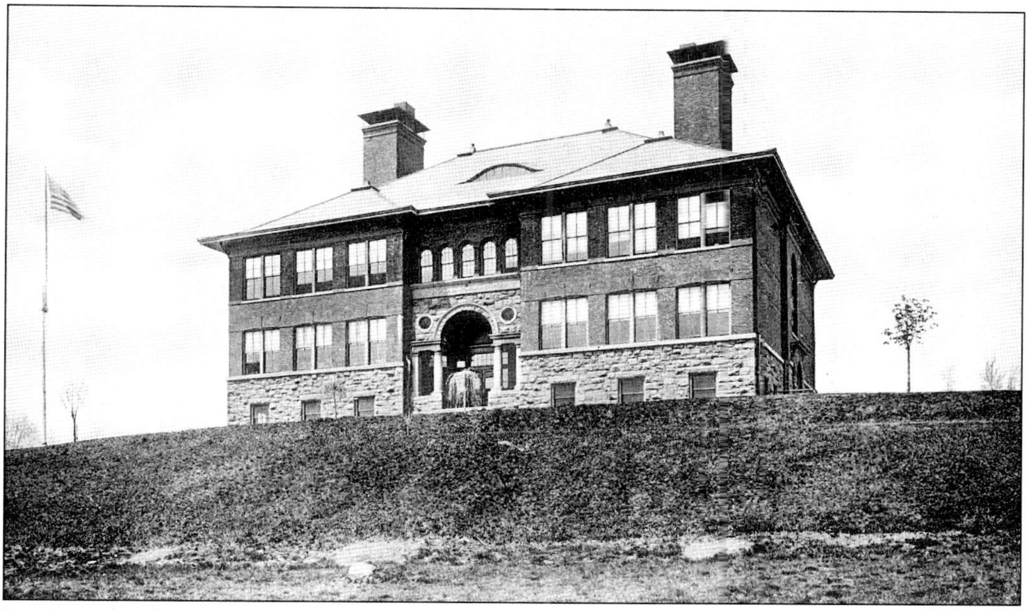

In 1902, the first part of Yantacaw Public School was constructed. The large square towers on top of the school were ventilator shafts for the rooms. Many in town fondly remember this little school building prior to its 1929 addition, which completely changed its look.

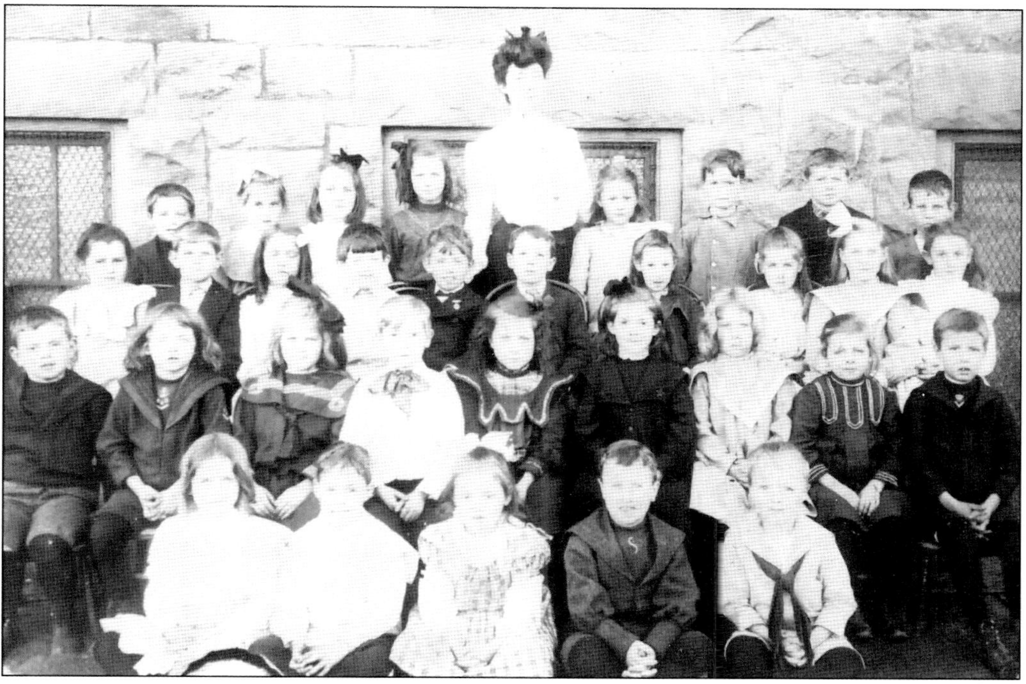

Somewhere in this photograph is second-grader Lloyd Adams, of West Nutley. His name, plus the date November 17, 1903, were penciled on the back of this photograph. The teacher's name is given as Miss Laura Stager; the picture was taken at Yantacaw School, which was built the year before.

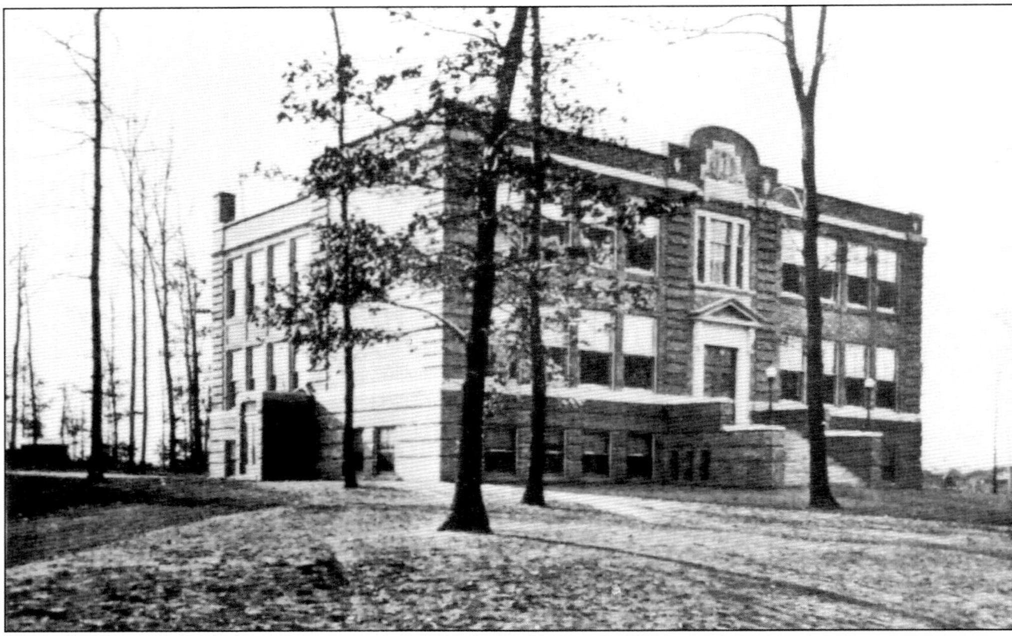

The first section of Lincoln School was built in 1915 for around $50,000 and only contained eight classrooms. In 1920, for another $90,000, the school had its first addition. In 1929, it was decided that the school would have to be added to again. This photograph was taken *c.* 1916.

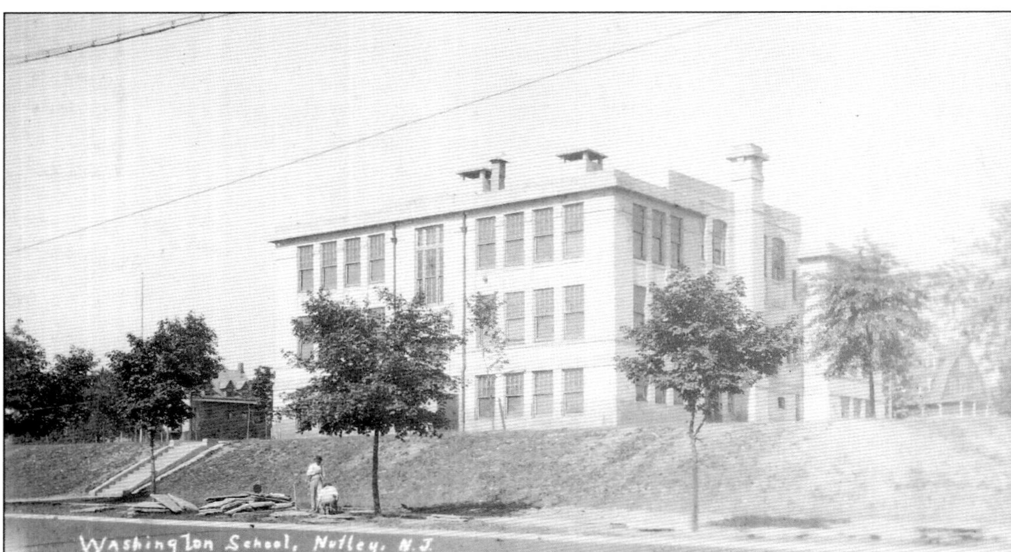

The workmen in this photograph are laying a new slate sidewalk by Washington School. Built in 1911, it was pretty unique for a Nutley school, due to its extensive use of poured concrete. The original school was added to in 1927, and the main entrance is now on Washington Avenue.

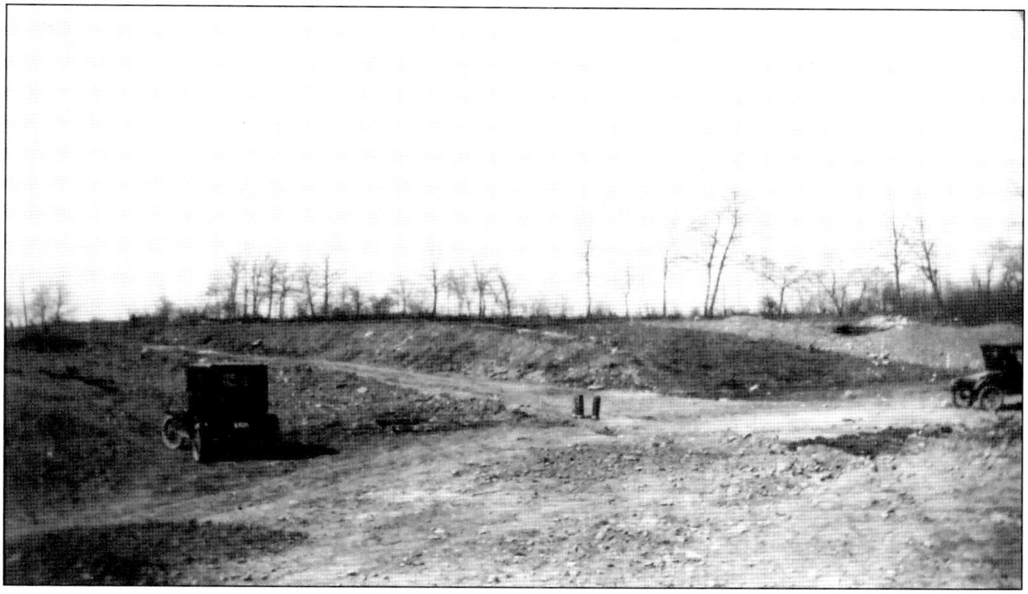

The building stakes in the middle of this picture mark the intersection of North Spring Garden Avenue and School Lane. The view is looking toward Alexander Avenue and was taken around 1917, the same year that Spring Garden School was being built.

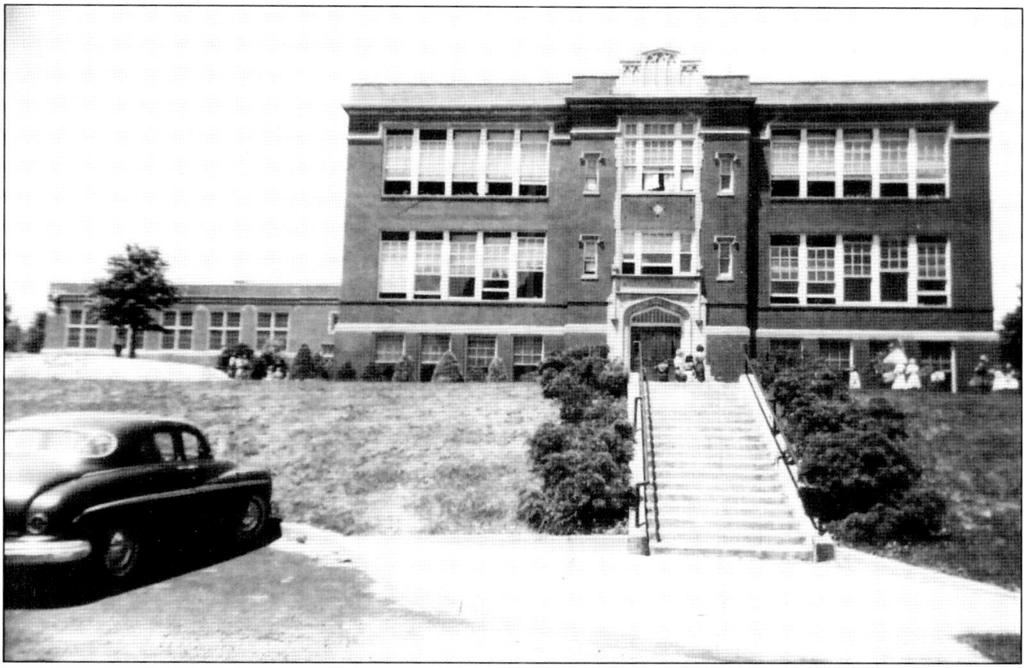

In 1917, a school was built in the Spring Garden section of town, which was one of the last development projects that the Nutley Realty Company would undertake. This photograph of Spring Garden School, taken in 1957, shows the expanded school with its 1927 addition.

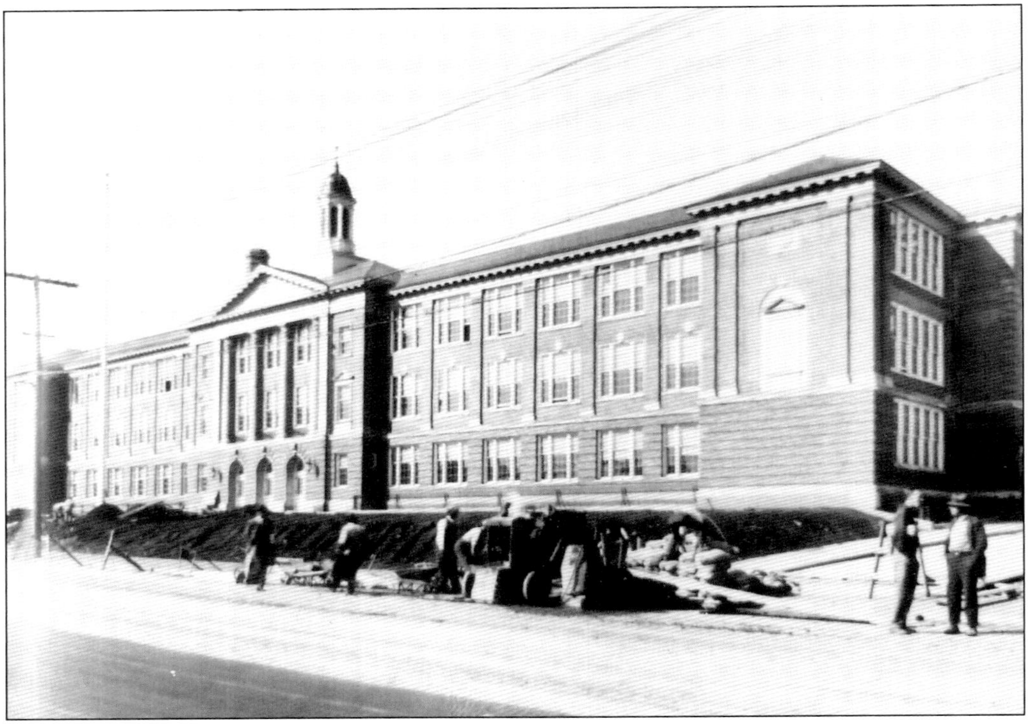

This building was originally designed to be used as a high school when it was built in 1926. The junior high school was across the street at the Park School building. In 1959, it was decided to switch the arrangement, and this became the Franklin Middle School.

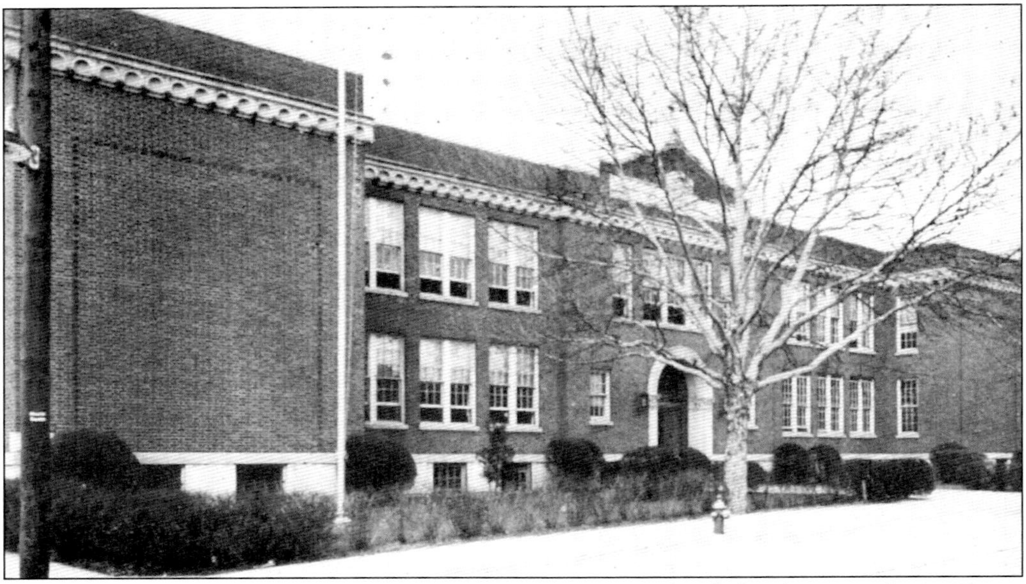

To satisfy a need for a Catholic school in town, Saint Mary's decided to have one built. This is a *c*. 1940 picture of Saint Mary's School; the 1921 building was expanded in 1926 and again in 1952. The school has since joined with Holy Family, to become Good Shepherd Academy.

Eight

Local Business

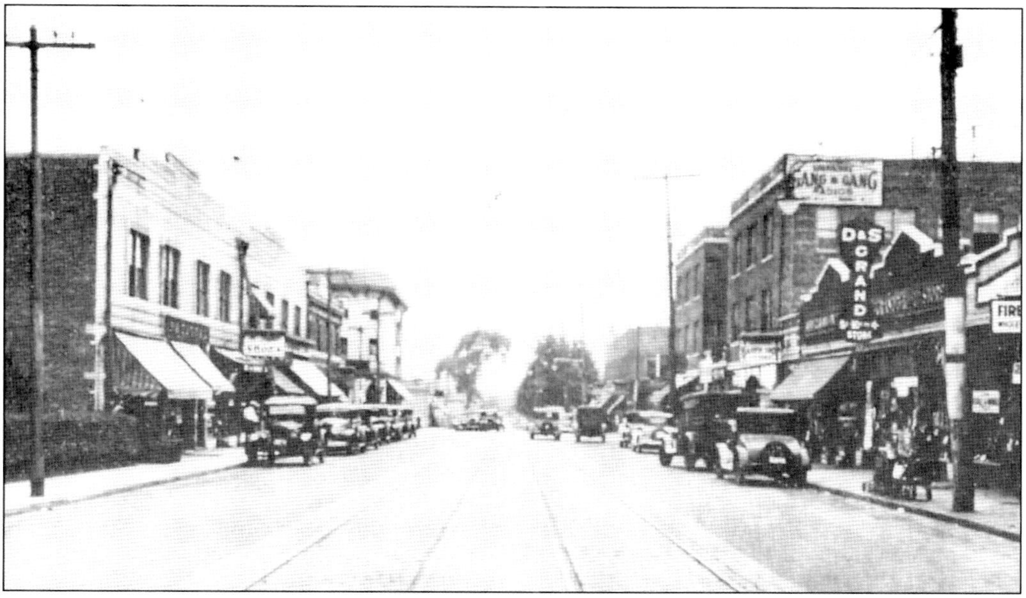

Here is an early 1930s view of Franklin Avenue, looking south toward Centre Street. This was the area that started Franklin Avenue's tremendous growth, and when this picture was taken, parking was still free. The trolley tracks were still running down the center of the road, but this would not last long. In 1937, the last trolley car passed down the street, never to return again.

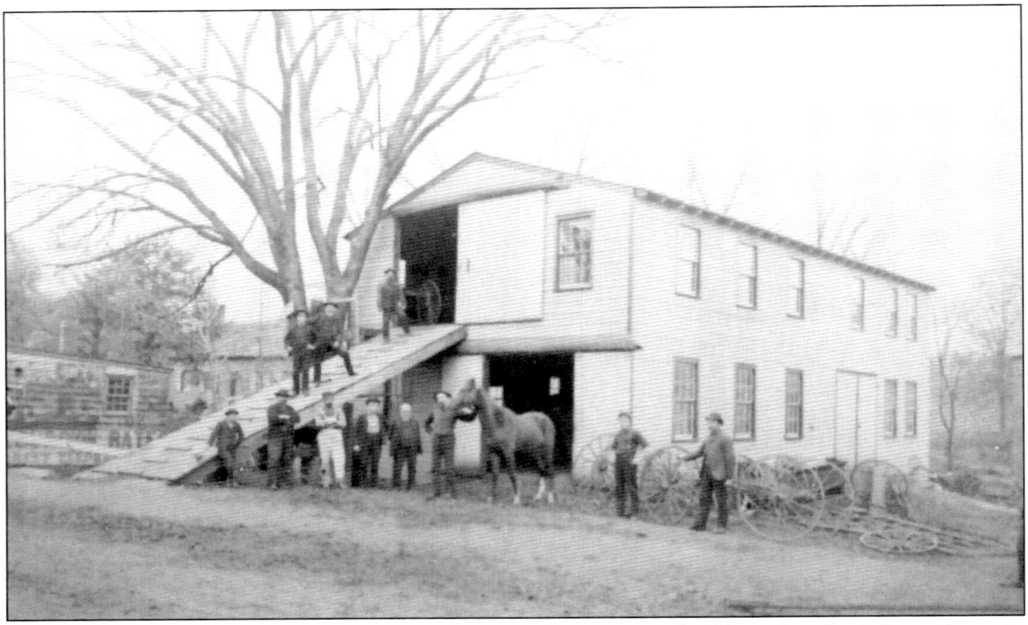

On the east bank of the Third River at Chestnut Street was a building that had three shops in one. Mr. Stirratt was a blacksmith, John Simpson was a wheelwright, and Thomas Brendreth ran a paint shop. The Vreeland homestead is visible on the other side of the river just behind the ramp. The building was used for storage by the town before being taken down.

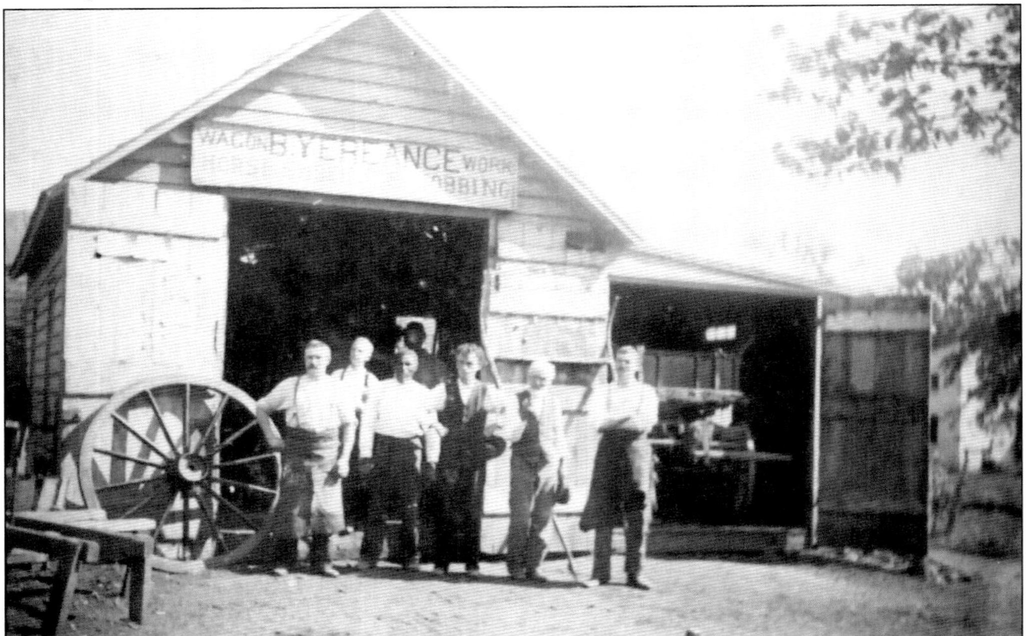

Bertram Yereance was the owner of a blacksmith shop located on Chestnut Street, where the Elks Club now stands. The blacksmiths were kept very busy in the old horse and wagon days, when the streets were very rough. Proper care of wagons was crucial to local businessmen, who relied on them for deliveries.

Thomas Hayes was one of several local plumbers to make his home and shop in Nutley. Indoor plumbing and central heating were becoming more standard features in homes, and Nutley's rapid growth kept many in the building trades occupied. Hayes ran his business for a time at 338 Passaic Avenue, at the corner of Chestnut.

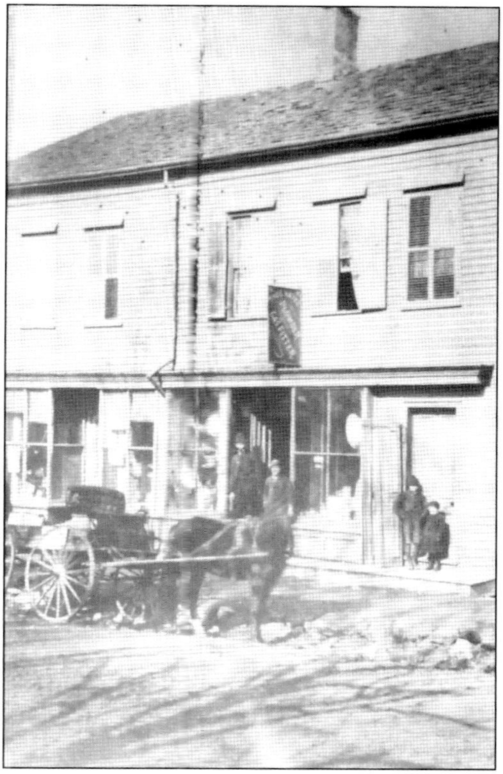

This is the inside of Hayes Plumbing shop at 338 Passaic Avenue. Mr. Hayes is seated here with his young apprentice, John Windheim, standing in back. On the left, a row of tubs, toilets, and sinks line the wall of the shop. Oddly enough, claw foot tubs are back in demand today.

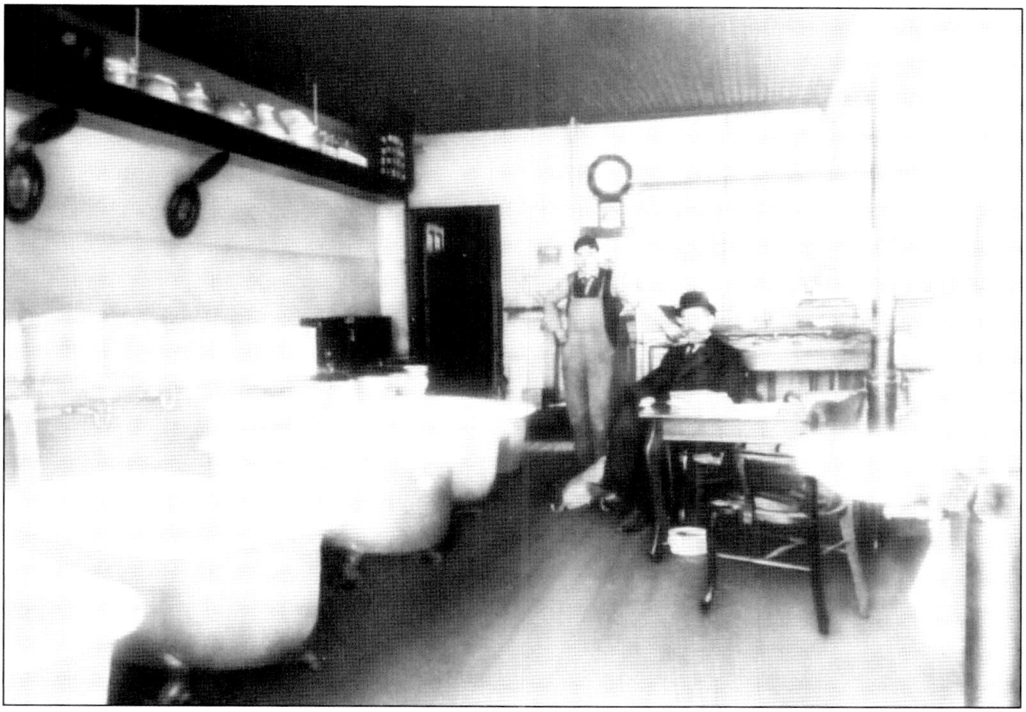

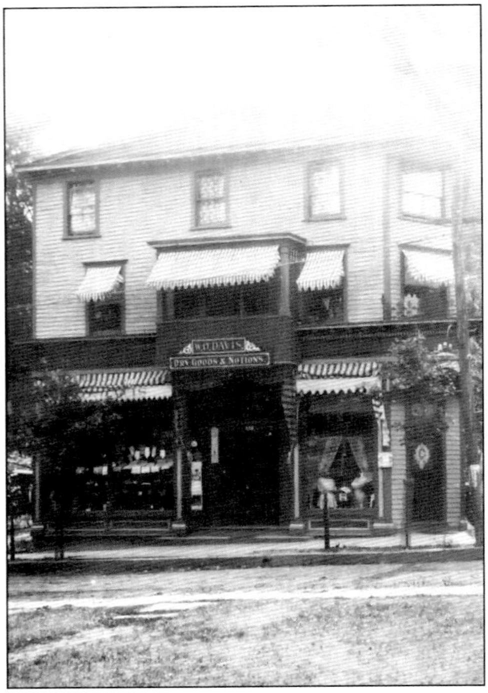

The W.O. Davis dry goods and notions store, at 350 Passaic Avenue, sits in the area that was a haven for local businesses. The white gloves and Victorian-style dresses date this picture, as does the horse-hitching post out front.

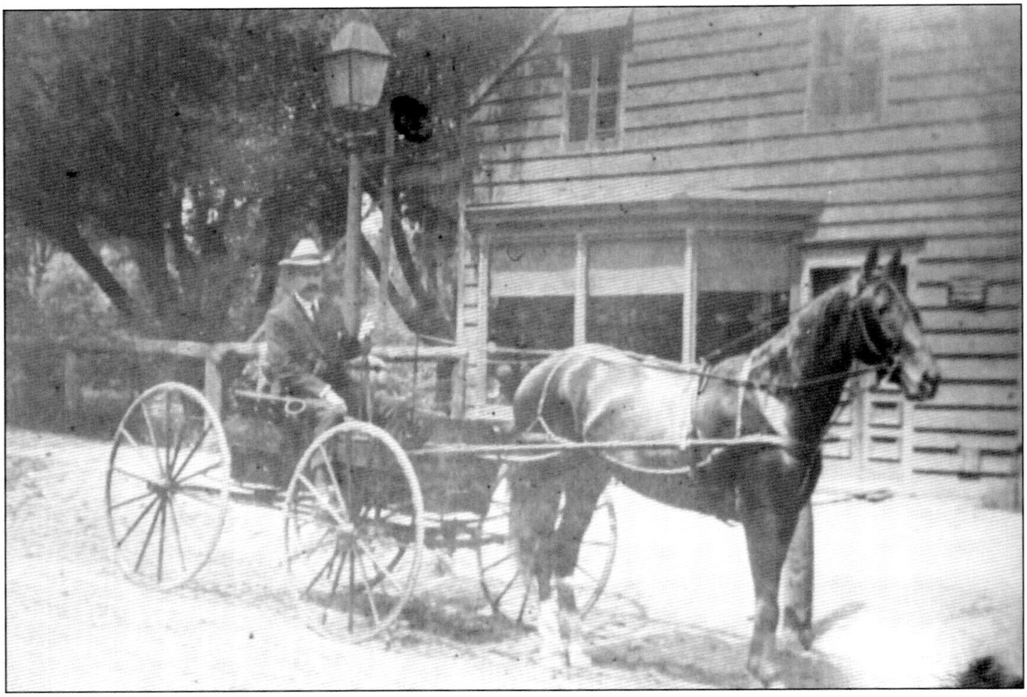

The house at 401 Passaic Avenue was once the office of Paterson-Passaic Gas and Electric, which eventually became Public Service Corporation. The building also housed a dry cleaners, and the storefront window was the scene for boxer training inside the house. The full-length glass is still encased in the wall section below the exposed glass on the house today.

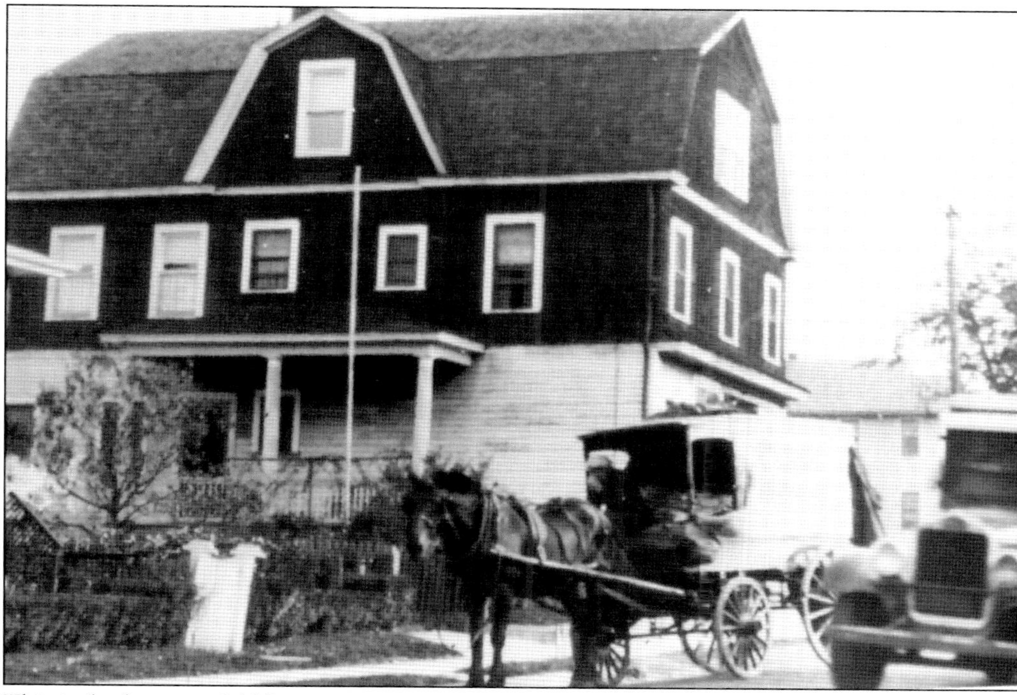

This is the house at 96 Harrison Street. Albert Stoppy had his shoe repair shop and then a confectionery store on the first floor. It is not certain what the horse cart out front was delivering, but it is plain to see that the automobile was already around. Horse-drawn wagons would soon become a thing of the past.

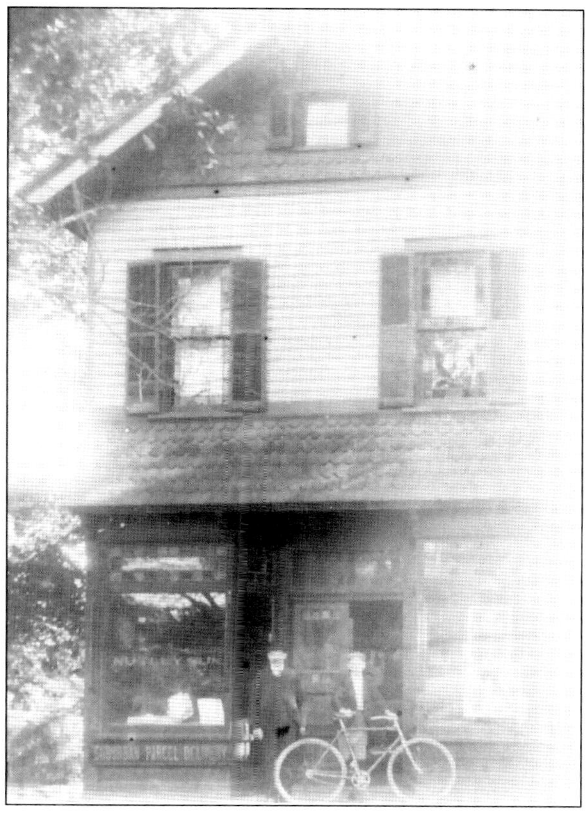

When Mr. Foy took over the *Nutley Sun* in 1900, he ran it from this building, which was on the east side of Franklin Avenue near Vreeland. Later operations moved across the street to 475 Franklin Avenue, right on the corner of Vreeland. That building still exists.

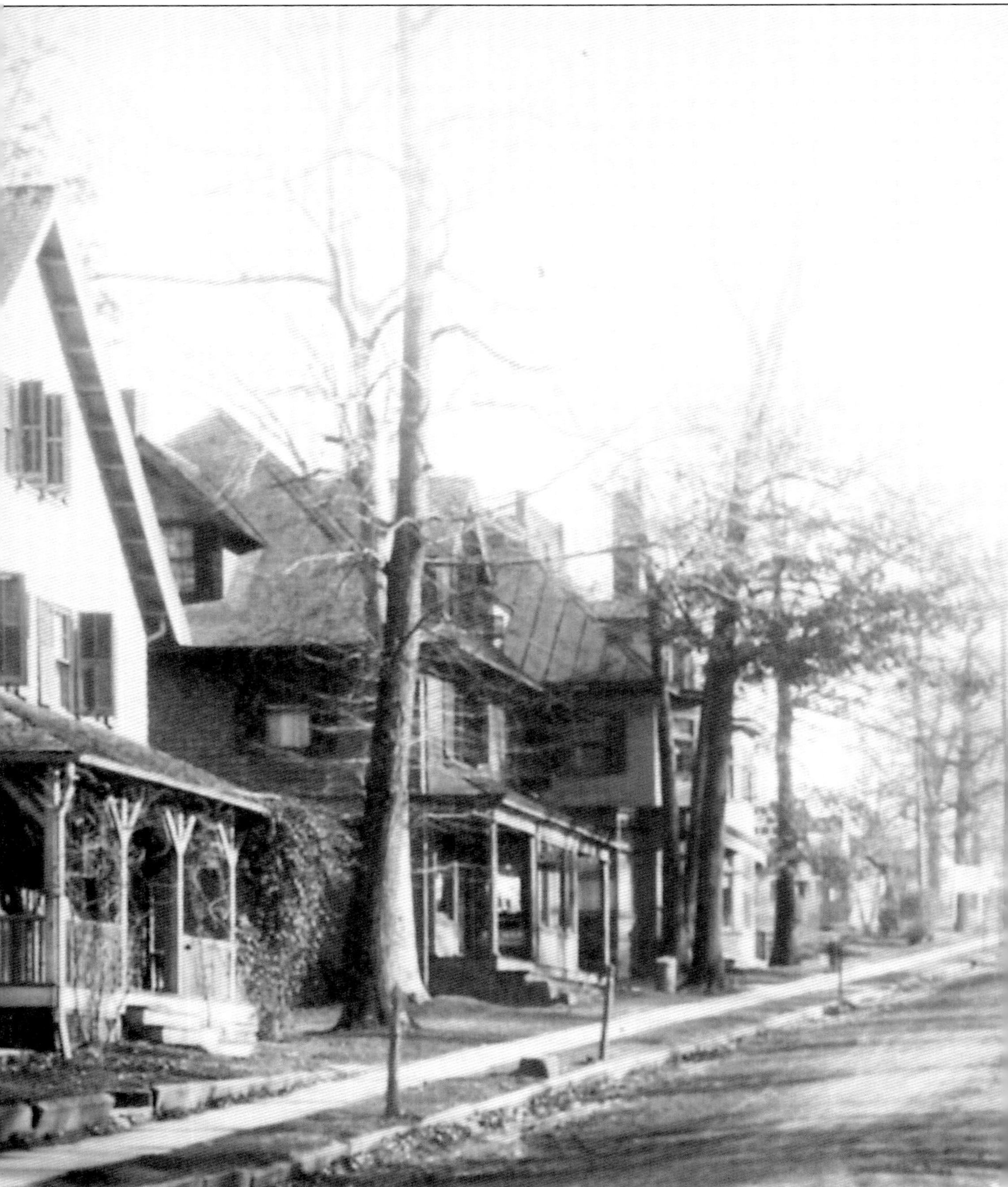

This is Highfield Lane, looking east from Passaic Avenue. On the left-hand side at the corner is Henry Connolly's meat market and hall, which was a post office branch during his time as postmaster. The next house up is P.F. Guthrie's confectionery store. Guthrie was the first person in town to have a public phone installed. Up from Guthrie's on the same side is the Columbia Building, which had apartments and business storefronts. On the right side, just

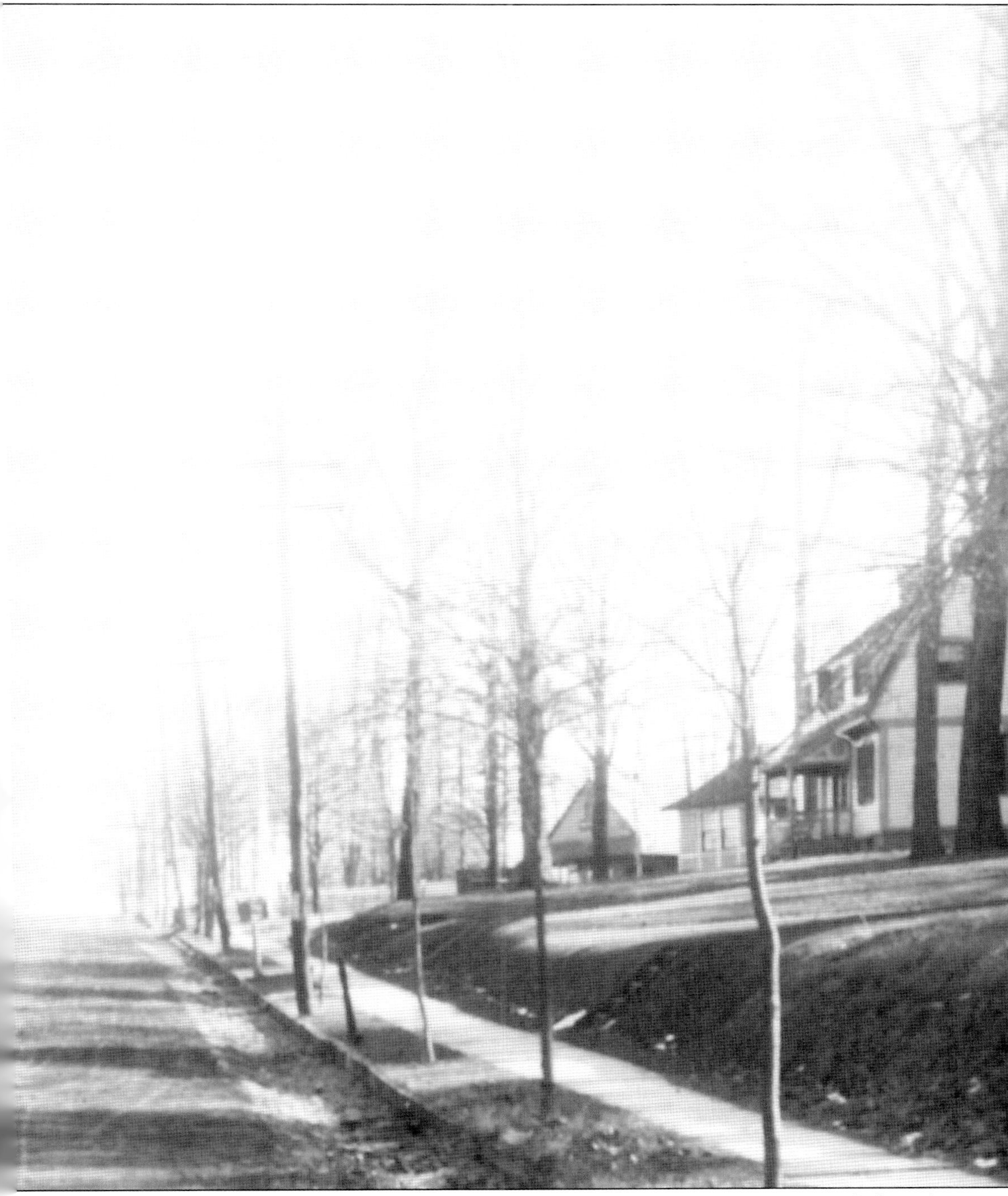

behind the house in the foreground, is a little building belonging to J.R. Hay. It is believed that a library of sorts was housed here prior to the construction of a more permanent library building. The last structure on the right is the Nutley Train Station, which serviced this part of town.

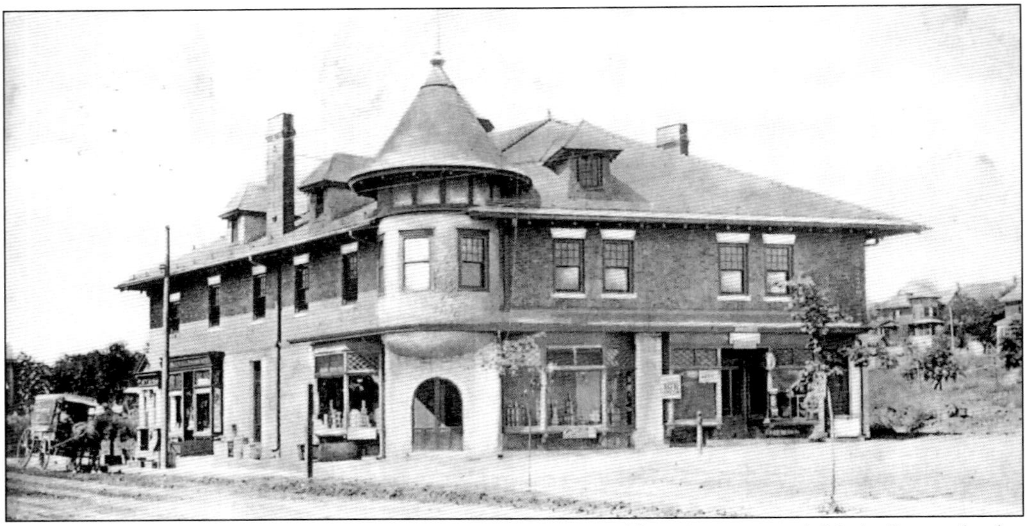

Built in 1904, the Masonic Hall on the corner of Franklin Avenue and High Street had a meeting hall on the second floor with storefronts below. During the showing of a movie in 1910, the film caught fire and burned the roof of the building. A third floor was added as part of the reconstruction work.

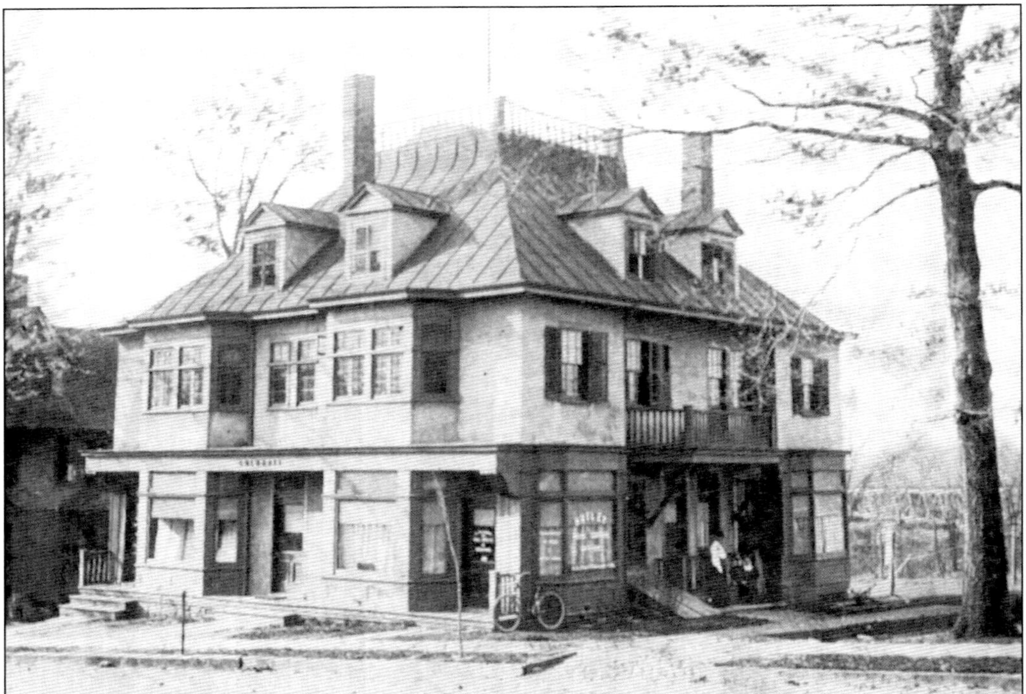

The Columbia Building was located at 288–290 Highfield Lane before it was demolished. It was an apartment building, with stores below owned by Dr. Satterthwaite. For a short period of time, the doctor donated a room to house the books of the future Nutley Library, which was built on Passaic Avenue in 1904.

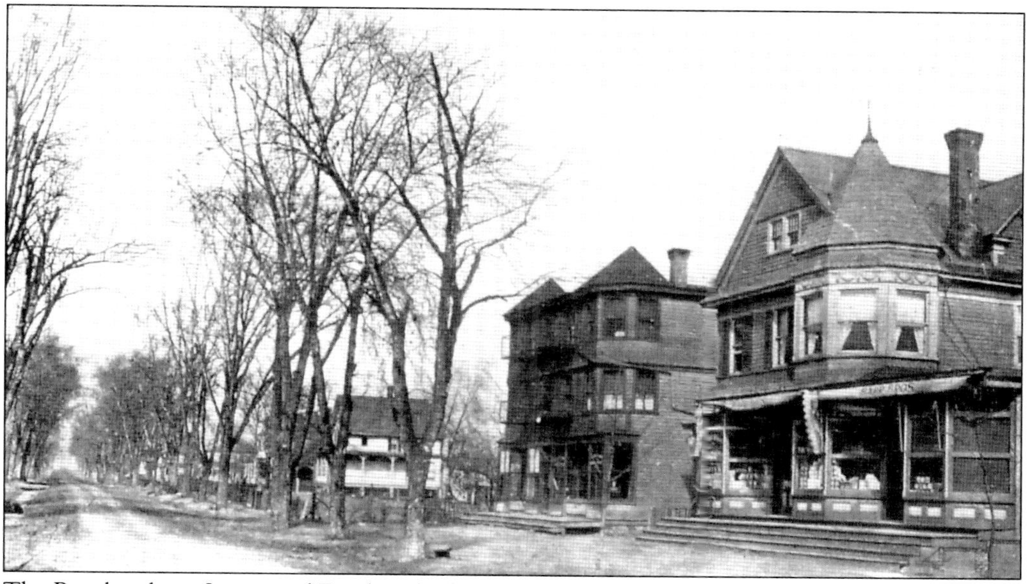

The Barr brothers, James and Frank P., had two store locations in town. One was at 474 Franklin Avenue and the other, pictured here, was at 92 Walnut Street near Park Avenue. This store sold groceries and meat, while the one on Franklin Avenue was a combination store and real estate office.

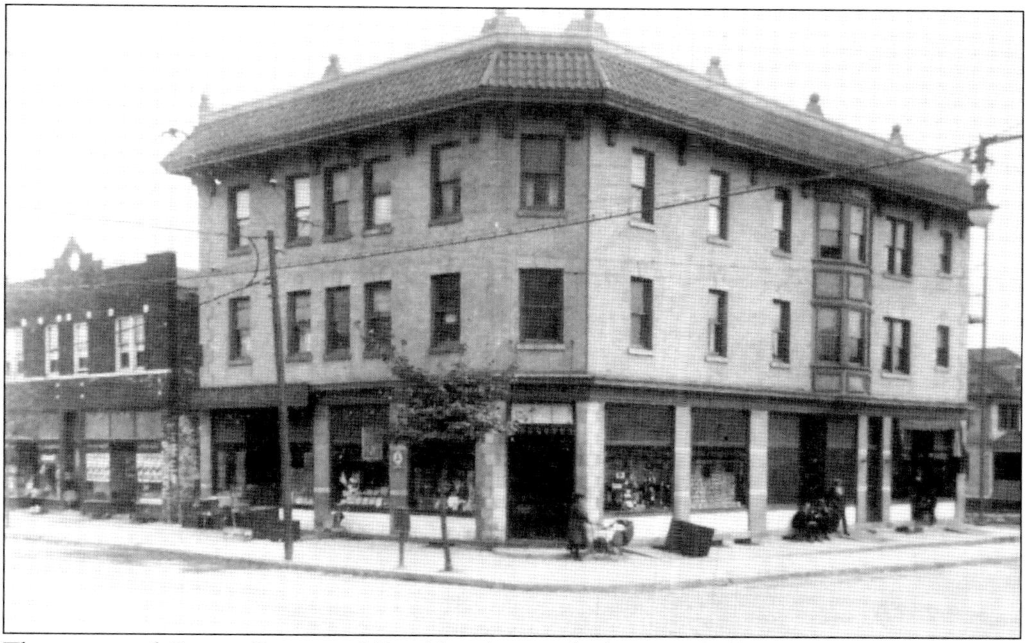

The corner of Centre Street and Franklin Avenue looks remarkably similar to this *c.* 1920s view, when the Great A&P Tea Company had one of its several Nutley stores here. It was at this corner that trolleys heading south on Franklin Avenue would turn left onto Centre Street to complete their trip toward Newark.

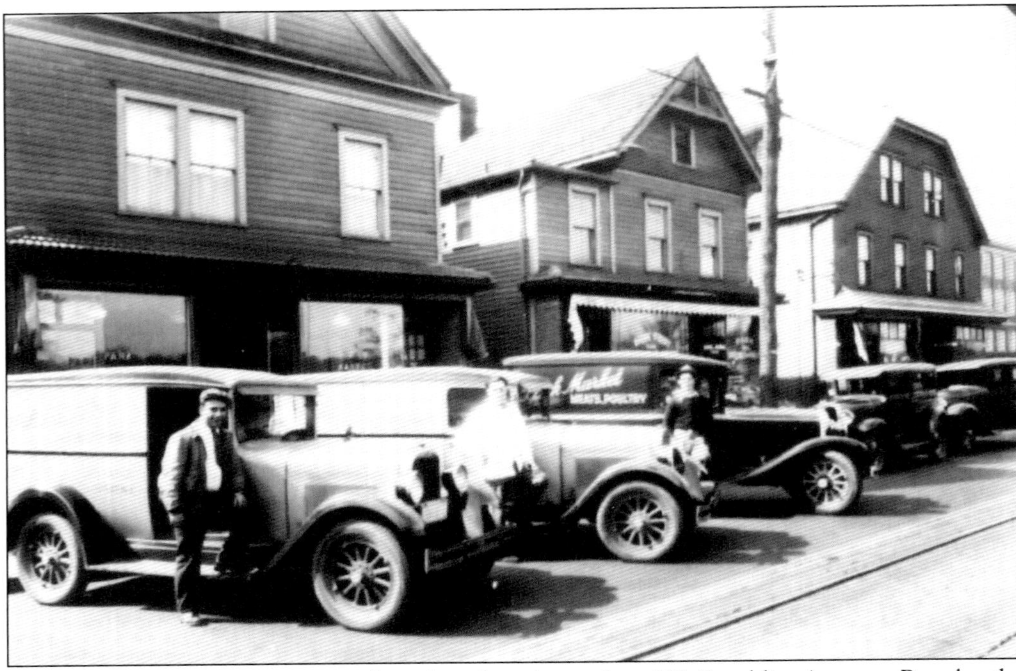

The Park Market was a meat and poultry shop located at 301 Franklin Avenue. Run by the Searle family, their fine fleet of delivery vehicles are shown here just a few feet from the trolley tracks. To the right was the Park Fruit Market at 305 Franklin Avenue and Wanner's sport shop at 307 Franklin Avenue. The edge of Nutley high school (now the Franklin Middle School) can just be seen on the far right.

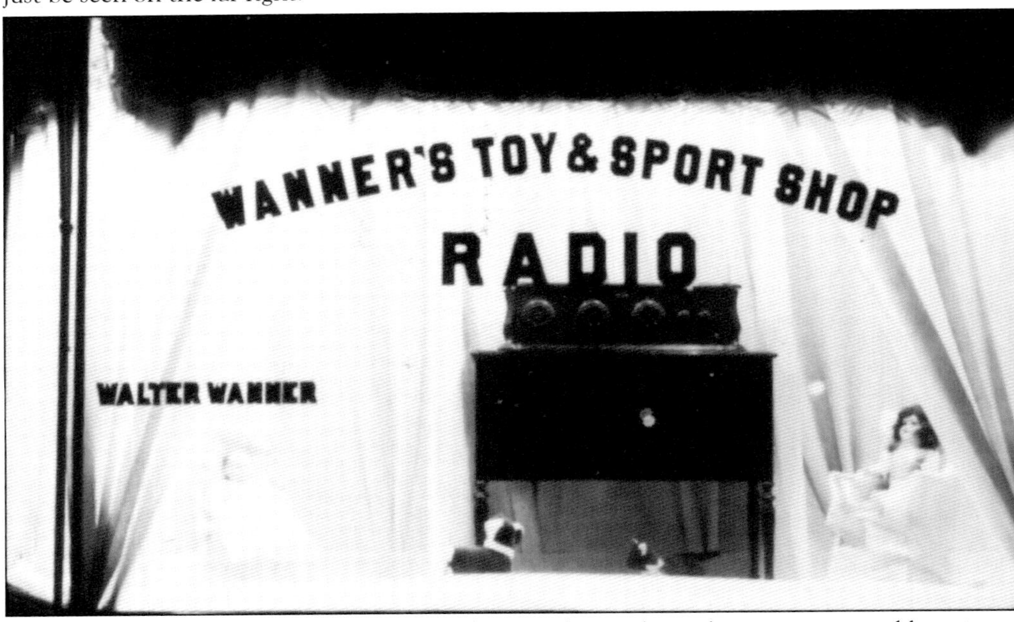

The storefront window of Wanner's Toy and Sport Shop is shown here at its original location at 307 Franklin Avenue. The window display had porcelain dolls and soft plush toys that any child would want. It also had the new grown-up's toy of the 1920s and '30s: the radio.

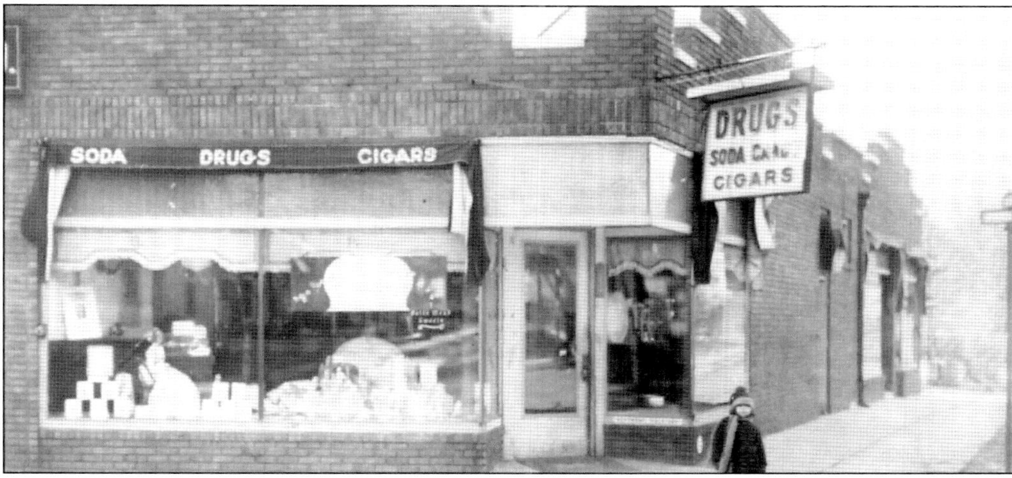

The corner of Park and Union Avenues was pretty lively on the night of March 9, 1926, when two armed men parked their running car on Weston Street and entered the pharmacy. They proceeded to rob the store and shot the owner in the shoulder during a struggle; the two men got away, and the owner recovered nicely.

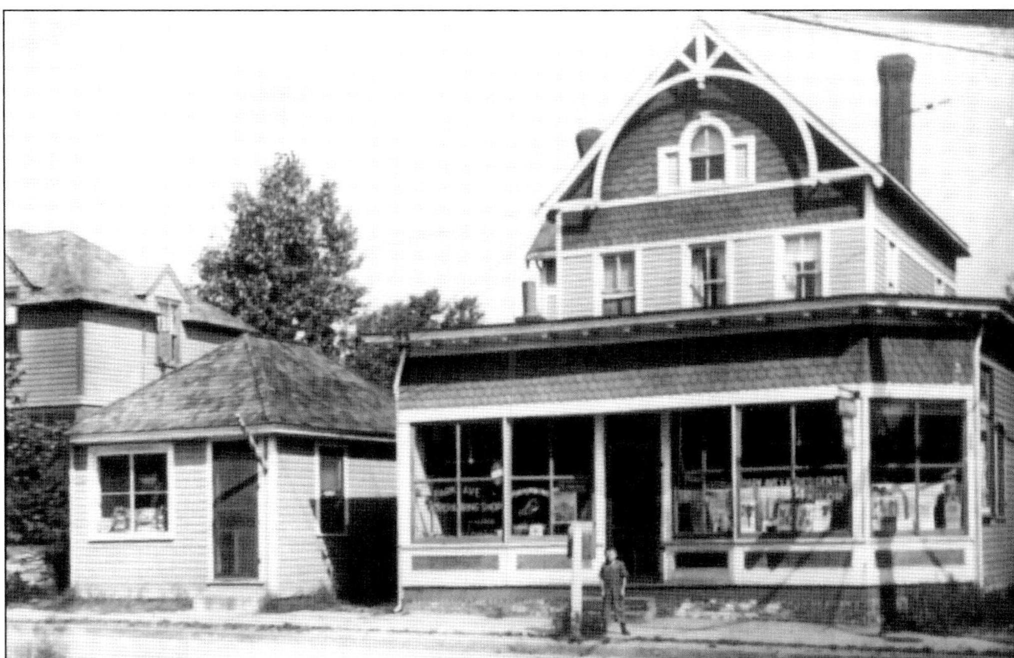
This house may look familiar, for it is the one pictured in Miss Ann Troy's book, with the original members of Avondale Hose Company standing out front. The same house (on Weston Street) was turned into a shoe repair and tailor shop before becoming a residence again.

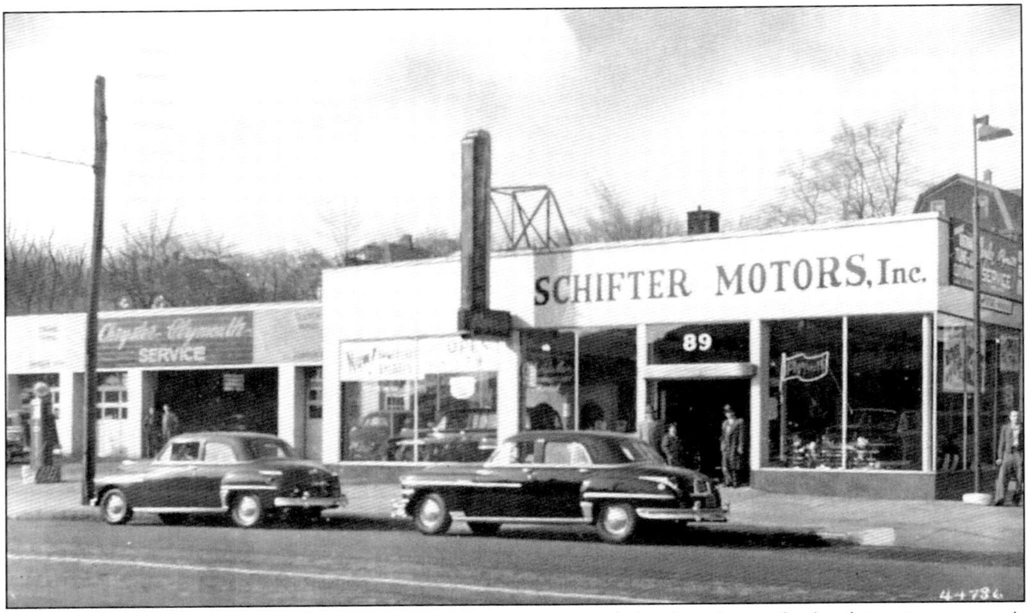

Schifter Motors, at 89 Washington Avenue, was one of the local car dealerships in town. A Chrysler-Plymouth dealership then, this building is the present location of Joseph Ricciardi Paints. The new shiny 1954 models in the window would be dream cars for any antique auto buff today.

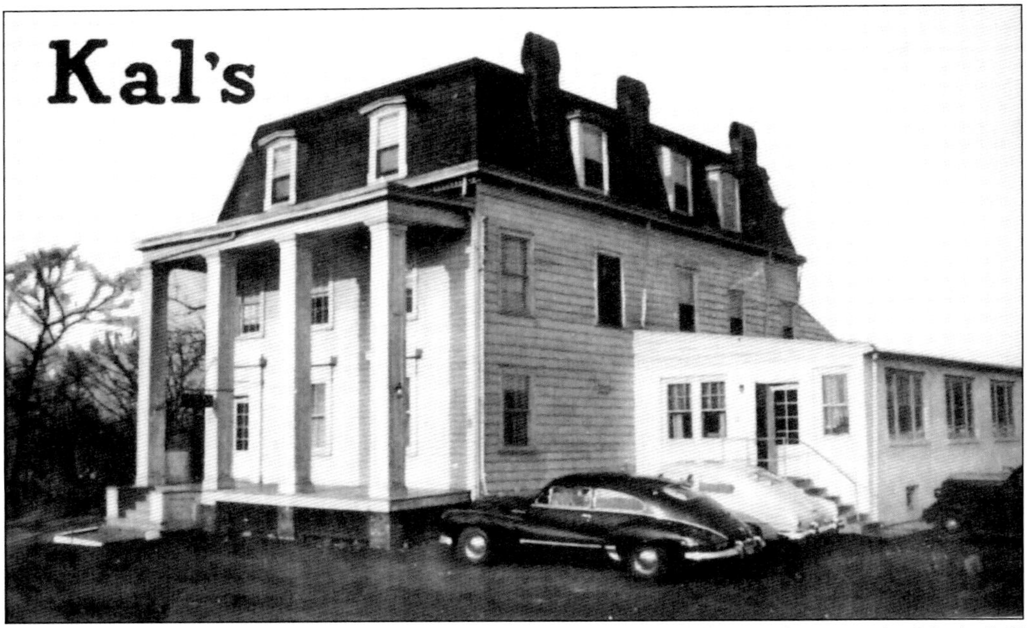

Off to the side of Harrison Street, where the Terrace Swim Club is today, was the Underhill home. Mr. Underhill was a mill owner. The house was purchased by one Mr. Kalakowski, who turned it into a bar and restaurant known as Kal's.

Nine

Trains, Tracks, and Trolleys

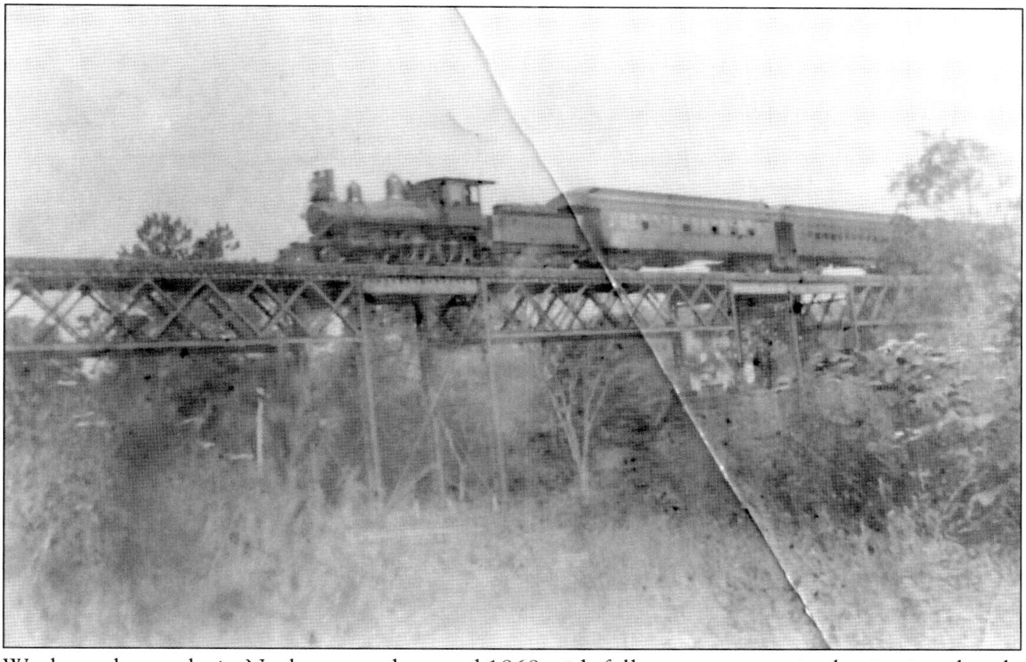

Work on the tracks in Nutley started around 1868 with full passenger service beginning shortly thereafter. This is a nice picture of the old steam train that ran through Nutley, crossing over Passaic Avenue. The short car behind the engine carried the coal used to fire the engine and bring up steam.

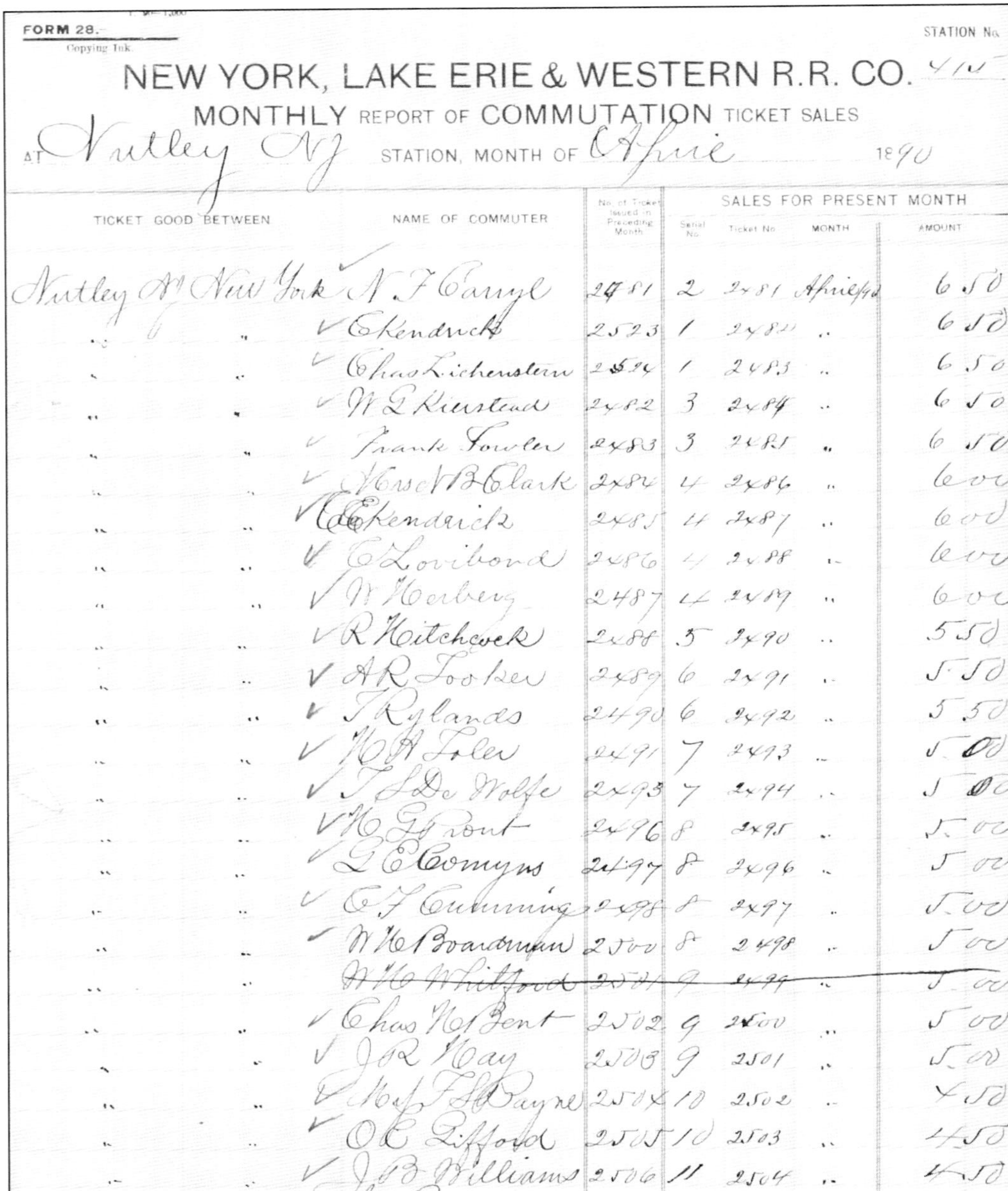

FORM 28.
Copying Ink.

STATION No. 415

NEW YORK, LAKE ERIE & WESTERN R.R. CO.

MONTHLY REPORT OF COMMUTATION TICKET SALES

AT Nutley NJ STATION, MONTH OF April 1890

TICKET GOOD BETWEEN	NAME OF COMMUTER	No. of Ticket issued in Preceding Month	Serial No.	Ticket No.	MONTH	AMOUNT
Nutley & New York	N F Caryl	2481	2	2481	April 90	6 50
" "	E Kendrick	2523	1	2482	"	6 50
" "	Chas Lichenstein	2524	1	2483	"	6 50
" "	W G Kierstead	2482	3	2484	"	6 50
" "	Frank Fowler	2483	3	2485	"	6 50
" "	Mrs N B Clark	2484	4	2486	"	6 00
" "	E Kendrick	2485	4	2487	"	6 00
" "	E Lovibond	2486	4	2488	"	6 00
" "	W Harberg	2487	4	2489	"	6 00
" "	R Hitchcock	2488	5	2490	"	5 50
" "	A R Tooker	2489	6	2491	"	5 50
" "	T Rylands	2490	6	2492	"	5 50
" "	H A Foler	2491	7	2493	"	5 00
" "	T S De Wolfe	2493	7	2494	"	5 00
" "	H G Prout	2496	8	2495	"	5 00
" "	L E Comyns	2497	8	2496	"	5 00
" "	E F Cumming	2498	8	2497	"	5 00
" "	W H Boardman	2500	8	2498	"	5 00
" "	~~W H Whitford~~	~~2501~~	~~9~~	~~2499~~	"	~~5 00~~
" "	Chas N Bent	2502	9	2500	"	5 00
" "	J R Hay	2503	9	2501	"	5 00
" "	Mrs F H Bayne	2504	10	2502	"	4 50
" "	O E Gifford	2505	10	2503	"	4 50
" "	J B Williams	2506	11	2504	"	4 50

Pictured here is an official train manifest for the New York, Lake Erie & Western R.R. Co., whose tracks ran through Nutley. It was filled out by the Nutley station manager, local resident John Donaldson. It lists all those who purchased tickets from Nutley to New York in April of 1890. Many of the names can be recognized as people who were associated with Nutley's early growth. The names of Frank Fowler, H.G. Prout, J.R. Hay, and W.G. Kierstead are a few that stand out on this list. The train was an important transportation tool for the business man, and it allowed people to go shopping in New York and return with relative speed. School age children who were being educated in New York could purchase special discounted monthly passes. Alternative forms of transportation ended passenger service on the Erie almost one hundred years after it began.

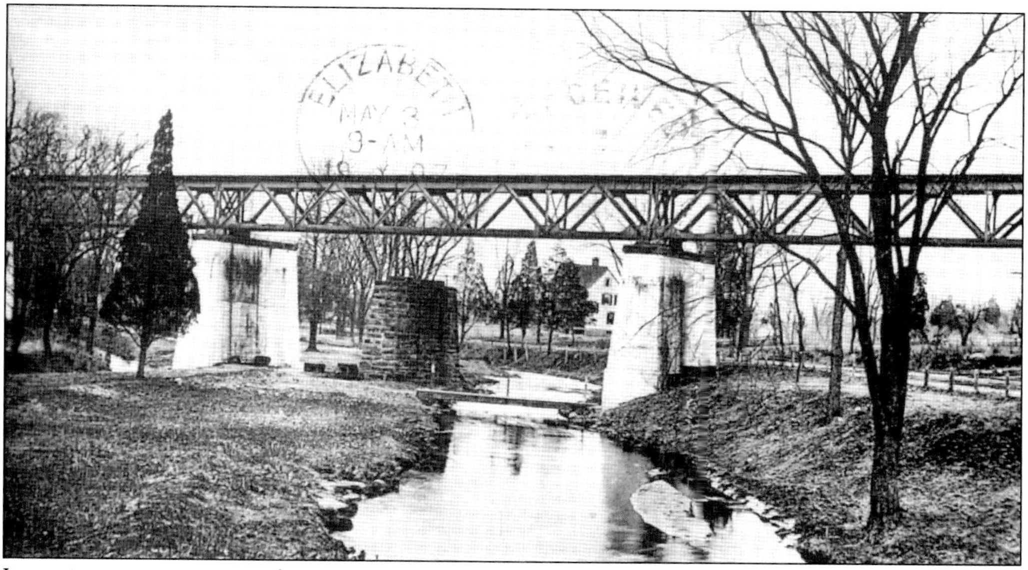

Later in time, more sturdy concrete piers were installed for the trestle over Passaic Avenue. For a while, the old piers remained unused below. The new piers were of double width for the accommodation of a potential second set of tracks, which were never built.

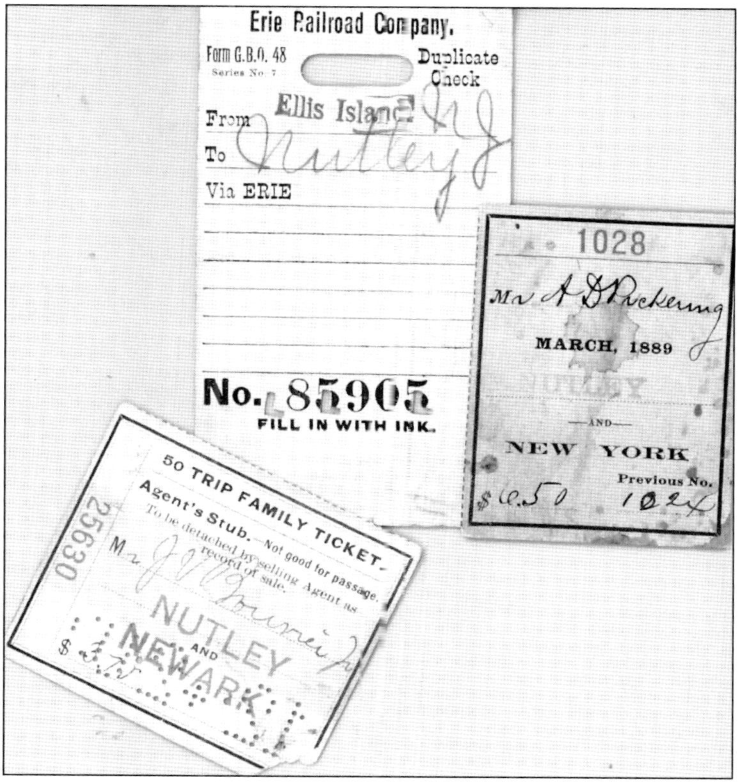

When train service was at its peak, Nutley was a bustling town. Shown here are several early Erie rail stubs. One is an early ticket from 1889. There is also a later stub used by J.V. Bouvier (Jacqueline Kennedy's grandfather) who lived in town. Also shown is a baggage claim check stub from Ellis Island to Nutley.

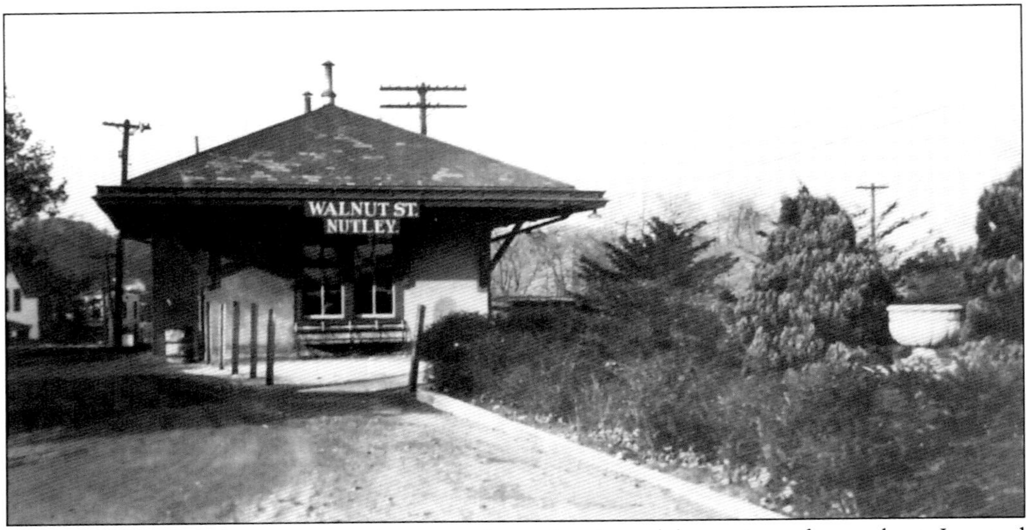

The Walnut Street Station served the people in the Avondale section of town best. Located right behind the old Saint Mary's Church, passengers from New York would get their first glimpse of Nutley at this station.

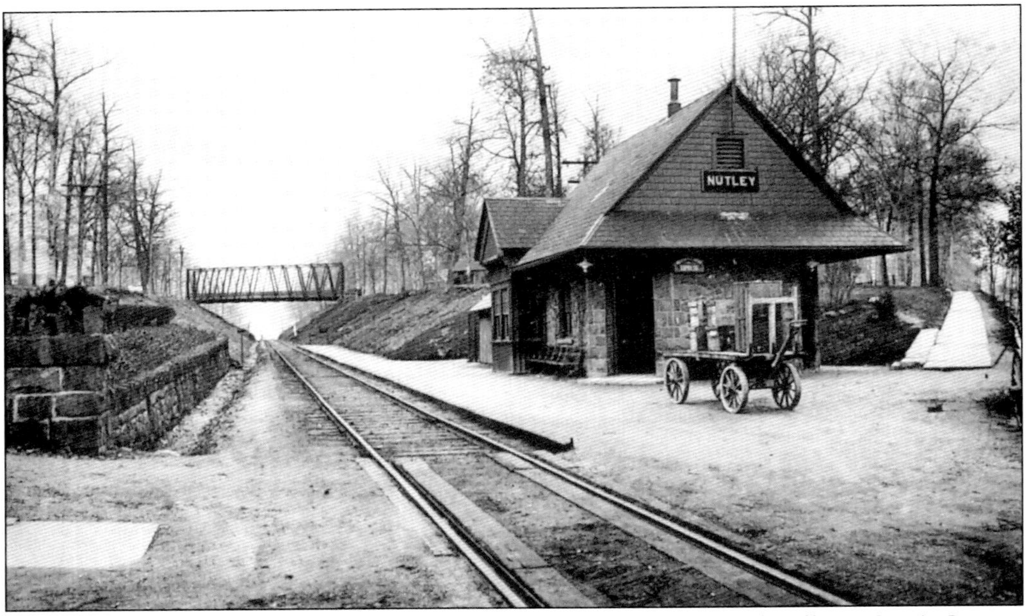

This was by far the station most used by Nutley residents. Known locally as Stitt's Station (Stitt's Mill was just a short walk away), Nutley Station was located at the southeast corner of Highfield Lane and Whitford Avenue. It was the second stop in town for a westbound traveler.

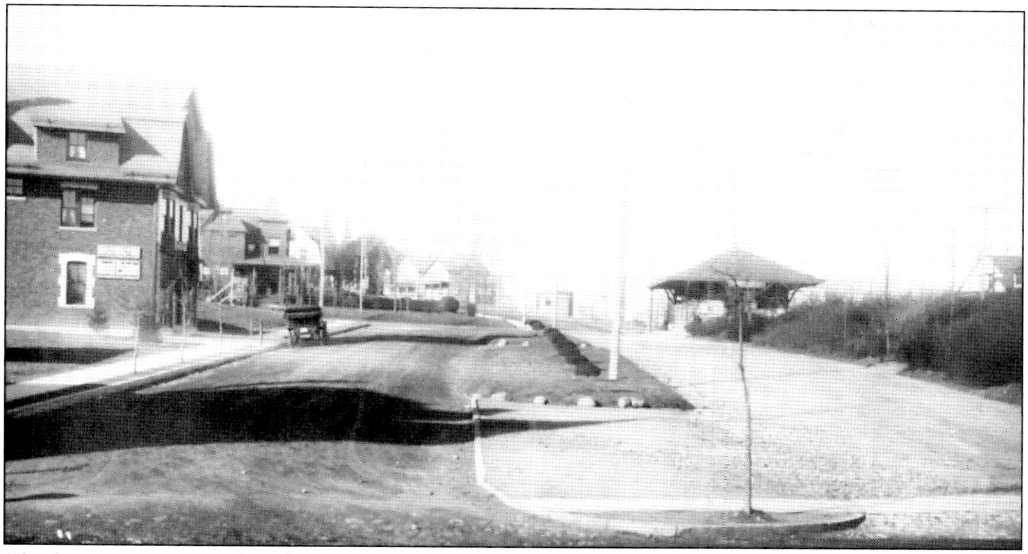

The last stop in town, heading west on the Nutley line, was the West Nutley or Franklin Avenue Station. Located on High Street near Franklin Avenue, it was right across the street from the offices of the Nutley Realty Company. The station and plaza were redone in 1901 to impress potential buyers of Nutley property.

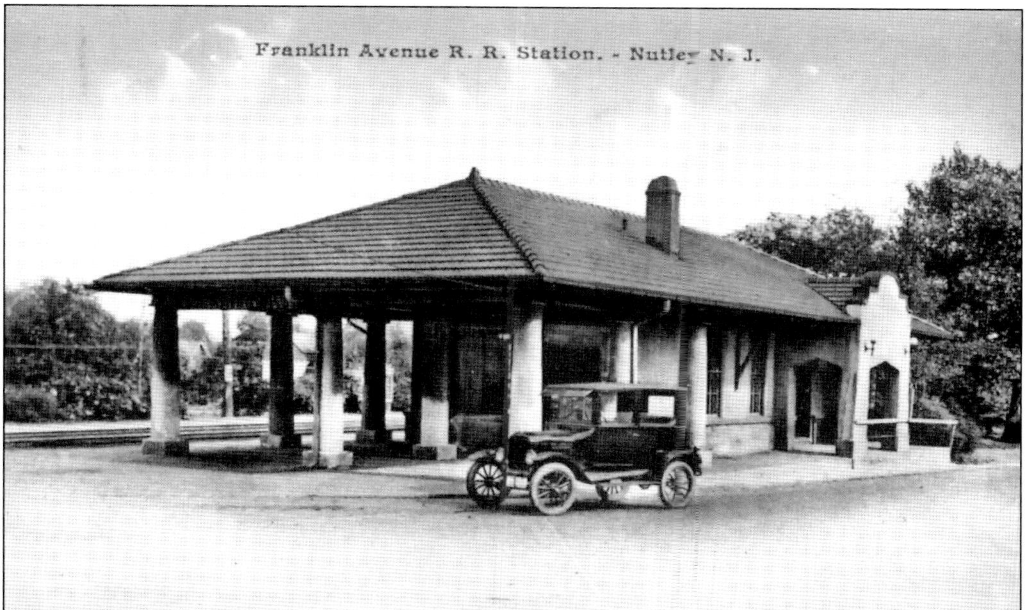

After another remodeling job, this is the Franklin Avenue (West Nutley) Station that most people in town remember. It is said that Nutley Realty owner William Lambert would always have a car ready at the station to give guided tours of properties for sale by his company.

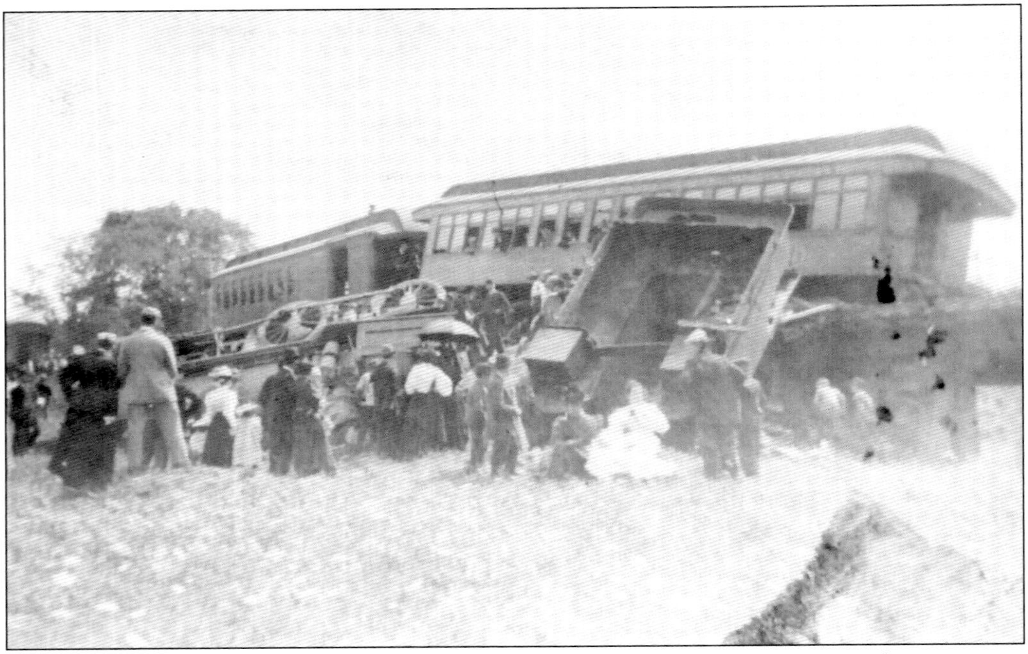

Tossed about like toys, these train cars were part of the only serious train accident to occur in town. In 1902, a train that was too long for the siding at the Franklin Avenue Station left several cars hanging out on the main line. Before the engineer could cut his train back, a milk train heading the opposite way hit head-on with the first train.

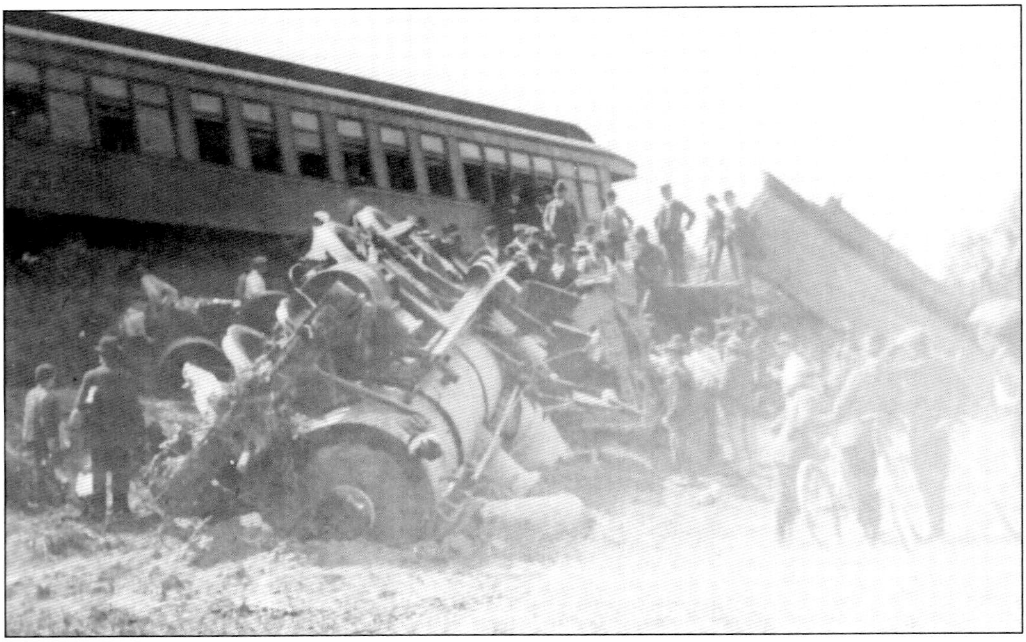

Here is another view showing the derailed engine and cars at the Franklin Avenue Station. The two engineers were both killed in the wreck, but luckily no one else was seriously hurt. It took a couple of days before regular commuter service was restored in town.

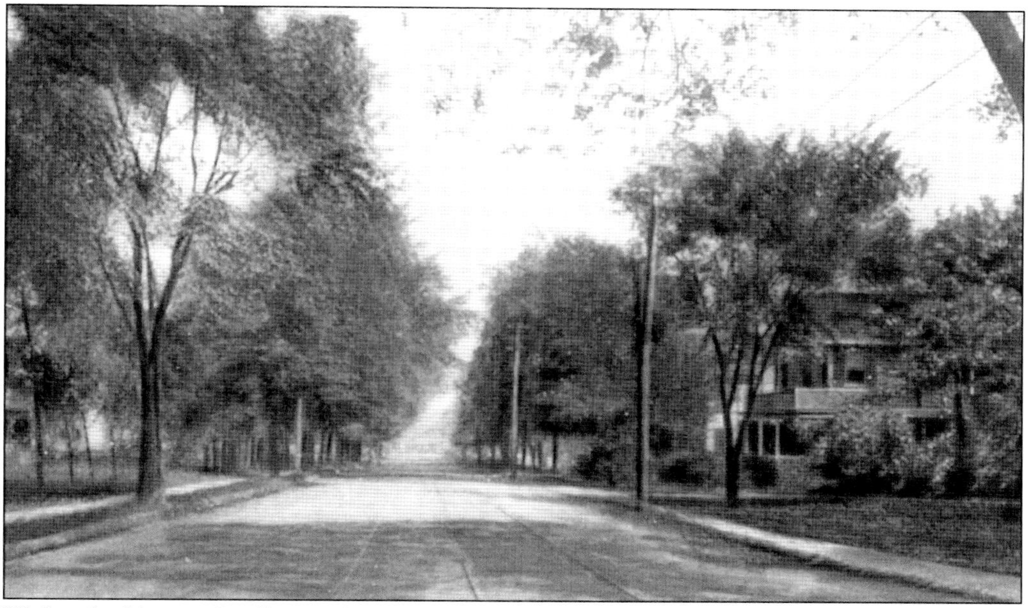

With a double set of trolley tracks running down the center of the street and the private homes on either side, this would be a hard view to recreate today. It is said that before Franklin Avenue was widened, the trees could canopy the whole street.

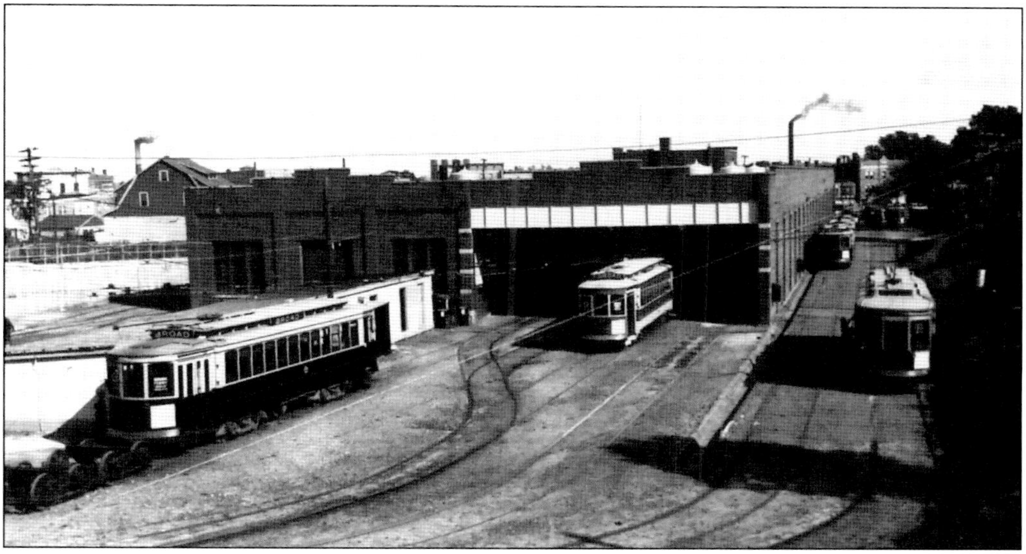

Nutley had two trolley lines that shared the same set of tracks through town. The #17 line ran from Paterson to Newark and the #13 line went from the Glendale loop in Nutley to Irvington via Broad Street. Cars on these two lines would frequently be held at Public Service's Big Tree Garage, at the corner of Washington Avenue and Hancox. Trolley service ended completely in 1937.

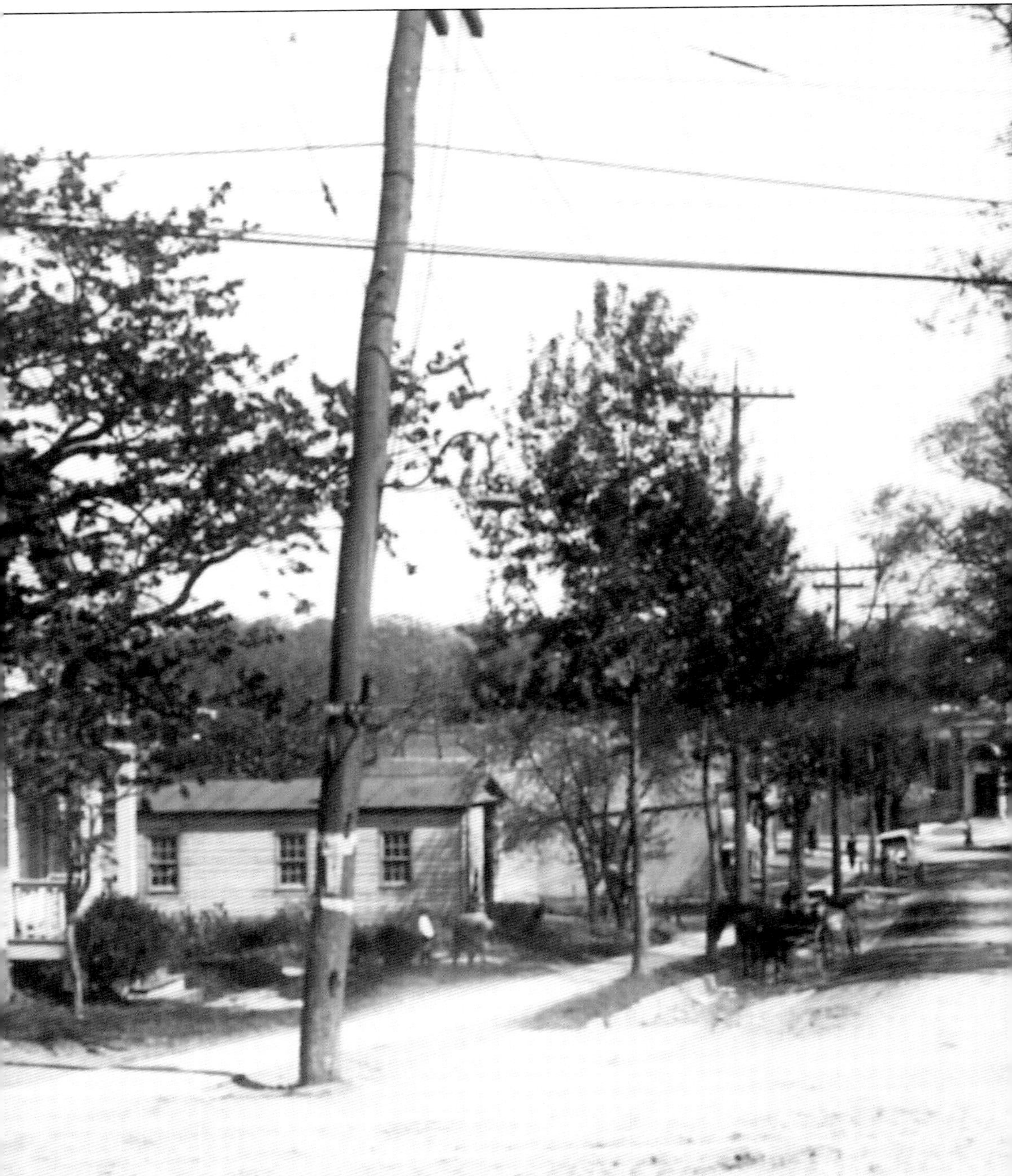

There is a lot of town to see in this postcard view of Chestnut Street from Lee's Park Pharmacy, at the corner of Chestnut Street and Franklin Avenue, *c.* 1914. The New Bank of Nutley, which was built in 1909, is straight ahead. On the right is the town hall with its relatively new dormers and cupola, which were added after the 1904 fire that damaged the roof. Behind the town hall is Vincent Methodist Church, which was dedicated in 1910. To the extreme left is

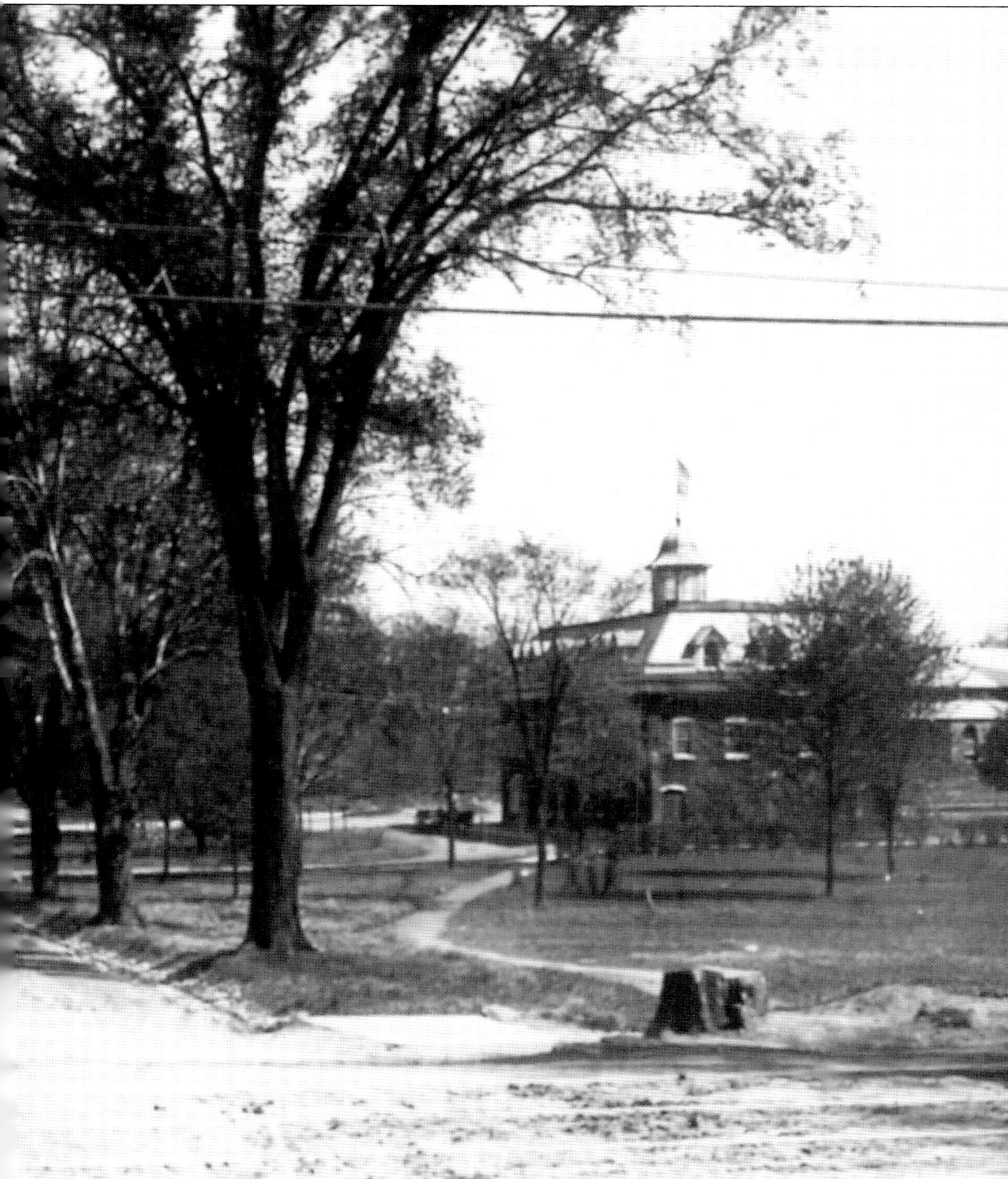

the Abraham and Warren Vreeland house, which was built in 1838; this is the house that was cut in half and moved to the enclosure (#51) in the mid-1920s to allow the construction of a new Bank of Nutley building. The trolley tracks can also be seen running down the dusty streets of Franklin Avenue.

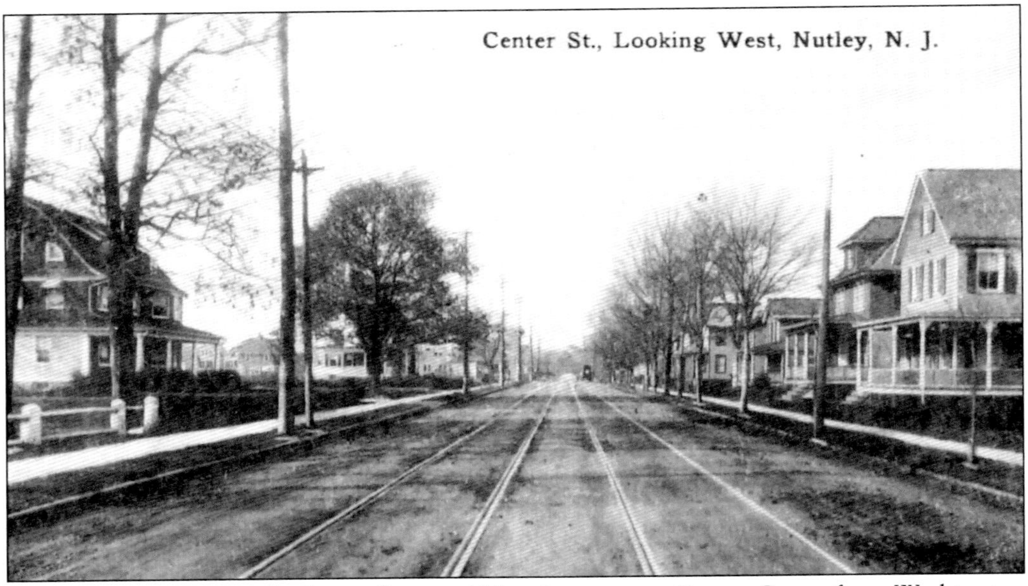

Coming up from Newark, the trolley would head west onto Centre Street from Washington Avenue. This view looks west from the Centre Street Bridge toward Franklin Avenue. The house on the left is the Di Biasi law office at 345 Centre Street, which is one of the few houses remaining today from this picture.

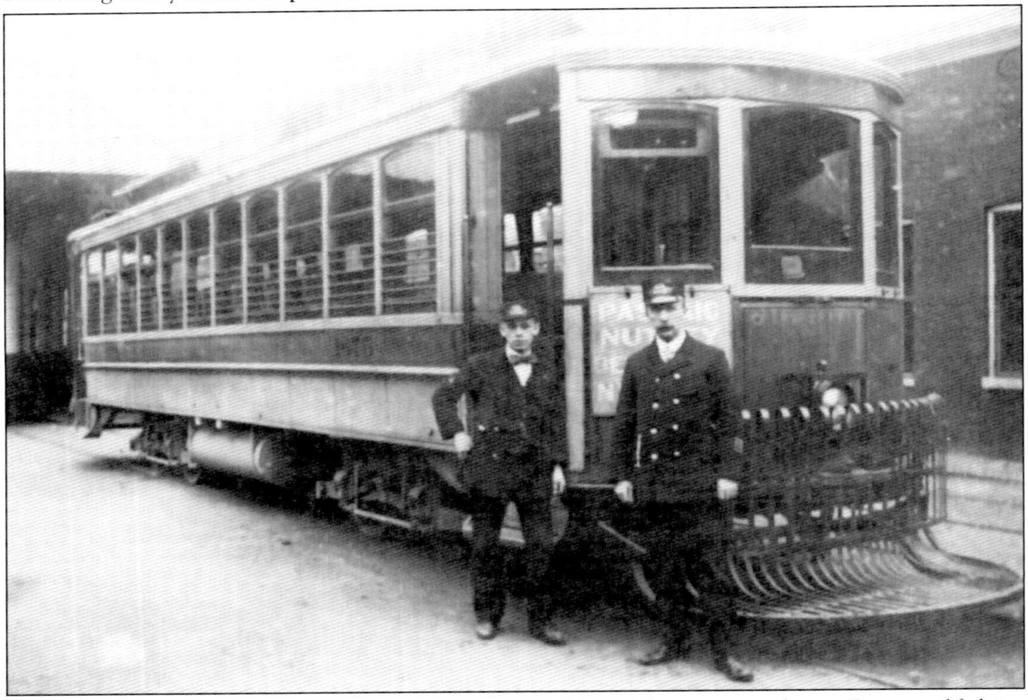

In the early days of trolley transportation, there were two rail men on each car. One would drive the trolley, and the other would be the fare collector. In 1923, this practice was stopped for economic reasons. This trolley ran on the Newark-Paterson (#17) line through town. Note the large "cowcatcher" device on this early car.

Ten

Houses and Buildings

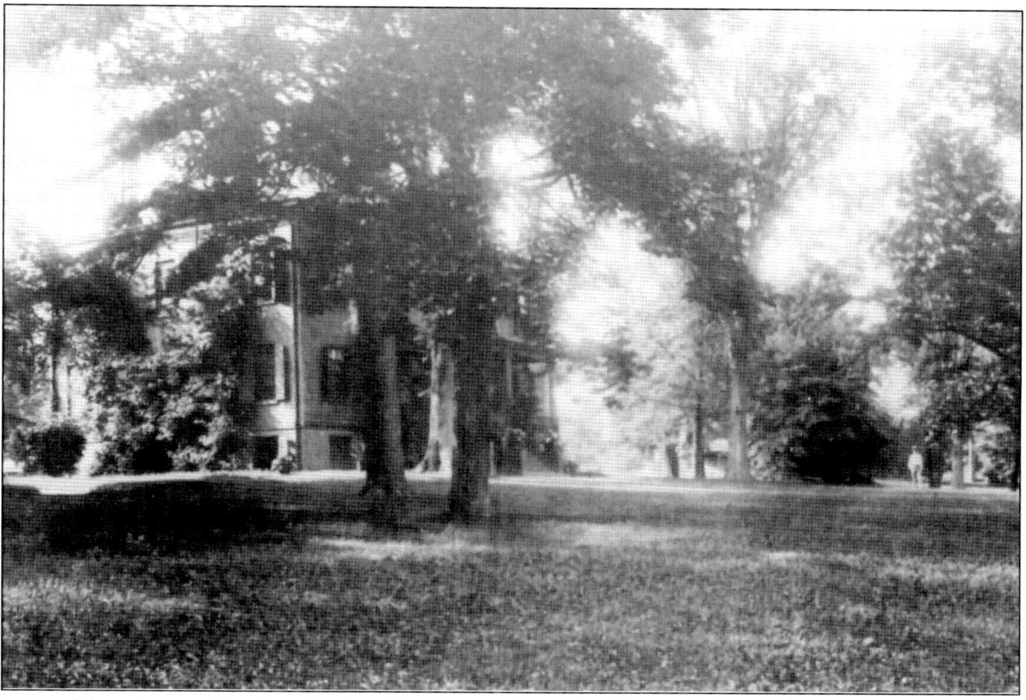

Legend has it that Nutley obtained its name from this house. The old Nutley Manor house (supposedly named for the variety of nut trees on the property) was built in 1828. It became part of the Satterthwaite estate in 1844 and was located near the southern end of the former ITT property on River Road.

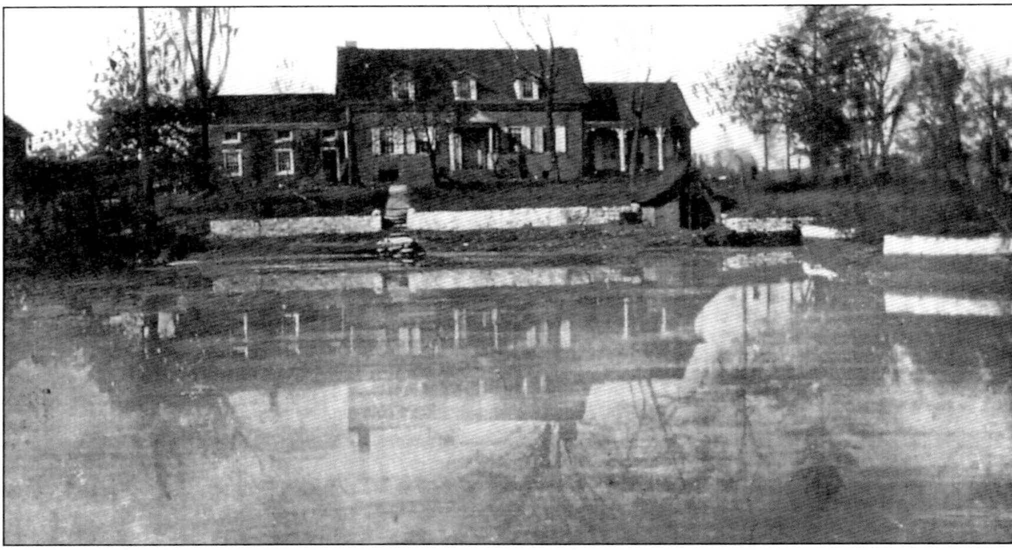

The first section of the Kingsland Manor that was built dates back to the late 1700s. It was once occupied by J. Kingsland near his gristmill. Kingsland also made wooden curbing for New York City streets from his lumber mill. The house was expanded in the 1800s and had a speakeasy in the cellar during Prohibition.

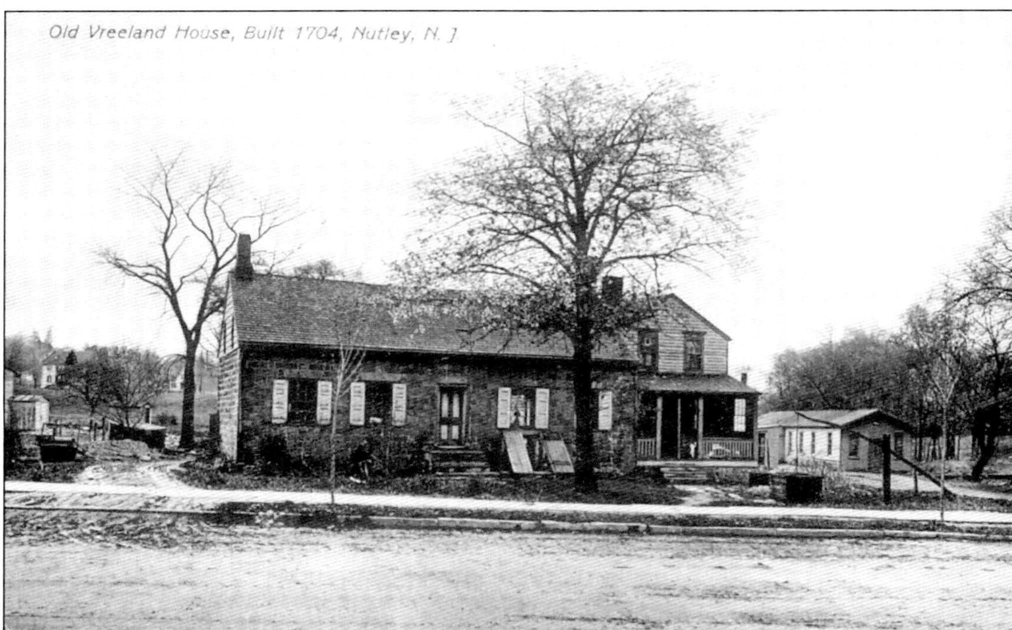

The Vreeland house was thought to have been built in 1702 and confiscated by the government during the Revolutionary War because the owners were Tories; however, recent findings do not support this. The house was most likely built in the mid-1700s, and all sales related to it seem to have been private transactions, with the Vreelands having possession from 1783 to the early 1900s.

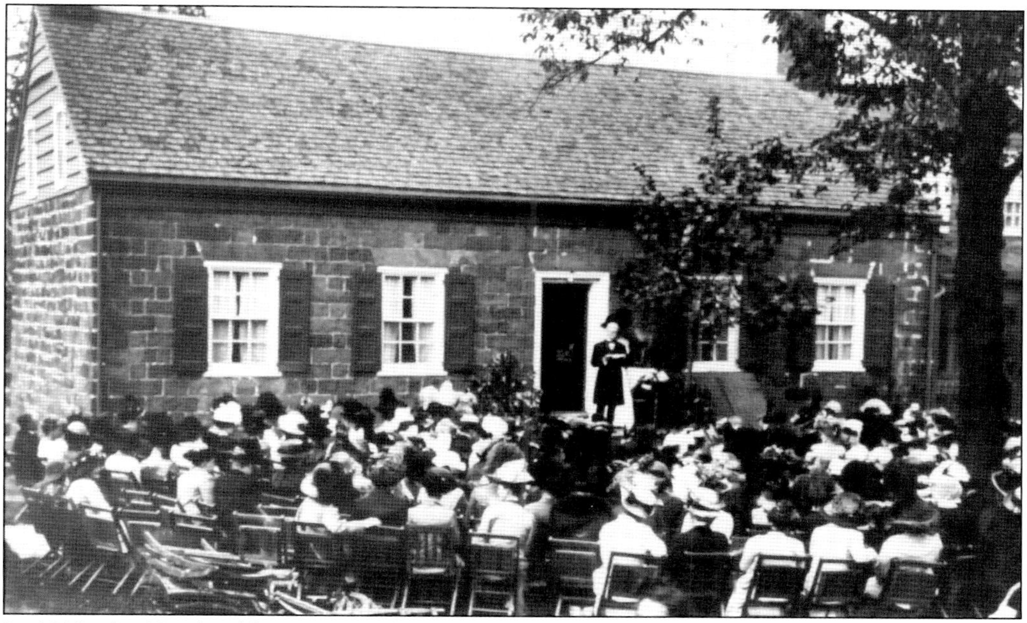

In 1912, the Vreeland house was taken over by the Woman's Club of Nutley. Pictured here is the opening day ceremony on October 3, 1912. The club is still run from this house today, and it remains an important part of Nutley's social life.

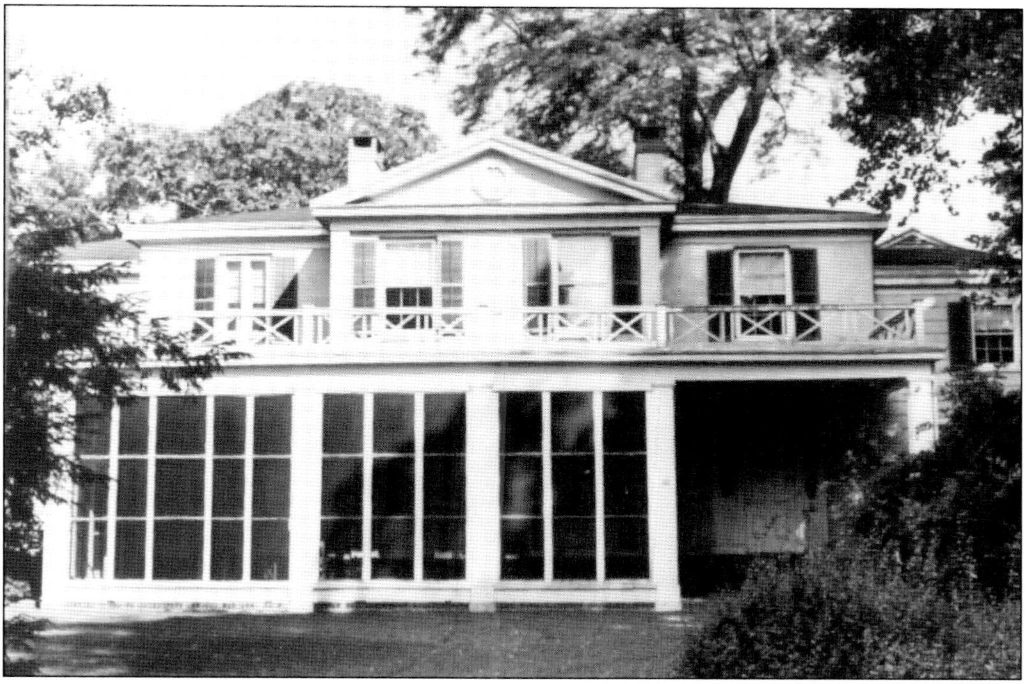

At one time, the cul-de-sac at the end of Enclosure had but one house. The Feland house was built c. 1840 around the same time that Belleville (which included the Nutley area then) separated itself from Bloomfield. The Felands, who resided here not too long ago, held elaborate garden parties for the League of Women Voters. The house was taken down c. 1967.

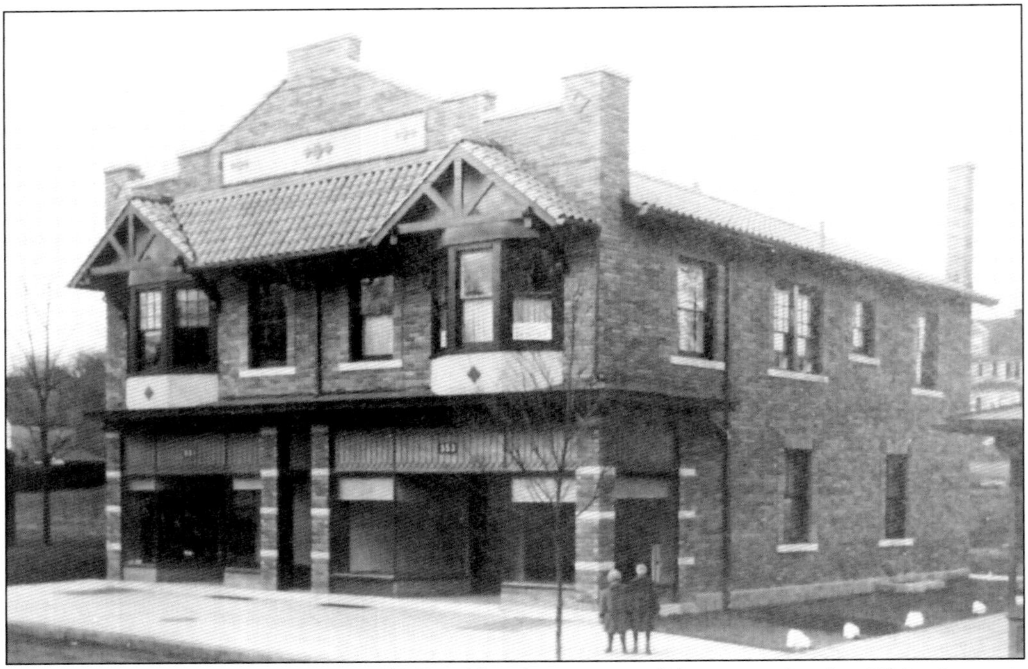

The commercial property at 551–553 Franklin Avenue is still being used today. This picture is on a postcard that belonged to Frank Speer. Written on the back, in his hand, it says, "Offered to me in 1945 by Nutley Realty Company for $8,000." That is probably the cost of the yearly taxes alone in today's market.

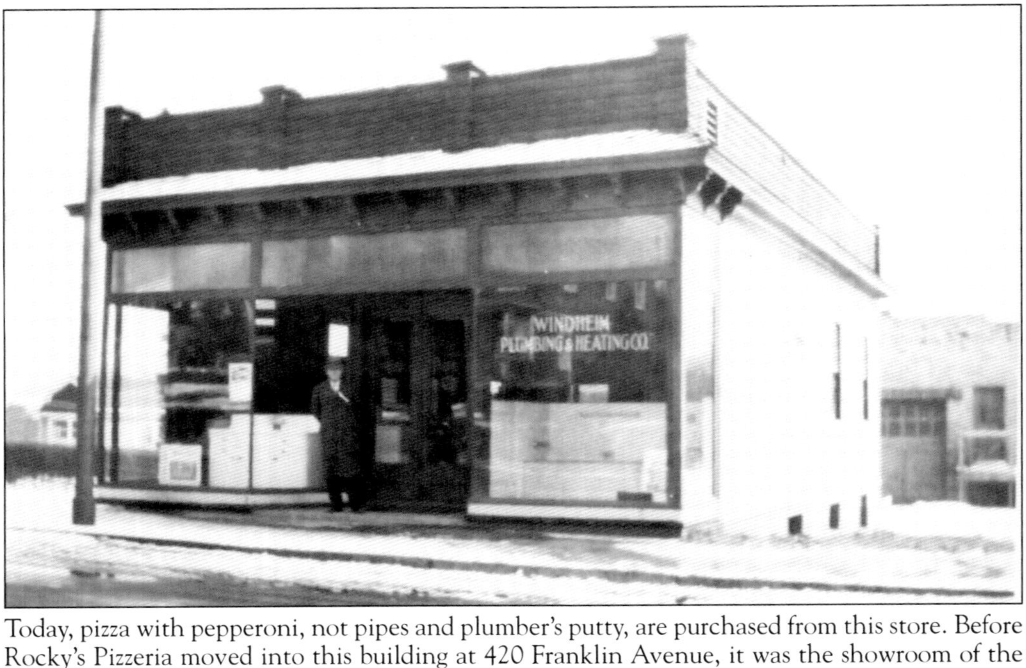

Today, pizza with pepperoni, not pipes and plumber's putty, are purchased from this store. Before Rocky's Pizzeria moved into this building at 420 Franklin Avenue, it was the showroom of the Windheim Plumbing and Heating Company. The business is now run from the building in the background of this photograph.

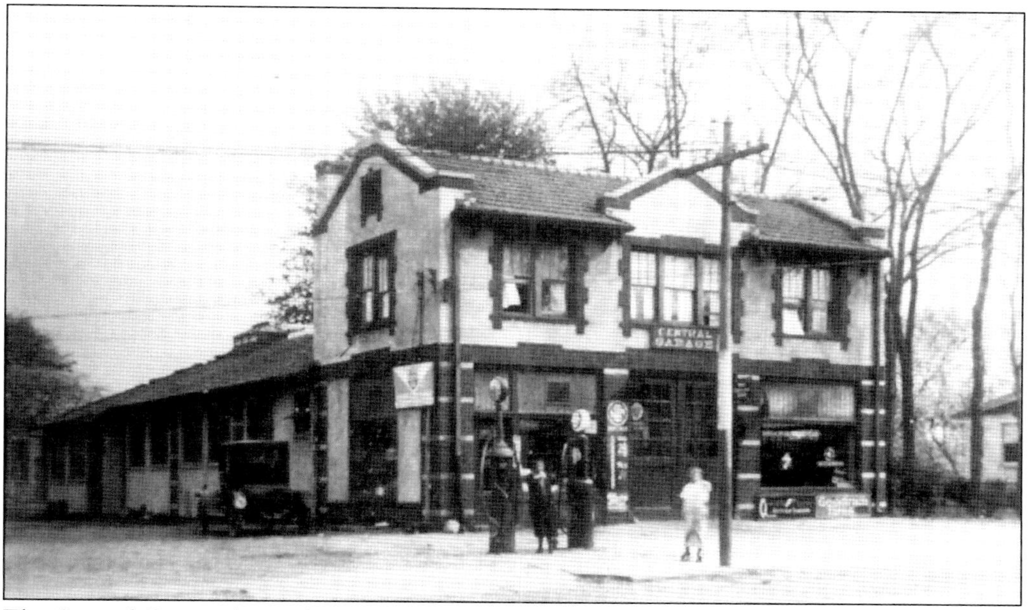

The Central Garage, located across the street from the Masonic Hall, at the southeast corner of Franklin Avenue and east High Street, is today's Buy-Rite Liquor Store. Back in the 1930s, it was a full service station for gasoline and auto repairs.

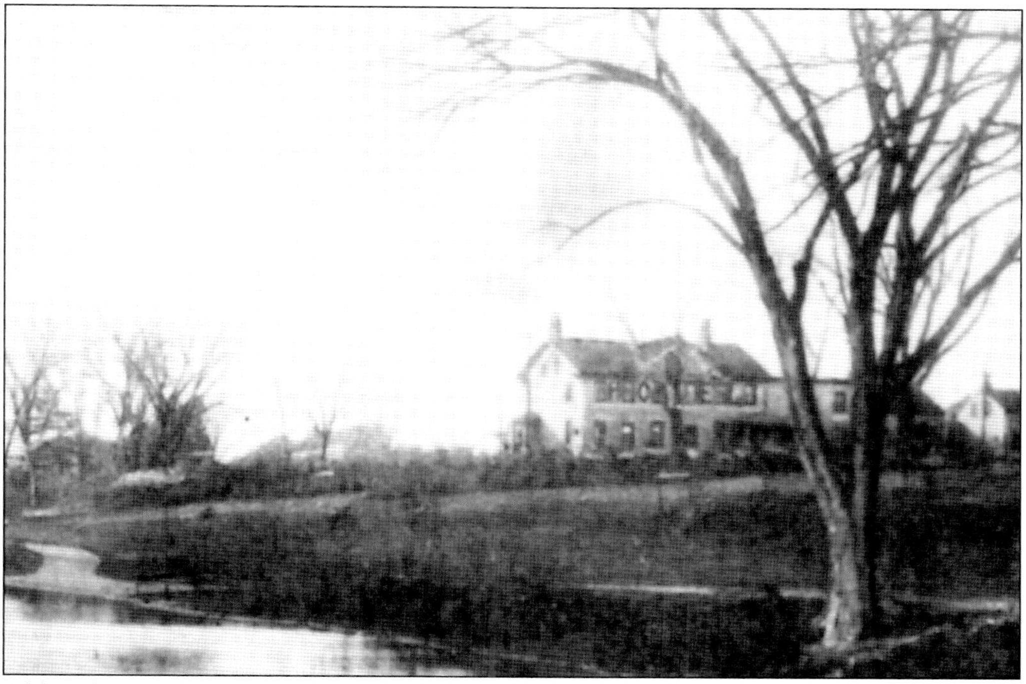

Although unconfirmed stories have dated this house to the late 1700s, it certainly was around for use as a training site for Civil War soldiers in the 1860s. Known as Old Military Hall, the building was called the Franklin Hotel in the early 1900s. It was located at the corner of New Street and Vincent Place before being razed by a fire.

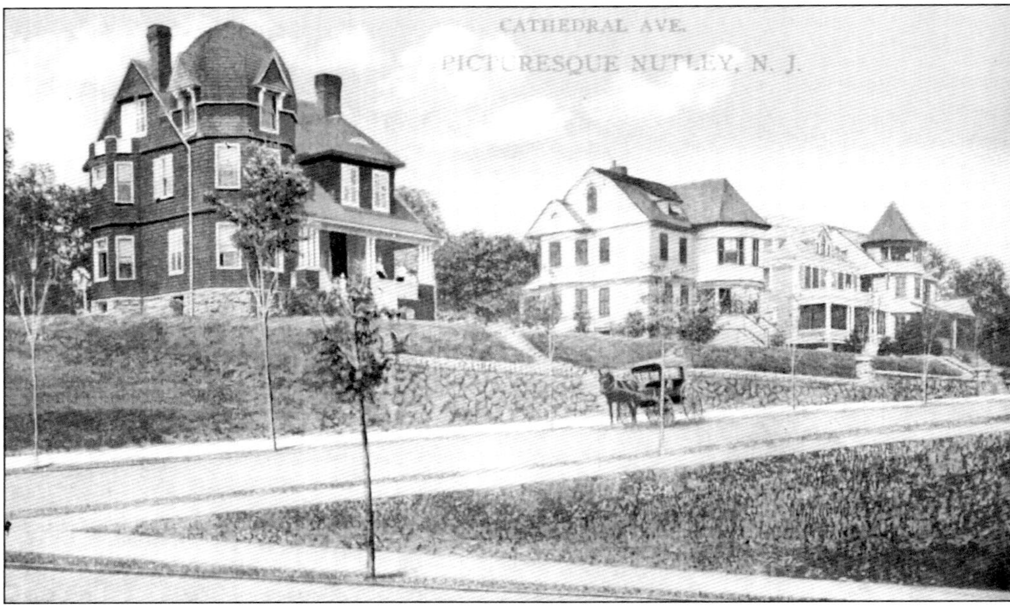

The house on the left in this view of Cathedral Avenue is near the intersection of Kingsland Avenue. It was the private residence of William Lambert, whose development of Nutley was not limited to building homes. Lambert also had a hand in the development of Nutley's 1915 post office, Saint Paul's Church, the Fortnightly Club, and the Franklin Avenue Train Station.

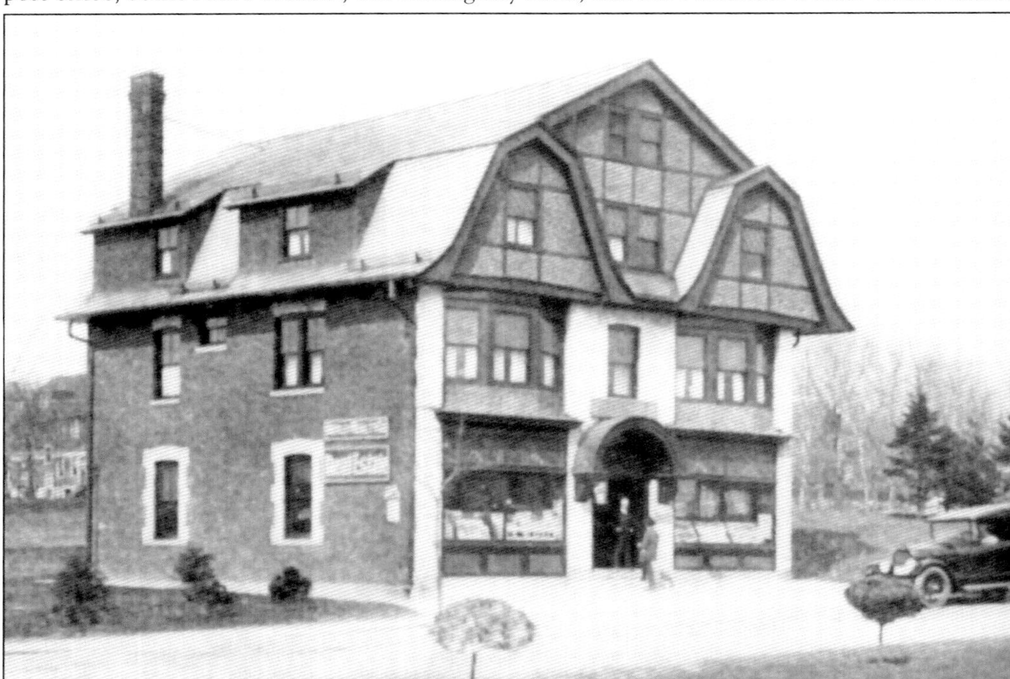

Just across from the previously mentioned station was the New Jersey office of the Nutley Realty Company. Its location was not by accident; the company president knew that by keeping in close proximity to visitors coming in on the train, sales would increase.

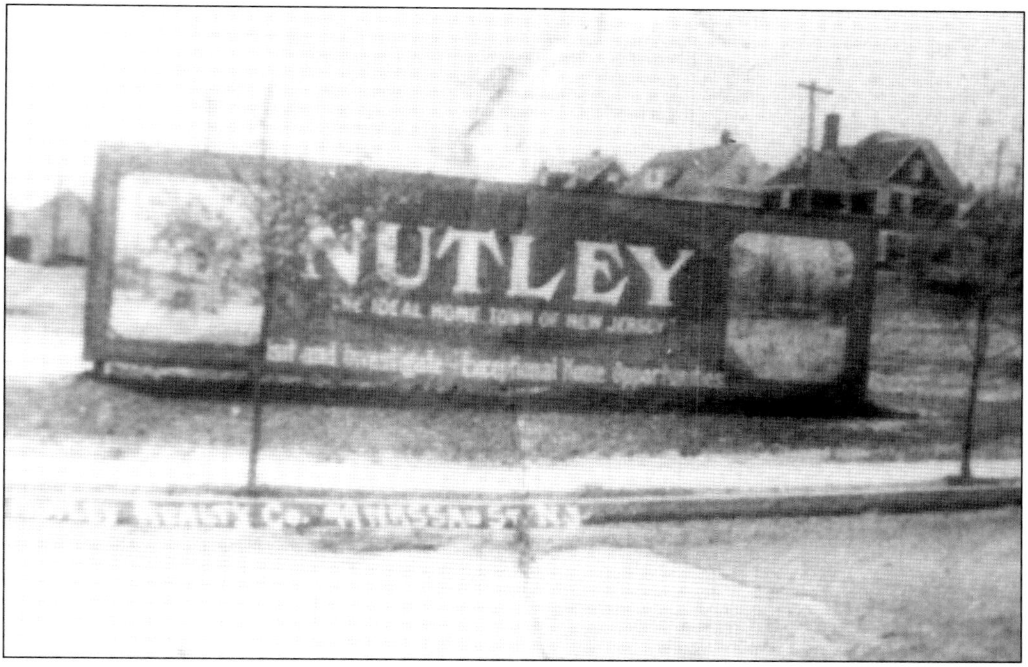

On High Street, just to the left of the Nutley Realty building, was their real estate sign. This ground-level billboard, c. 1910, pictures two Nutley views and states, "Nutley the ideal home town of New Jersey—visit and investigate exceptional home opportunities."

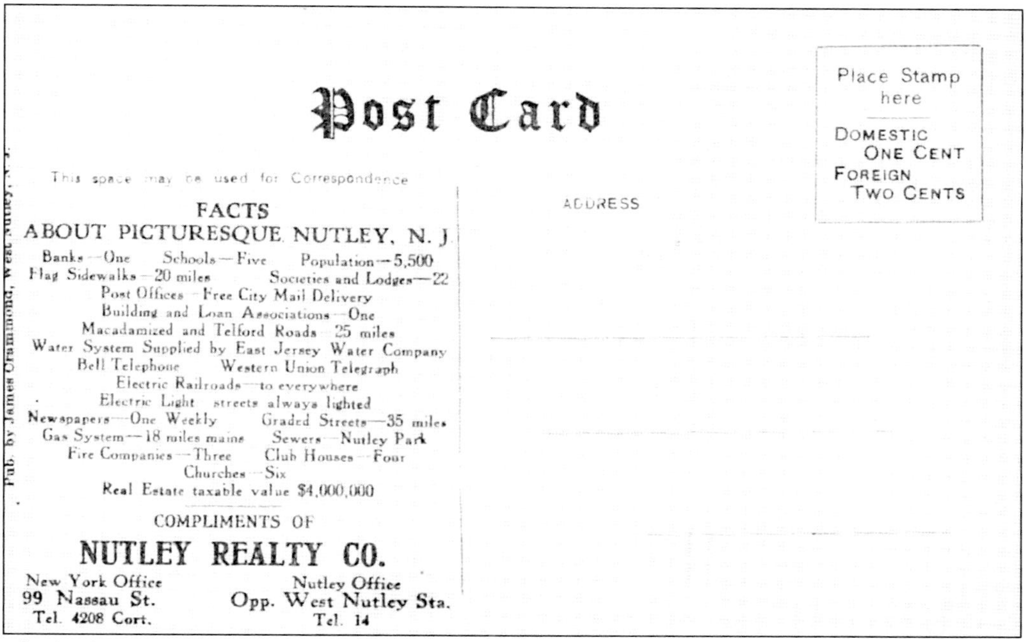

Post Card

Place Stamp here

DOMESTIC ONE CENT
FOREIGN TWO CENTS

This space may be used for Correspondence

ADDRESS

FACTS
ABOUT PICTURESQUE NUTLEY, N. J.

Banks—One Schools—Five Population—5,500
Flag Sidewalks—20 miles Societies and Lodges—22
Post Offices—Free City Mail Delivery
Building and Loan Associations—One
Macadamized and Telford Roads—25 miles
Water System Supplied by East Jersey Water Company
Bell Telephone Western Union Telegraph
Electric Railroads—to everywhere
Electric Light streets always lighted
Newspapers—One Weekly Graded Streets—35 miles
Gas System—18 miles mains Sewers—Nutley Park
Fire Companies—Three Club Houses—Four
Churches—Six
Real Estate taxable value $4,000,000

COMPLIMENTS OF

NUTLEY REALTY CO.

New York Office
99 Nassau St.
Tel. 4208 Cort.

Nutley Office
Opp. West Nutley Sta.
Tel. 14

Pub. by James Crammond, West Nutley, N. J.

The back side of many Nutley Realty postcards carried facts about the town. W.A. Lambert, the company president, was very adept in promoting the little town both here and in the New York offices. The population given on this card is 5,500, dating it c. 1910.

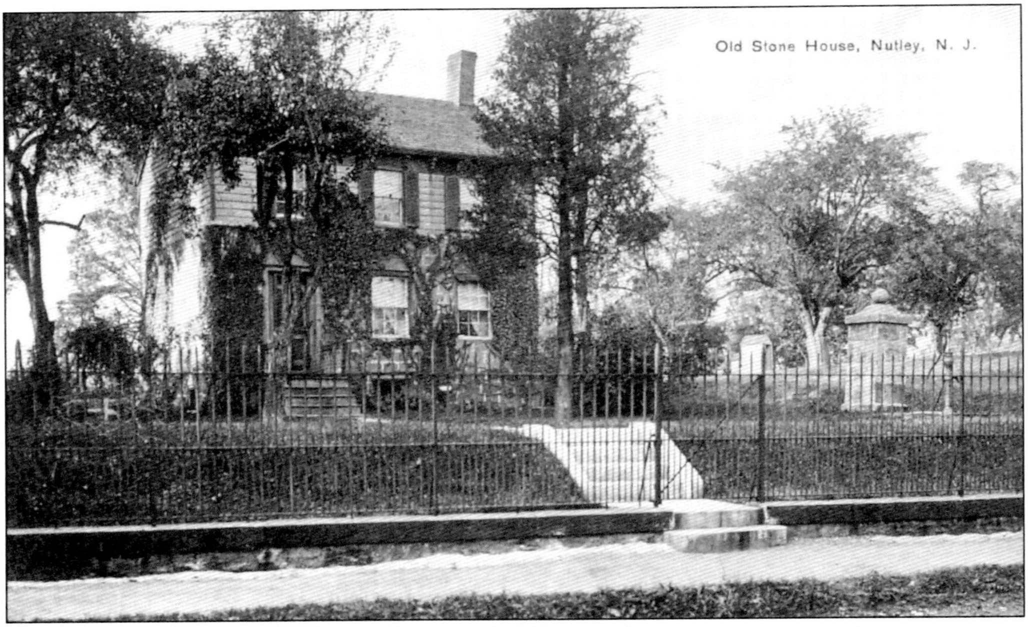

Built in the mid-1700s, the Stone House at 213 Passaic Avenue was once used as a parsonage for the original Methodist church in Nutley, which was just to the left of it. The church has moved to become our new Vincent Methodist, but the house and cemetery remain.

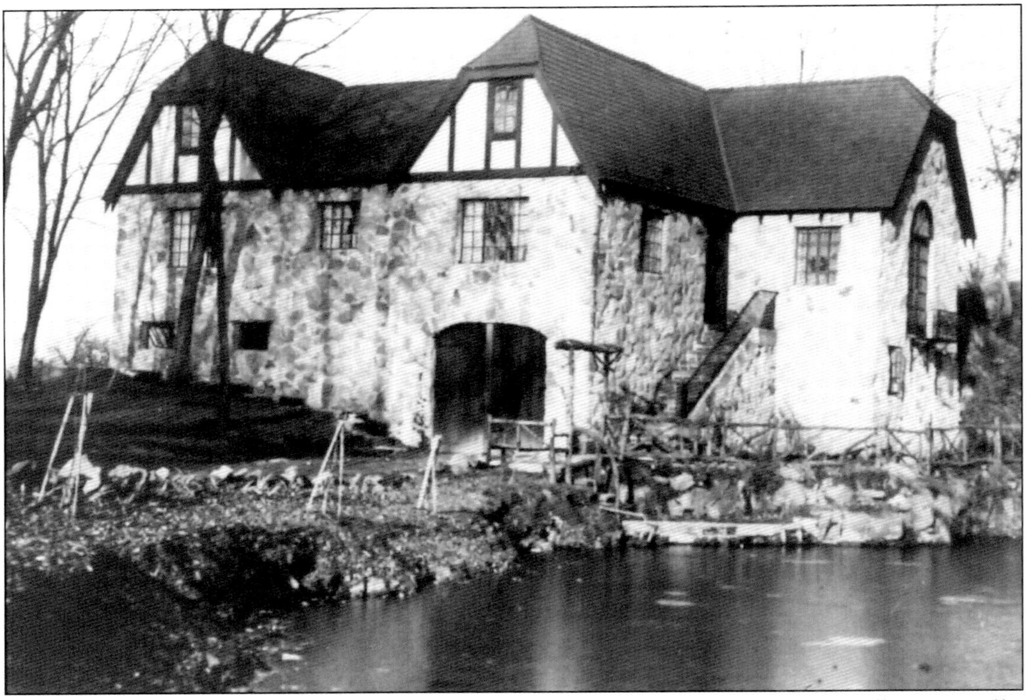

At the edge of the quarry belonging to circus man Eaton Stone was the home of Albert F. Scully, a local homebuilder. The Eaton Stone quarry was on Kingsland Avenue in the area where the Hoffmann La Roche complex is now. This photograph was taken c. 1929.

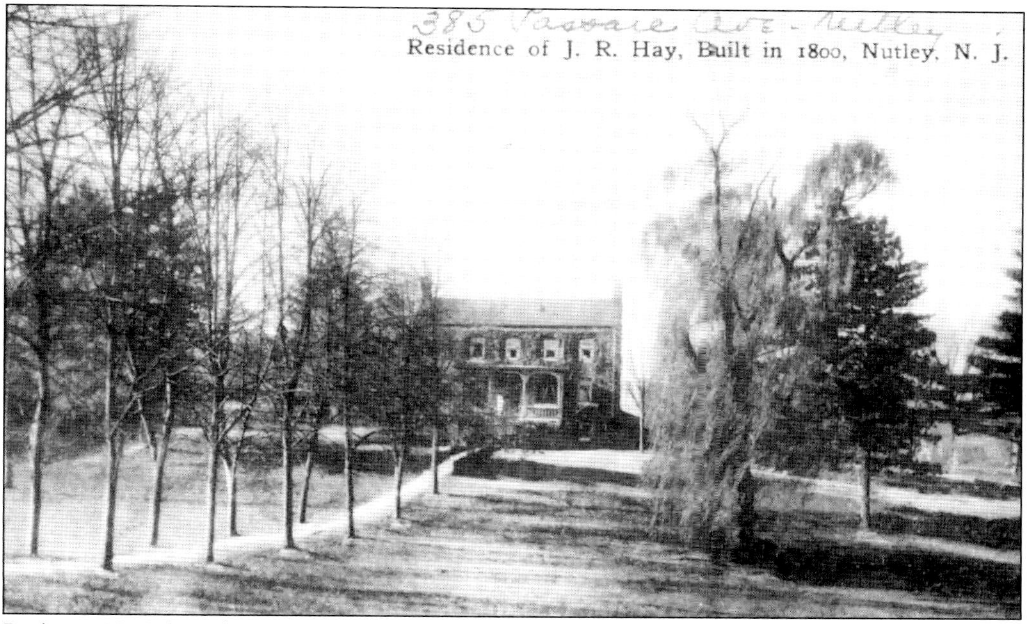

Built in 1812 by John Mason, this house overlooked the cotton mill that operated in the park area near the Mudhole. The house was lived in for years by J.R. Hay, an early real estate developer in town. It is located at the end of Calico (a cotton term) Lane.

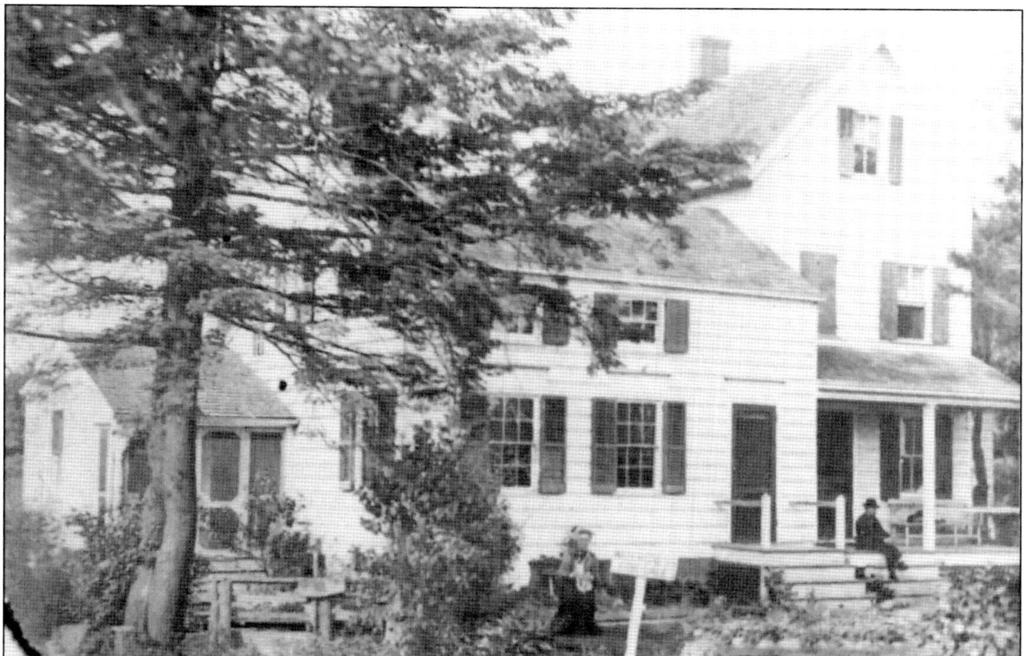

In the area where Bloomfield Avenue runs, from Centre Street north toward Kingsland Avenue, was a stretch of water known as Baskin (bearskin) Brook. Some of the people living along the brook would grow watercress, which thrived in it. Long-time resident John Stager had one such patch in his yard.

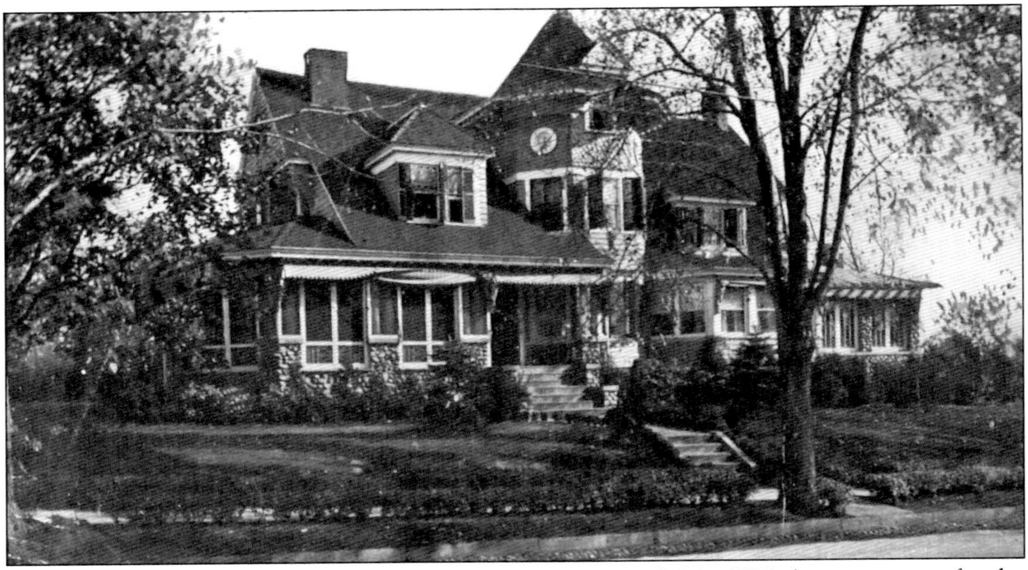

This beautiful house was once the home of Thomas J. O'Neil. Mr. O'Neil was secretary for the Kingsland and La Monte paper manufacturing companies and was vice president of the Bank of Nutley in 1906. The house still stands today at 142 Brookfield Avenue.

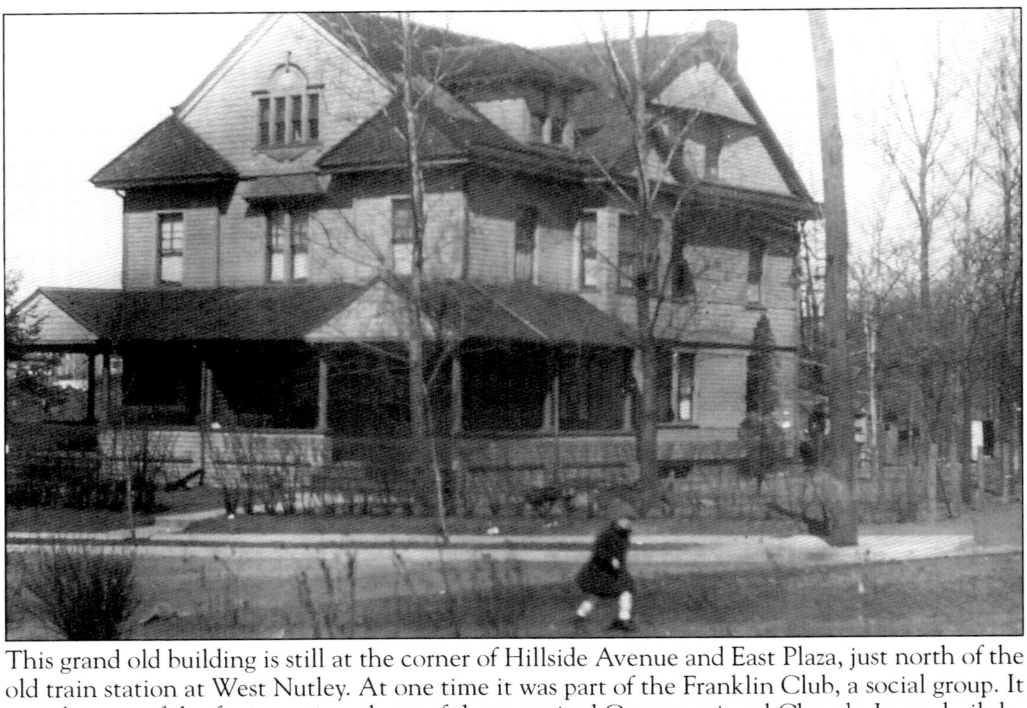

This grand old building is still at the corner of Hillside Avenue and East Plaza, just north of the old train station at West Nutley. At one time it was part of the Franklin Club, a social group. It was also one of the first meeting places of the organized Congregational Church. It was built by William Lambert, who called it "The Hillside."

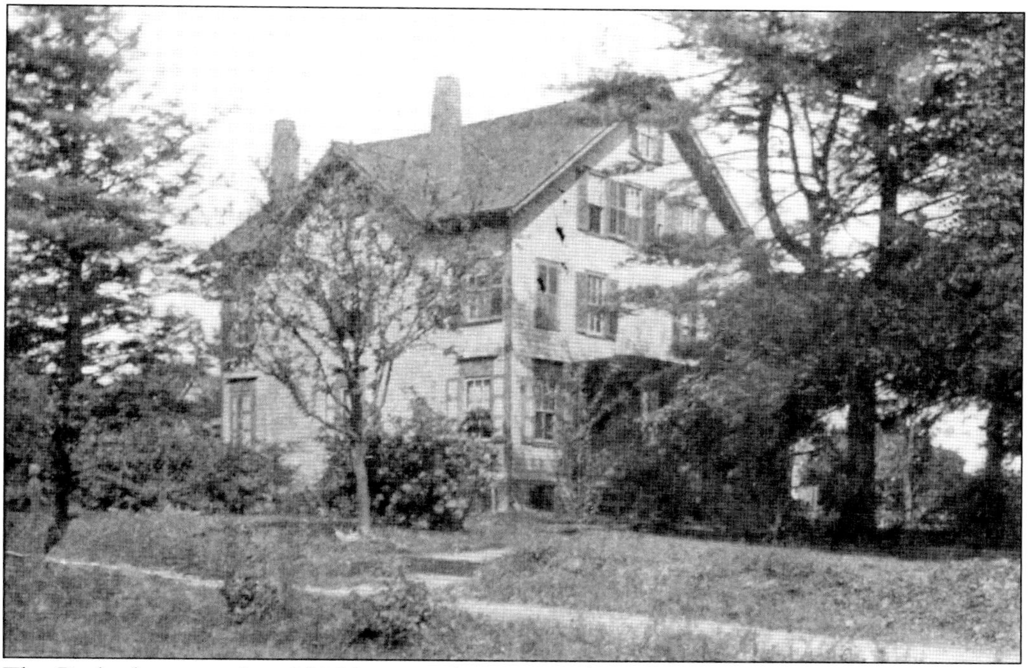

The Rusby homestead at 254 Harrison Avenue was home to several members of the Rusby family, including John Rusby. John was a contributor to the Board of Education in Nutley. A merchant by trade, he was instrumental in obtaining the old Duncan Mill property on Chestnut Street for public and school use.

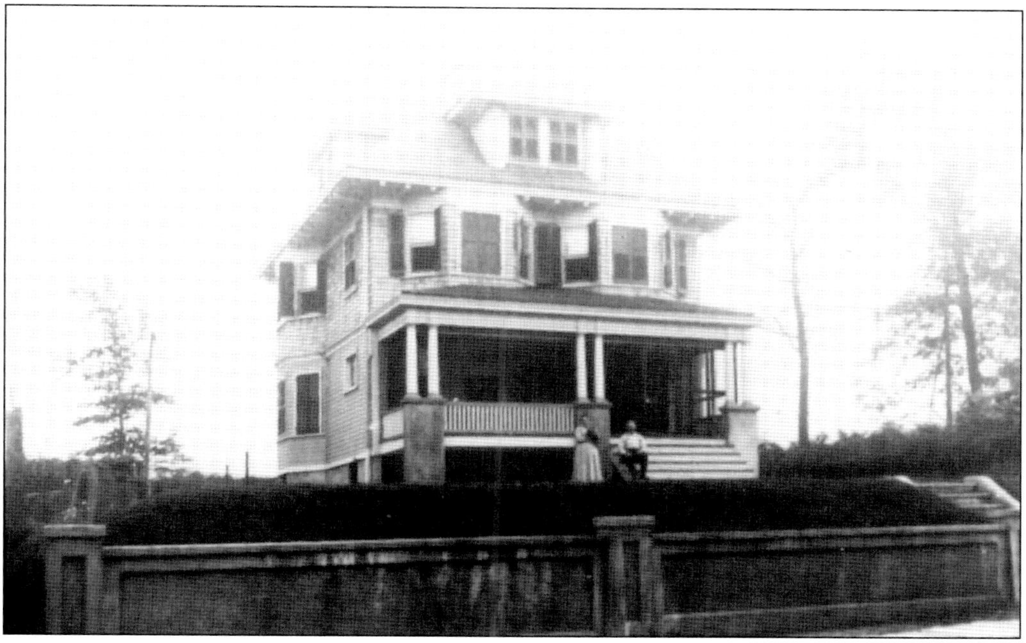

This is 145 Centre Street, which was the home of E.P. Cook, a local painter, and his family. Only a small section of the retaining wall remains today, as it became common to subdivide the large land lots, allowing newer homes to be built between older ones.

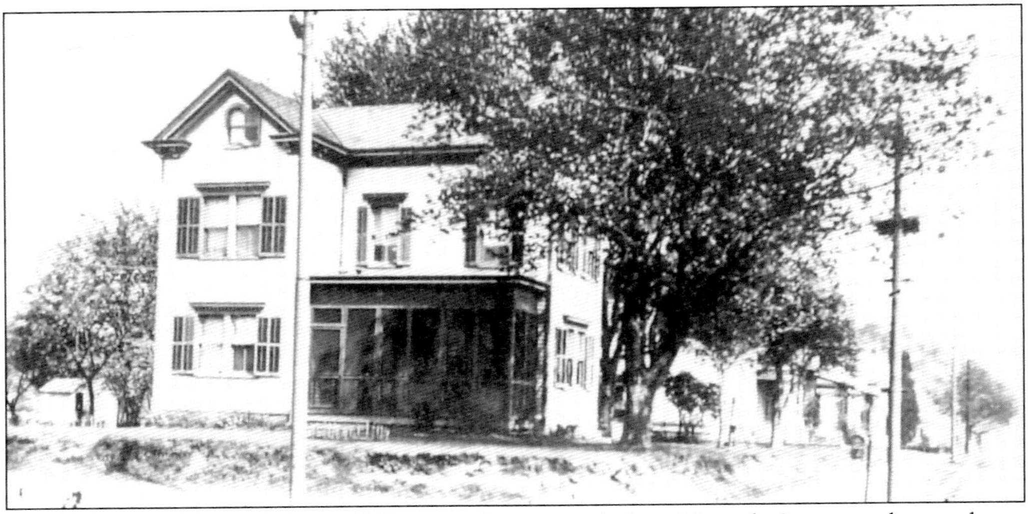

This house belonged to George F. Brown, who was a clerk in Newark. It sat on the northeast corner of Franklin Avenue and Centre Street. When it became obvious that the intersection there was going to be the new business center of town, the house was removed and a larger commercial building was built.

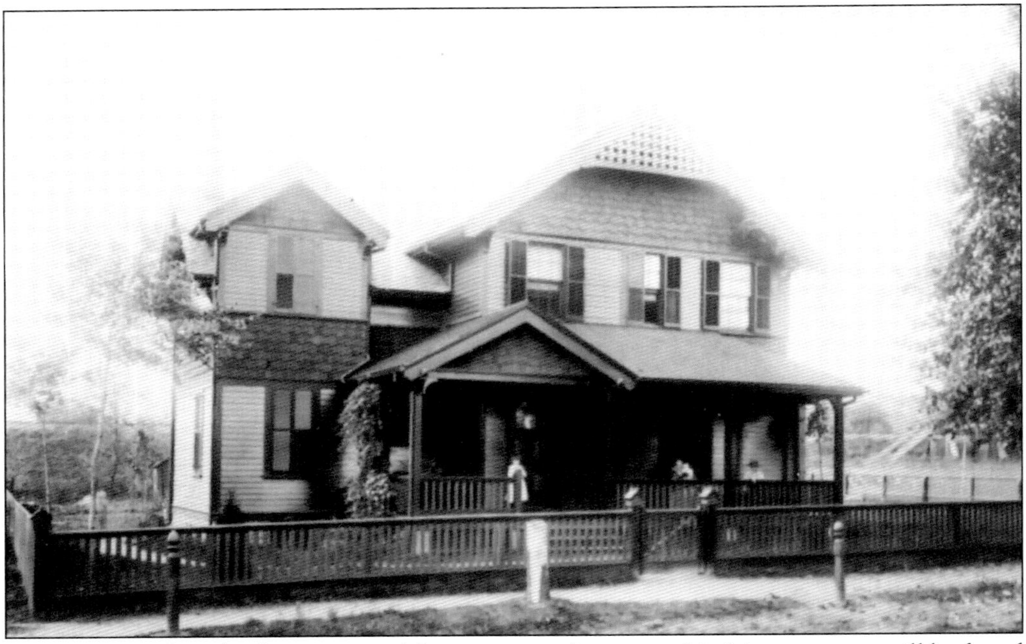

This home, with its birdhouse-topped fence posts and cast-iron hitching post, can still be found at 131 Brookfield Avenue. It was once the home and shop of a Mr. Whitfield, who built some of the houses in the Erie Place district (the tracks can be seen in the background).

Eleven

Sports and Recreation

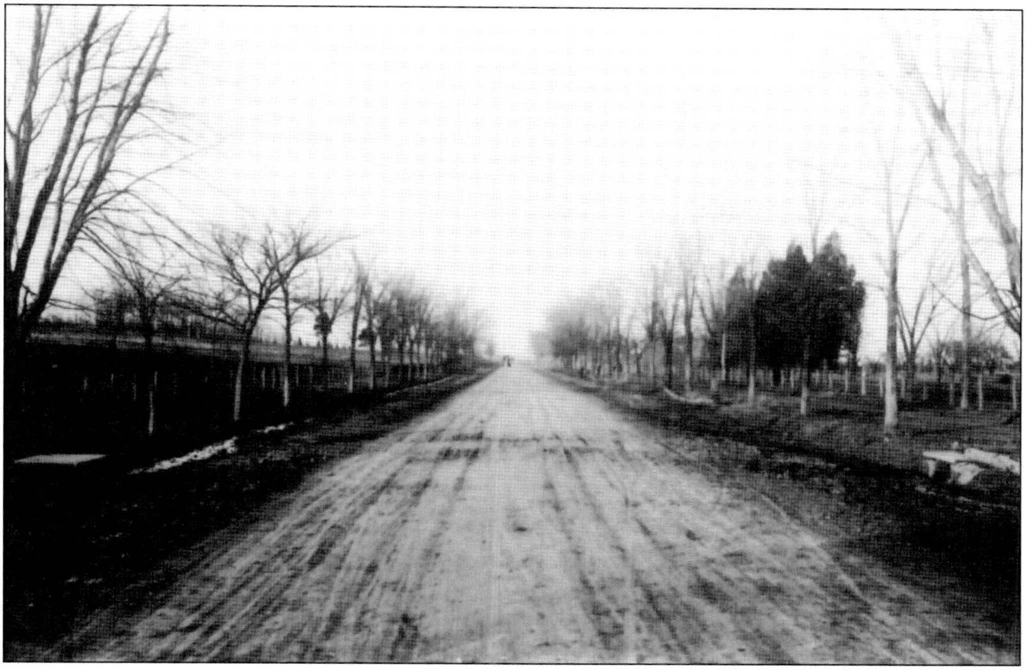

The Mile Stretch was famous for its horse-and-buggy races on Sundays. It started on Washington Avenue near Kingsland Avenue and ended somewhere around Grant Avenue near Goreman's Hotel. The races were allowed by the local churches as long as they did not interfere with Sunday services, but had to be stopped when horses and automobiles started to share the road.

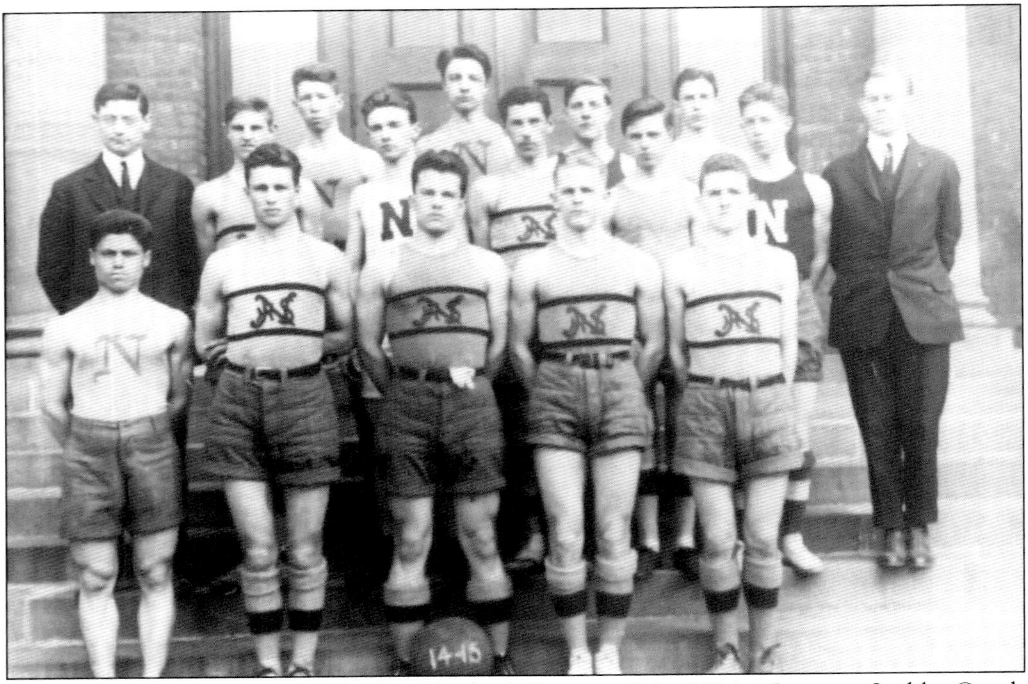

Pictured here are members of the boy's basketball team of the 1914–15 season. Led by Coach Olson, the team started strong by winning its first two games, but they finished up the season with a 12–13 record. During one game against Montclair Normal School, the team won with an amazing score of 75 to 2.

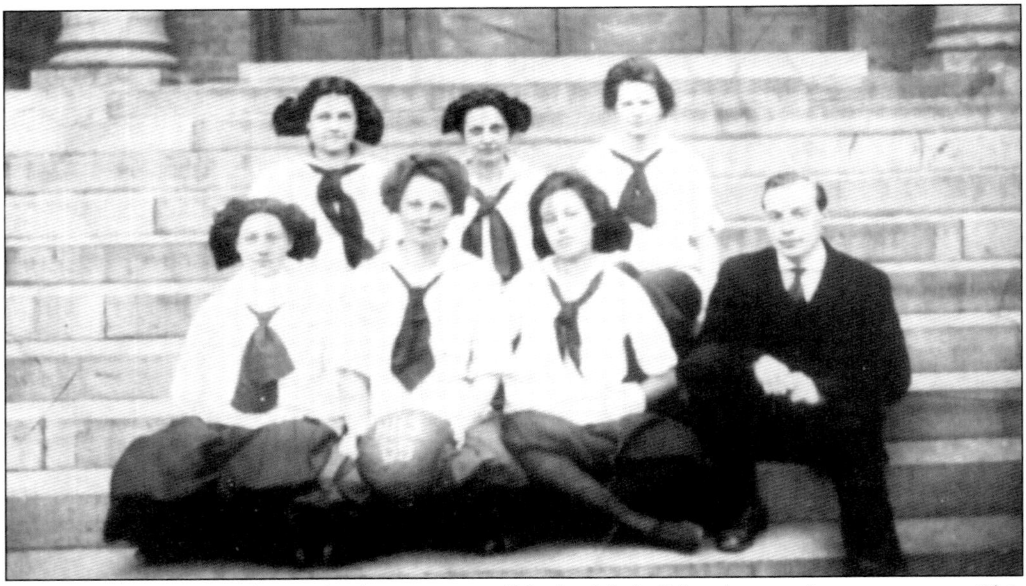

Girl's basketball teams have also been a part of Nutley High School sports for many years. This photograph from 1909 shows how few girls were taking part of the program. Even as late as 1915, it was still difficult to get players; for example, the pictured team only has six members on the roster.

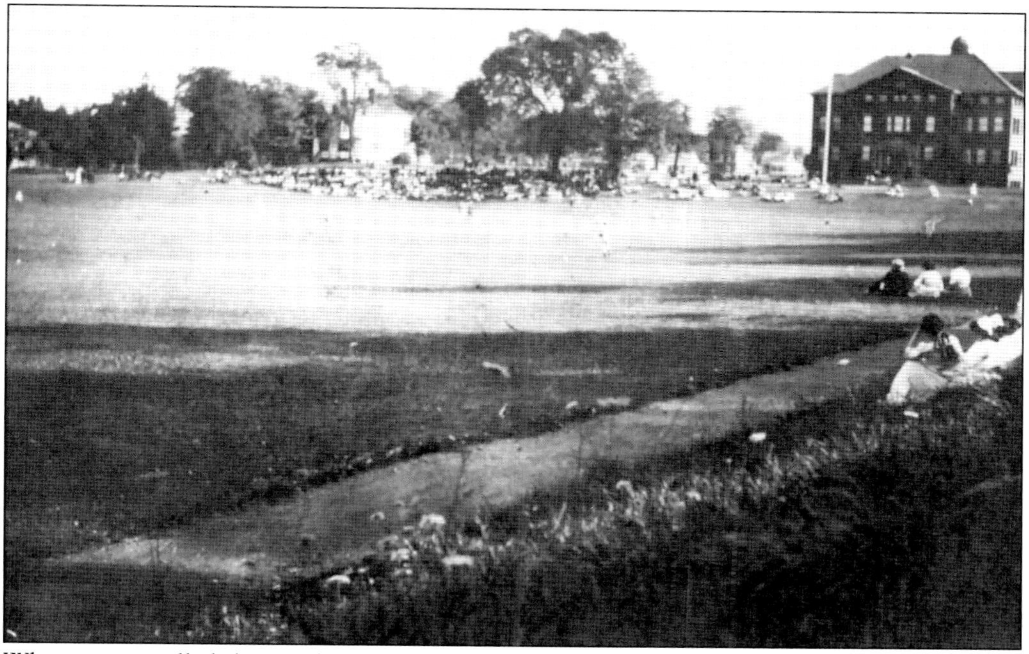

What is now called the Oval was once known as the Park School campus. All of the biggest sporting events in town were held here. During the early 1900s, baseball was an extremely popular sport in town. Nutley had several local teams from the high school to the semi-professional level.

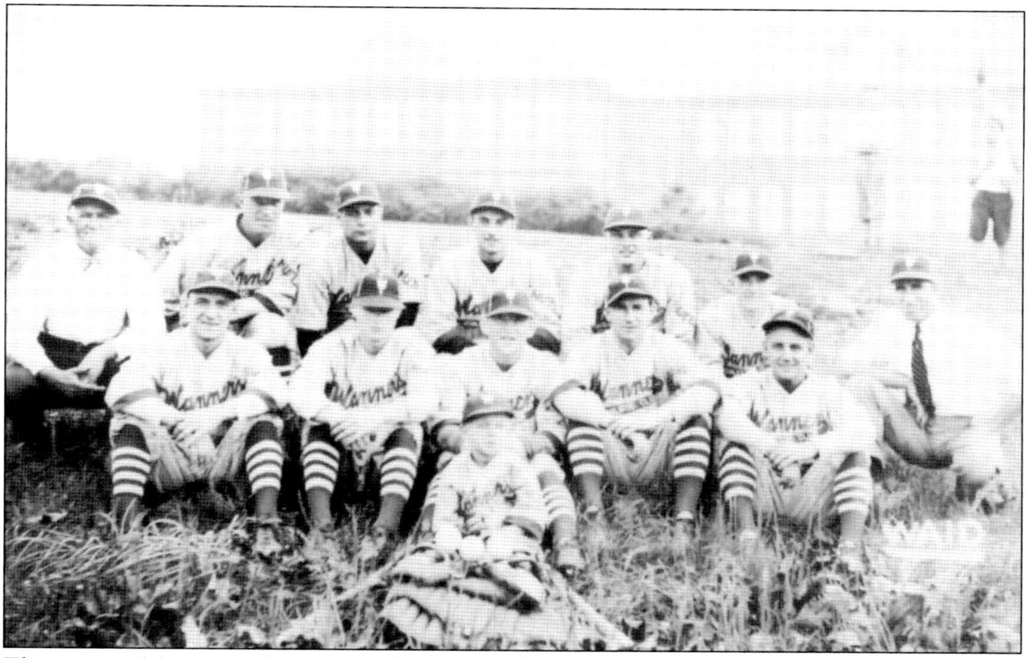

This is one of the privately sponsored teams from Nutley. They are pictured here on Park campus at the side of Park School (which used to be the high school), and were sponsored by Wanner's Toy and Sport Shop from 307 Franklin Avenue.

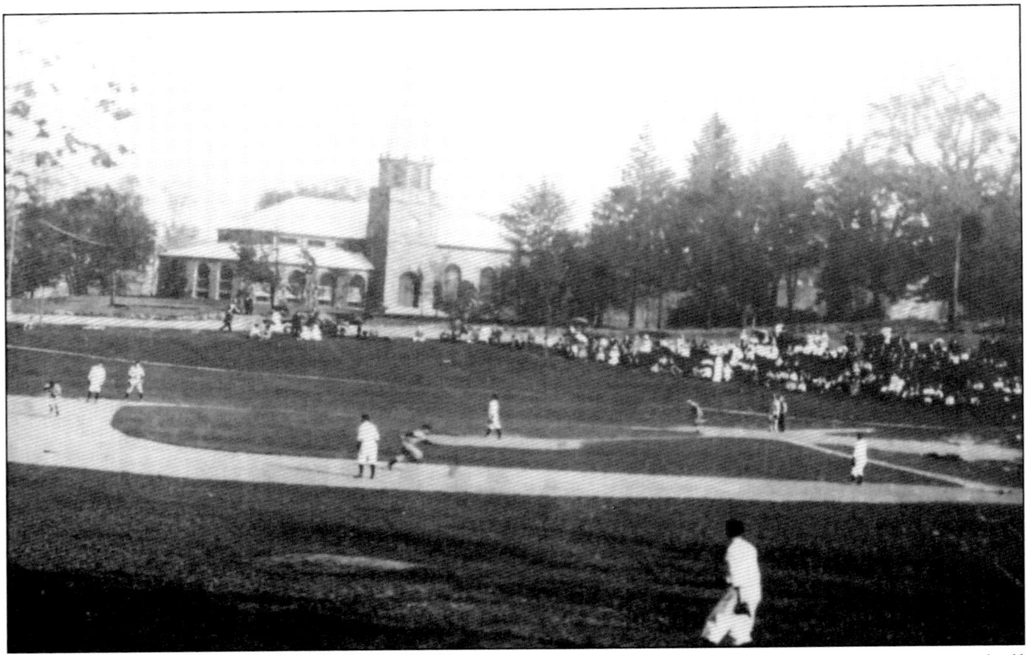

The Nutley Pleasure Club also sponsored a baseball team, whose 1916 record was 16–8. Baseball was started by the club in 1912, under the name "the young men's club," but was dropped due to a lack of interest. In 1915, it was started up again with a lot more success.

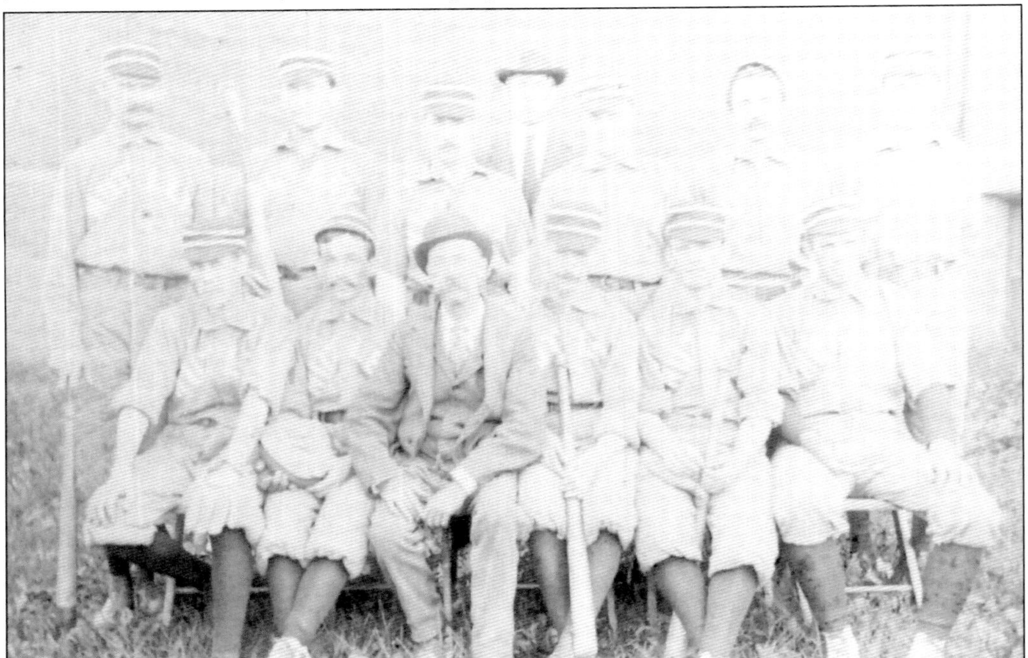

This faded photograph was part of Nutley historian Frank Speer's collection. It is one of the earliest sports-related images the author has seen in connection to Nutley. It appears to have been taken next to the wall of Park School, which would date it no earlier than 1894.

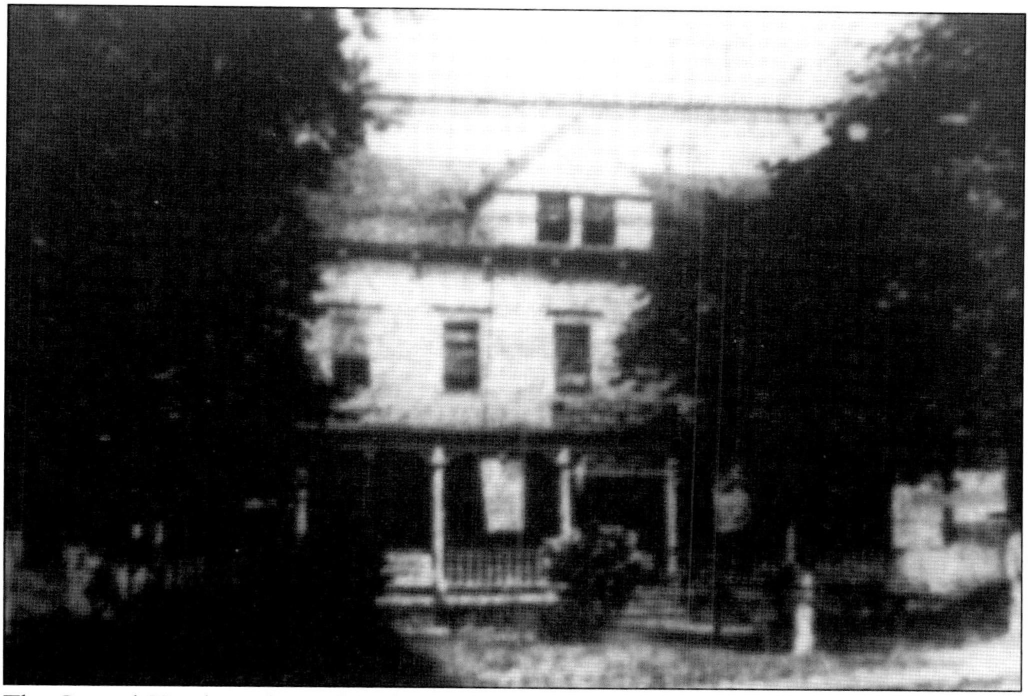

The Central Hotel was located at the corner of Hamilton Place and Chestnut Street. It was famous for its bowling alleys, which were used by several local teams for tournaments. Originally a house owned by Texan Colonel Rowan, it was taken over and converted by hotel owner/manager L.C. Rubin.

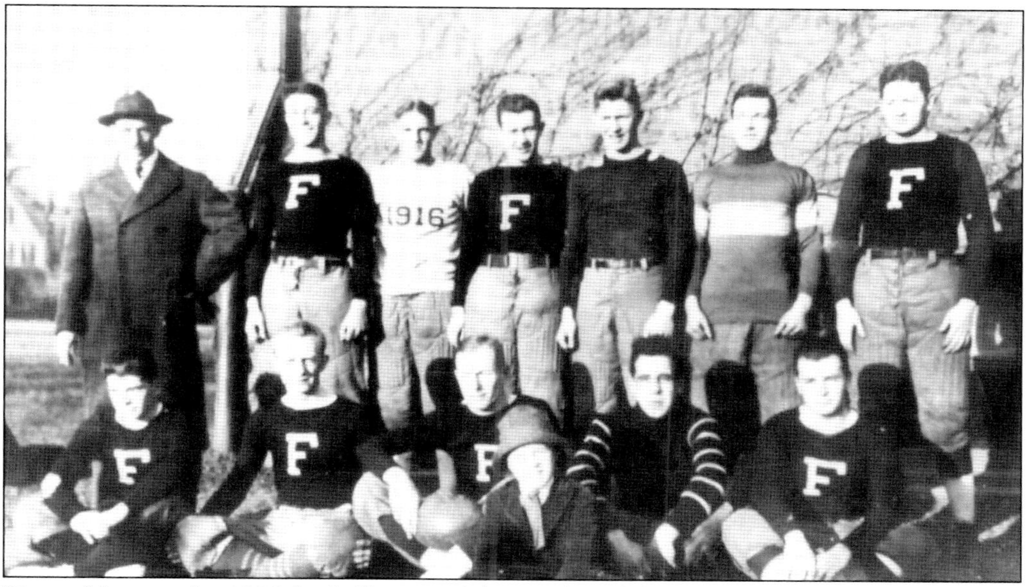

Pictured here is the 1916 football team of the Nutley Club. The Nutley Club was formed in 1911 by the Franklin Reformed Church to promote social and athletic character. In its 1916 season the team was 5–1–2, with its only loss going to Paterson YMCA. The boys were led to their victories by coach Milton Witbeck.

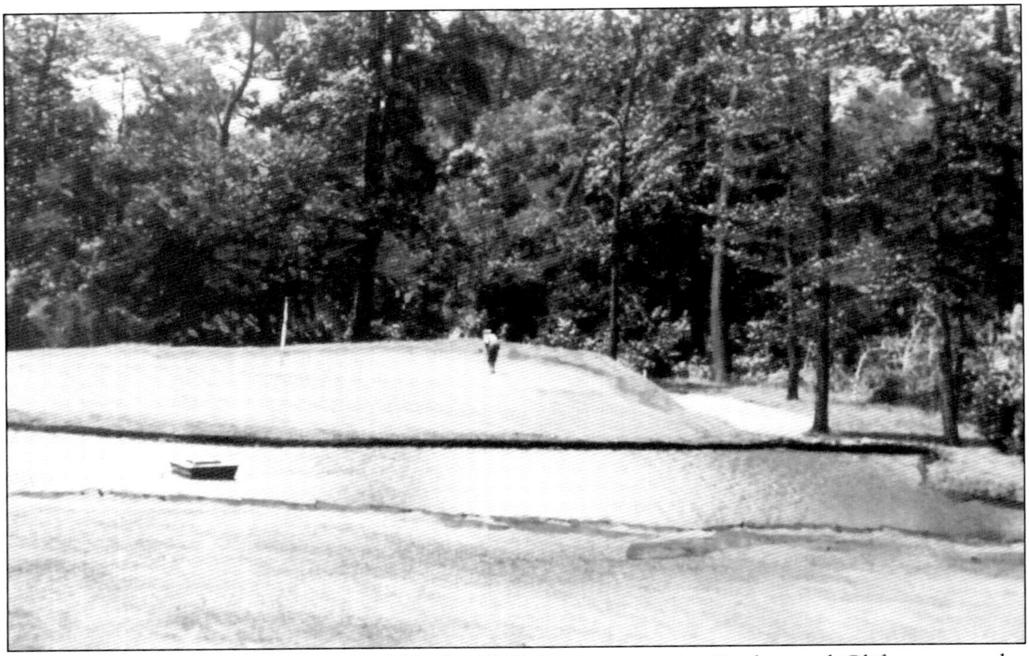

On the property formerly occupied by the ITT Corporation in Nutley and Clifton were the greens and clubhouses of the Yountakah Country Club. The club's 18-hole course featured sand traps and artificial water hazards. Taken about 1929, this photograph captured a golfer on one of the greens during a fine spring day.

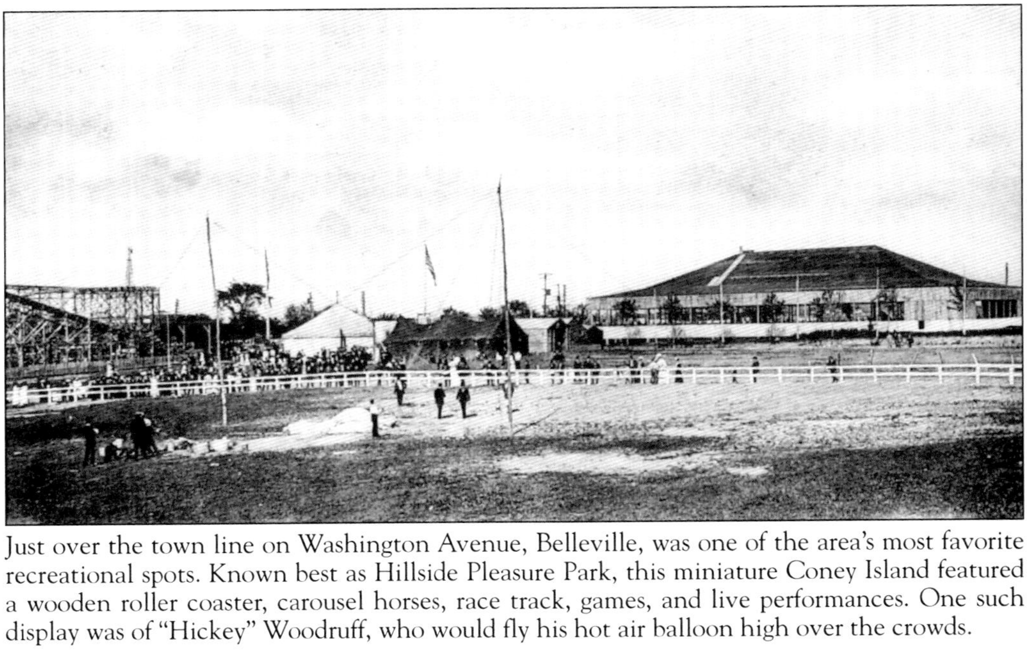

Just over the town line on Washington Avenue, Belleville, was one of the area's most favorite recreational spots. Known best as Hillside Pleasure Park, this miniature Coney Island featured a wooden roller coaster, carousel horses, race track, games, and live performances. One such display was of "Hickey" Woodruff, who would fly his hot air balloon high over the crowds.

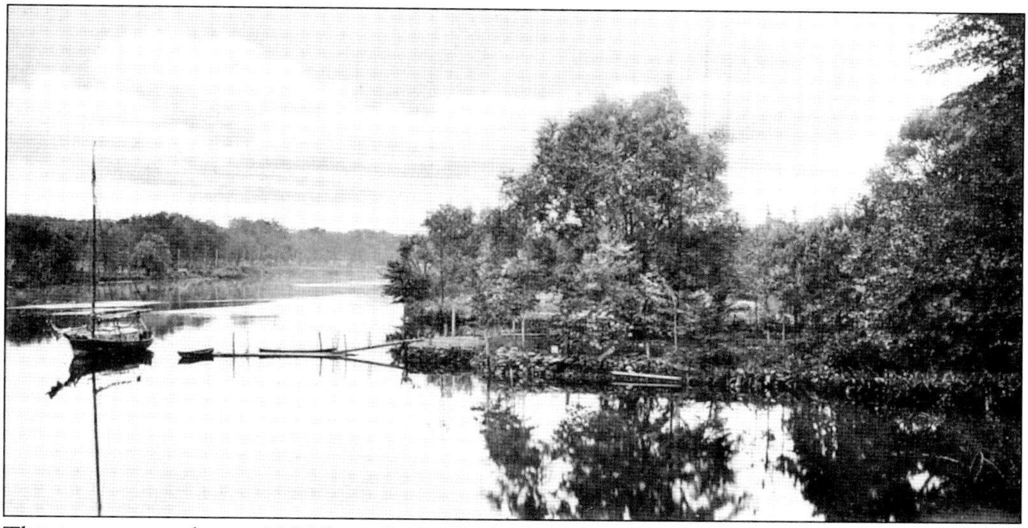

This image was taken c. 1906 from the bridge looking south. The Passaic River was often dotted with small sailboats, like the one shown here. Many River Road residents could easily enjoy a daily sail from their own docks. This postcard was part of a series that focused on the Avondale section of town.

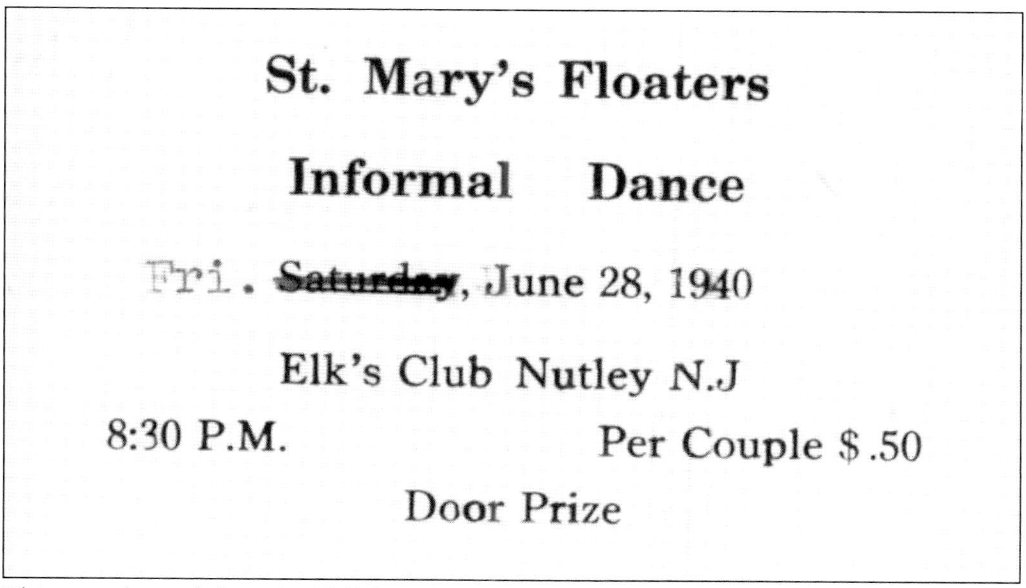

St. Mary's Floaters

Informal Dance

Fri. ~~Saturday~~, June 28, 1940

Elk's Club Nutley N.J

8:30 P.M. Per Couple $.50

Door Prize

This is a ticket stub from the 1940 Saint Mary's Dance, which was held at the Elks Club. Dances were very popular social events and a fun way to spend an evening. While people still enjoy dancing at clubs or parties today, it is a much different style than the old dance hall days.

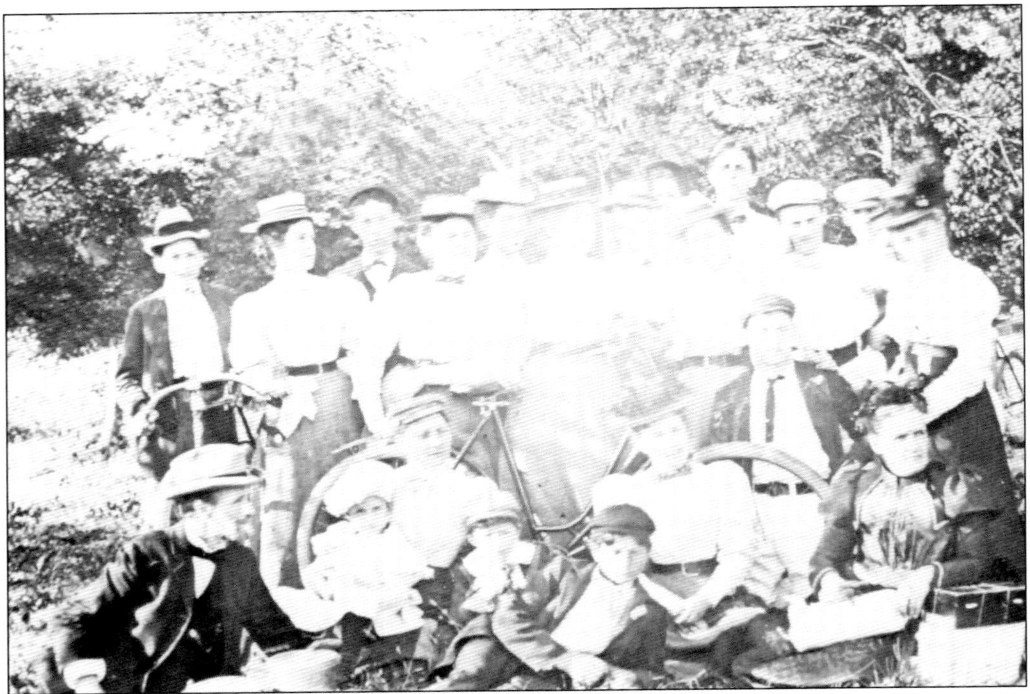

A bicycle picnic in Nutley is shown here sometime during the early 1900s. When the members of this group decided to spend some time outdoors, some of them brought along their bicycles. Biking in Nutley must have been very enjoyable around that time, for not only was there very little traffic, but Nutley was still largely undeveloped with plenty of scenic landscapes.

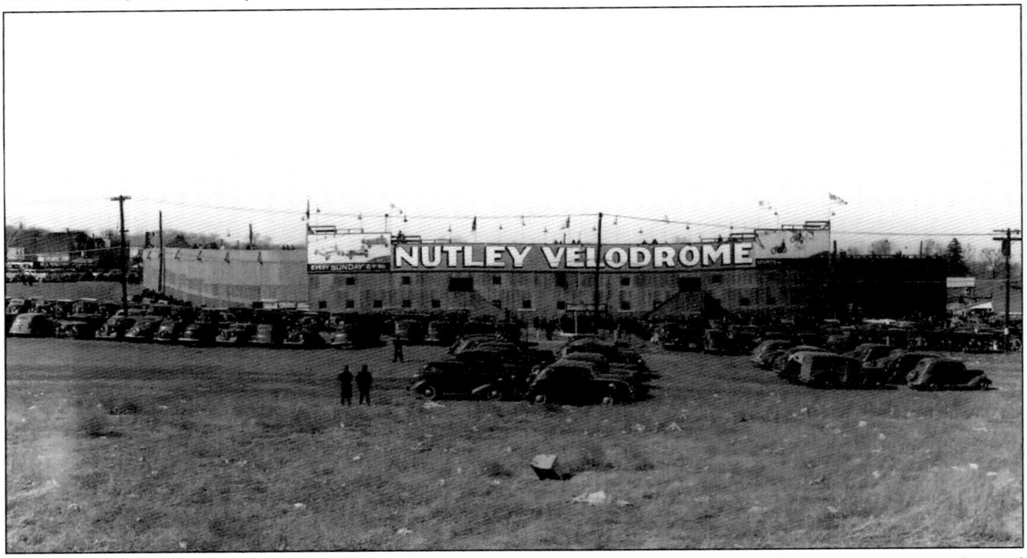

The Velodrome was built by Joe and Anthony Miele near the site of the present park and recreation building on Park Avenue. It was a saucer-shaped track, made completely of wood and clad with galvanized sheets on the outside. Built initially for bicycle racing, each lap was 1/7th of a mile. Opening day was June 4, 1933, with a packed house of 12,000 people and Mayor Reinheimer firing the starting gun.

The Management requests its patrons to kindly be sure and step on all matches, cigars and cigarettes after discarding them.

NUTLEY VELODROME

PARK AVENUE, Between Washington Ave. and River Road

OFFICIAL 10c PROGRAM	Races Conducted Under Permit of National Cycling Association	OFFICIAL 10c PROGRAM

SUNDAY, JULY 2, 1933 — 8:30 P. M.

OFFICIALS

REFEREE—FRANK L. KRAMER

Judges—Wm. R. Drake, Edward Christopherson, Alfred Freiensehner, Joseph R. Abell, George Stanford.

Starter—Gabriel J. Abieneste

Scorers and Timers—Charles Caufield, Leo Callman, Herman Hillenbach, William Goss, Herbert A. Grives.

Clerk of Course—Jo Fogler

Announcer—William Sullivan

NOTICE: When in Doubt About the Weather or to Reserve Tickets Call NUTLEY 2 - 0752 or NUTLEY 2 - 0753

Shown here is a Nutley Velodrome racing schedule for Sunday, July 2, 1933. Races were held every Wednesday night and Sunday afternoon. Built in 1933, the Nutley Velodrome was well known among the international racing circuit. At that time, bicycle racing was just at its peak in the United States. Tickets cost 55¢ originally, but prices were soon lowered to 40¢ with an additional 10¢ charge for a program. The track was built without a concrete foundation, for it was on top of the old quarry site, which was filled with decomposing trash. This shifting land base made it necessary for carpenters to literally lift and shim the track on occasion. When cycle racing started to die out as a spectator sport, the velodrome found new life as a track for miniature car races. Several deaths at the track, lack of attendance, and local complaints finally ended the Velodrome's role in Nutley's history; after remaining idle for a couple of years, it was dismantled in 1942.

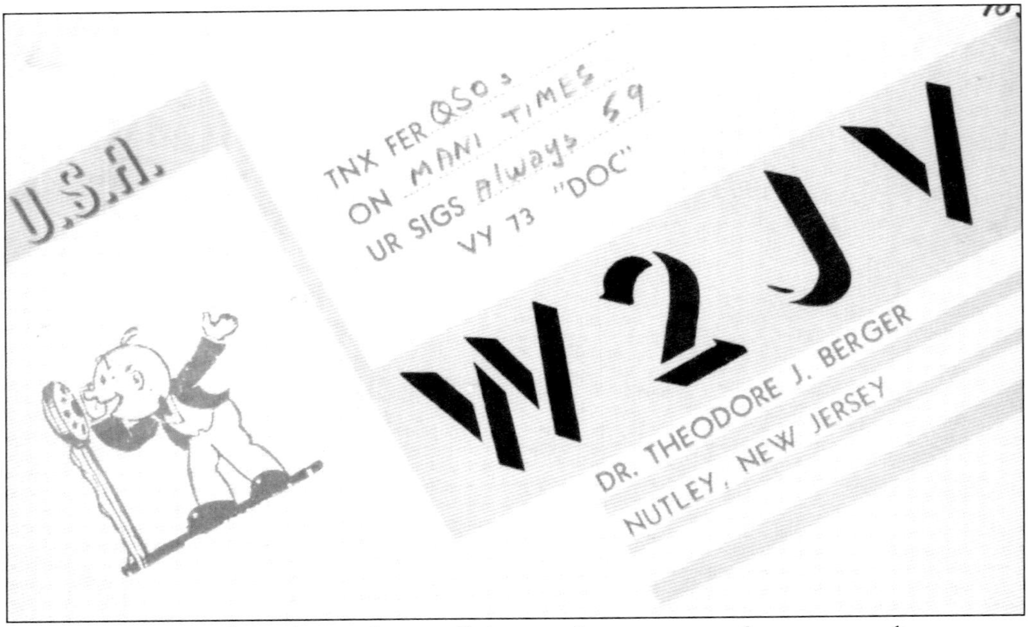

During the 1940s and '50s, ham radio was all the rage. It was common for amateur radio operators to have QSL postcards made giving their name, location, and the technical characteristics of their equipment.

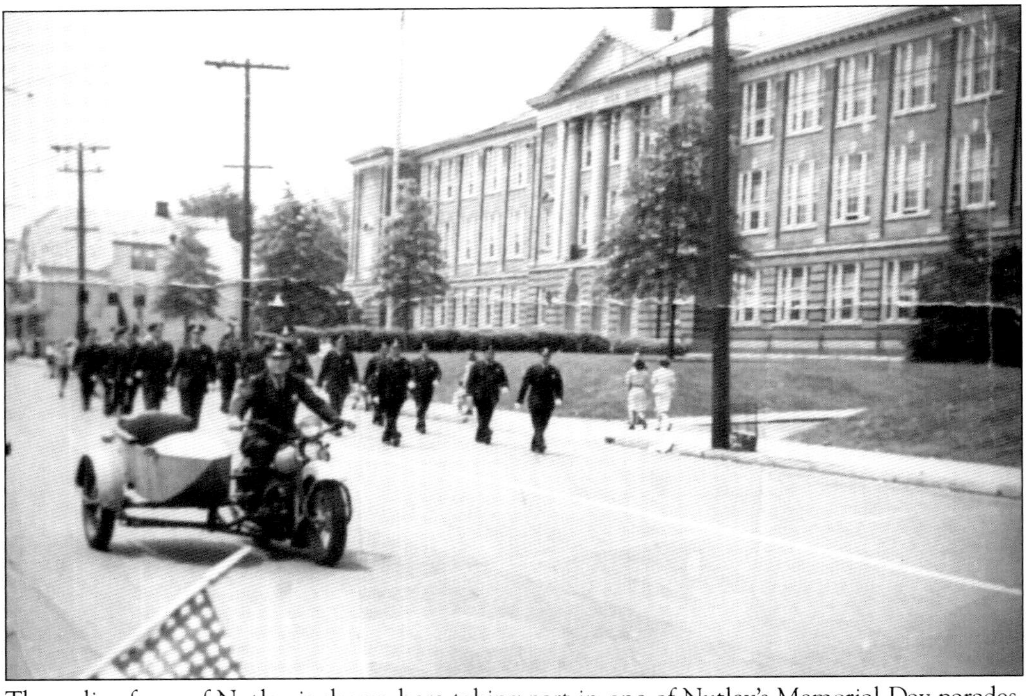

The police force of Nutley is shown here taking part in one of Nutley's Memorial Day parades. The photograph was taken c. 1950, at which time the building on the right was still used as the Nutley High School. Police Officer Ritacco is seen here riding the motorcycle with the side car.